HEAVY
TRAFFIC

HEAVY

30 Years of Headlines

and Major Ops from

the Case Files of the DEA

TRAFFIC

DAVID ROBBINS

CHAMBERLAIN BROS.
a member of Penguin Group (USA) Inc.
New York
2005

CHAMBERLAIN BROS.
Published by the Penguin Group
Penguin Group (USA) Inc., 375 Hudson Street,
New York, New York 10014, USA
Penguin Group (Canada), 10 Alcorn Avenue, Toronto, Ontario M4V 3B2,
Canada (a division of Pearson Penguin Canada Inc.)
Penguin Books Ltd, 80 Strand, London WC2R 0RL, England
Penguin Ireland, 25 St Stephen's Green, Dublin 2, Ireland
(a division of Penguin Books Ltd)
Penguin Group (Australia), 250 Camberwell Road, Camberwell, Victoria
3124, Australia (a division of Pearson Australia Group Pty Ltd)
Penguin Books India Pvt Ltd, 11 Community Centre, Panchsheel Park,
New Delhi–110 017, India
Penguin Group (NZ), Cnr Airborne and Rosedale Roads, Albany, Auckland
1310, New Zealand (a division of Pearson New Zealand Ltd)
Penguin Books (South Africa) (Pty) Ltd, 24 Sturdee Avenue, Rosebank,
Johannesburg 2196, South Africa

Penguin Books Ltd, Registered Offices:
80 Strand, London WC2R 0RL, England

Copyright © 2005 by Chamberlain Bros., a member of Penguin Group (USA) Inc.
All rights reserved. No part of this book may be reproduced, scanned, or
distributed in any printed or electronic form without permission. Please do not
participate in or encourage piracy of copyrighted materials in violation of the
author's rights. Purchase only authorized editions.
Published simultaneously in Canada

An application has been submitted to register this book
with the Library of Congress.

ISBN 1-59609-007-3

Printed in the United States of America
10　9　8　7　6　5　4　3　2　1

This book is printed on acid-free paper. ∞
Book design by Jamie Putorti

While the author has made every effort to provide accurate telephone numbers and Internet addresses at the time of publication, neither the publisher nor the author assumes any responsibility for errors, or for changes that occur after publication.

CONTENTS

Introduction | *vii*

Foreword | *xi*

The Early Days | *1*

1973–1974 | *7*

1975–1980 | *13*

1981–1985 | *28*

1986–1990 | *44*

1991–1994 | *54*

1994–1998 | *67*

1999–2000 | *88*

2001–2002 | *119*

Drugs and Terrorism | *145*

2002 | *155*

Shadows on the Wall | *199*

2003 | *207*

2004 | *260*

The Challenge for the
Future | *277*

Appendix A
Wall of Honor | *281*

Appendix B
Crack Cocaine | *293*

Appendix C
Sinister Brotherhoods | *297*

Appendix D
Foreign Terrorist
Organizations | *315*

Addendum: Drug Trends
and the Future | *327*

Sources | *333*

Acknowledgments | *337*

Index | *339*

INTRODUCTION

I know a little something about the stories in this book, and about the extraordinary and courageous work carried out each and every day, in the United States and around the globe, by the men and women who represent the DEA. You see, I'm a onetime juvenile delinquent who grew up to become an original member of the DEA's legendary Group 93, founded in 1990 to target the Colombian drug cartels. I've witnessed firsthand the ravages of illegal narcotics; I've seen the bloody results of the war on drugs. I've lived it. So I guess I have a clearer understanding than most as to why this is an important book, and why you should care about its message.

The drug trade in the United States, I'm sorry to report, is still driven primarily by massive demand. We're talking about basic economics: if there were no demand, there would be no real profit motive for the drug cartels. I can vividly recall a clandestine meeting with Freddie Herrera, the nephew of Cali kingpin Helmer Herrera. I was working under deep cover at the time, posing as a wealthy drug trafficker who cared only about lining his own pockets. Herrera's fractured moral compass was revealed when he told me that he felt no guilt about his chosen career path. "The young gringos use this stuff," he said with a laugh. "We only sell it, and that's why we are getting rich—on poisoning your youth."

Fighting the war on drugs is a monumental task. One serious problem faced by the United States is the fact that the Colombian cartels are masters of importation; they know how to penetrate the weakest points in our borders and smuggle tons of drugs into our country. They do it every day. The cartels' leadership is nothing if not smart and practical. About ten years ago, they realized that heroin might be a more marketable and cheaper product than cocaine, which had been their primary source of income. So they quickly brought in chemists from Southeast Asia and began processing Colombian heroin, which is about 95 percent pure. Seemingly overnight, the Colombian cartels began dominating the U.S. market and flooding it with heroin. What we see today—a staggering number of young intravenous drug users—is the result. Pure, deadly Colombian heroin is enslaving our children and stealing their innocence right before our eyes.

I've often been asked whether we are winning the war on drugs. That's a tough question, and I can answer it only in this fashion: yes and no. This is a never-ending battle, and while we are making progress, it's nearly impossible to win a war that is perpetually underfunded. The United States needs to vigorously and enthusiastically fund the drug war if it wants to emerge victorious. But that is merely the beginning—a prerequisite, if you will. Specifically and tactically, there are a number of things that need to be done.

One is to develop a thicker diplomatic skin, so to speak. We can't be overly concerned with not offending the sensibilities of countries and governments that are involved in smuggling drugs into the U.S. There is no gray area in this matter. There is only right and wrong. The trafficking of drugs on a wide scale is nothing less than a form of domestic terrorism. It kills our youth and shatters our collective spirit.

Along those same lines, we need to punish governments that fail to stop the flow of drugs out of their own countries, regardless of where the drugs are headed. How do we do this? With strength and resolve—by cutting off all aid immediately, and then, if necessary, by using special operations personnel to infiltrate jungle laboratories and put the lowlifes out of business. If that sounds harsh, well, so be it. This is not a game for those with weak stomachs. As a matter of fact, it's not a game at all. It's a matter of life and death.

Drugs breed violence; drugs provide fuel to crime at all levels of society. No one is left untouched. Street crime is driven by the user, the desperate junkie hooked on heroin who can't help himself because the craving is so powerful. He cares about one thing and one thing only: the next fix. When the addict reaches bottom—and eventually he *always* reaches bottom—when he gets to a point when he can't afford to buy drugs, he will invariably turn to criminal activity to feed his habit. Burglar, thief, prostitute—these are job descriptions for the junkie.

But the problem is not confined to the saddest segments of society, to the poor and uneducated. Larger, more widespread crime is created by the disruption of law enforcement against the cartels. Police can intercept money or drugs from a simple car stop on the highway or as a result of a major investigation. Thus begins a violent and deadly spiral. The cartel bosses don't want to hear about the mistakes that led to an interruption in the flow of cash. Someone, naturally, has to pay. Mistakes are punished by murder. Lost money is replaced through any means necessary. The drug business is a brutal business, populated by the worst that mankind has to offer. They are heartless killers, and they must be taken down.

I'll be honest. I was an adrenaline freak. I was driven largely by the action—by the thrill of trying to infiltrate and shatter the cartels. But I also believed that I could make a difference. And I think that most of the men and women who are fighting the war on drugs are similarly motivated. They believe in what they are doing. They honestly feel that they can make a substantial impact on society by waging this battle.

It is true that there are DEA agents who become frustrated by the international corruption and lack of adequate funding. Some crumble beneath the weight of the job. They move to the mountains and isolate themselves from the workaday world, leaving fractured families and broken dreams in their wake. Others—too numerous to count, really—fight on. They stand on the front lines, putting their lives at risk. Or they climb the ranks of the DEA administration and try to make an impact on a larger scale, by cutting through red tape and assisting the agents in their employ.

But they are all soldiers, deserving of our respect and support. And I am proud to call myself one of them.

Jerry Speziale is one of the nation's leading experts on narcotics smuggling and frequently lectures at the DEA Academy. He currently serves as the elected sheriff of Passaic County, New Jersey.

FOREWORD

America is under assault. The land of the free is being attacked on several fronts at once. Terrorists have declared war on the Great Satan, as they call her, and acts of terrorist violence have claimed thousands of American lives. Enemy nations do everything in their power to diminish America's influence and prestige abroad. Several actively work to develop nuclear weapons, elevating the danger to America a thousandfold.

Then there is the quiet front, the insidious front: an enemy that seeks to destroy America from within. An enemy that attacks young and old alike. An enemy that has caused more misery than all the terrorist attacks combined. An enemy already on America's shores and wreaking havoc with American society.

That enemy? Drugs. Substances proven harmful to those who use them and banned by law; that impair judgment and ravage the body. Substances that have caused an epidemic of random crime ranging from burglary to murder.

Scoffers say the drug problem isn't that serious. Statistics indicate otherwise. The evidence shows that the cost in suffering and ruined lives ranks as one of the greatest threats to America's well-being.

Drug offenses are now the leading cause of arrests in the United States. More than 1.5 million such arrests occur annually, and the numbers are climbing. Millions of Americans are addicted and succumb to a vicious cycle of need and abuse.

It was not always this way. Drug abusers comprised a small niche segment of the total population. But that changed with the drug boom of the 1960s, when the youth of America underwent a lifestyle transformation in which drugs played a key part.

The drug culture has seeped into all aspects of American society. Users run the full spectrum, from corporate business people to the homeless. CEOs responsible for the economic welfare of American industry are hooked on cocaine. Pregnant mothers live in hovels, spending every penny they have to feed their heroin or crack addictions, destroying two lives in the process.

But drug abuse is not the sole problem associated with drugs. Criminal enterprises have arisen that are devoted to supplying the illegal substances. Such enterprises are intrinsically violent by nature, and they are devoted to fostering the widespread use of drugs by any means necessary.

The problem has reached the point at which the number of people who die each year from drug-related violence is far greater than the number of people who die each year from using drugs. Thousands of lives are snuffed out on the altar of greed and addiction.

Statistics vary, but certain generally accepted figures bring the overall drug picture into even more glaring light. Over one-fourth of all high school students indulge in illegal drug use. Among college-age students, that figure more than doubles. About one-fifth of all crimes are committed to obtain money for drugs. Drug-trade-related murders number in the thousands yearly. Over 80 percent of all jail inmates report having used illegal drugs.

On and on it goes.

America is under siege from within. Unless the tide can be stemmed, it bodes ill for her future.

Into the breach have stepped a number of government agencies determined to do all they can to stop the spread. The problem is that, akin to the legendary multiheaded Hydra, drugs enter America from many directions at once. There is not just one drug syndicate, but many. There is not just one drug dealer; they are legion.

Law enforcement has gradually risen to the challenge. Local and state police organizations often have drug units of their own, and they can also look to the federal government for help in combating drug pipelines that span the globe.

The FBI, the U.S. Customs Service, the U.S. Border Patrol, Homeland Security, and others all strive diligently to stem the menace.

But one agency in particular is specifically and exclusively devoted to combating the drug trade. You could say that this effort is the sole purpose for the agency's existence.

The Drug Enforcement Administration is in the vanguard of America's defense against the illegal tide. What you are about to read is the DEA's own story, from its early days as a fledgling agency with little financing and few resources, to today, when the DEA has an annual budget of more than a billion dollars and the high-tech capability to deal with increasingly sophisticated drug rings.

It is a story of persistence and dedication; of dedication to duty and devotion to an ideal; of men and women who gave their very lives to end the drug blight.

America has awakened to the staggering social costs and the toll in human suffering attributable to illegal drugs. She is fighting back on every front. The war has not been lost. To win it will take years and much more sacrifice, but America has a history of rising to meet every threat and defeating it.

Enter the DEA.

THE EARLY DAYS

Federal drug enforcement evolved slowly over many years. In the 1800s, many drugs that are now illegal could be bought over the counter. The sale of opium was not restricted in any way. Popular patent medicines for every ailment under the sun contained opiates as main ingredients. Their use became so widespread that concern was voiced in official circles.

In 1906, the Pure Food and Drug Act was passed. Deemed by some as the first anti-drug law, all it did was require that opiates be properly labeled, and, incredibly, establish purity levels so that those who bought patent medicines and elixirs could be sure the opiates were of high quality.

More and more people, however, were using opium and its derivatives for other than medicinal purposes. Recreational use was on the rise, and in 1914, the Harrison Narcotics Act made headlines. Opium users, many of them addicts, could no longer purchase the drug legally. This act was the true launching pad for the federal effort to contain illicit drug use.

Enforcement fell to the Bureau of Internal Revenue because the act was a revenue measure, not a drug act per se. The act wasn't a ban on opiates so much as an excise tax, although it did limit possession unless it was for valid medical reasons.

It was at this point that one of the most crucial events in America's war on drugs occurred. Charges were filed against a number of doctors who had prescribed opiates for addicts. Ultimately, the Supreme Court was called on to decide if the federal government could or could not limit the use of certain drugs. The Court decided that it could.

Over the ensuing decades, various federal agencies were given limited drug-enforcement powers. At the start of the 1960s it was estimated that only about four million Americans had ever tried illegal substances.

Then came the explosion. The counterculture burst upon society with all the impact of a nuclear detonation. Values were turned topsy-turvy. Where before drug use had been frowned on and discouraged, it now became the vogue. Everyone was doing it, as advocates had it. Turning on and tuning out became a cultural movement. Drug abuse skyrocketed.

It soon became apparent that the federal government's fragmented attempts at curtailing illegal activity were not up to the task. Something better was called for. The federal effort needed to be unified.

In 1968, President Lyndon Johnson combined the Bureau of Narcotics and the Bureau of Drug Abuse Control and formed the Bureau of Narcotics and Dangerous Drugs, which was placed under the purview of the Department of Justice.

The BNDD, as it was known, made a valiant effort to

squash illegal drug use. It launched the first task force to coordinate efforts between federal, state, and local authorities. It set up nine foreign offices in countries that were funneling drugs into the United States.

The BNDD's efforts were made easier by a new law. In 1970, Congress passed the Controlled Substances Act, Title II of the Comprehensive Drug Abuse Prevention and Control Act. What this act did was replace and update more than four dozen other laws already on the books, establishing a single system of overview for the first time in United States history.

With the new law lending extra bite to its enforcement powers, the BNDD made significant gains. Undeniably, the most famous of its cases was the notorious French Connection.

As early as the 1930s, it was learned that heroin labs in France were trafficking in the drug on a global scale. Much of their product was bound for the United States. The raw material came from Turkey, was refined in Marseilles, and was then shipped to ports overseas.

One of those ports was New York City. In fact, the very first seizure was made in New York in February of 1947, when a Corsican seaman getting off a vessel from France was arrested with seven pounds of heroin in his possession.

It was the proverbial tip of the iceberg. In 1960, a major break occurred. Authorities learned that a Guatemalan ambassador was smuggling hundreds of pounds of morphine, the base for heroin production, from Lebanon to Marseilles. It gave them a fuller picture of the scope of the operation, and of what would be needed to stop it.

By the late '60s, French traffickers were supplying up to 90 percent of the heroin used in the United States. To make matters worse, their heroin was 85 percent pure. Addicts could literally not get enough.

In 1972, the BNDD went on the offensive. In January, working with French officials, the BNDD seized 110 pounds of heroin at the Paris airport. Two major figures in the French Connection were taken into custody.

In February, the French traffickers approached a United States Army sergeant with a lucrative proposition. They offered to pay him $96,000 to smuggle almost 250 pounds of heroin into the United States. They misjudged their man. The sergeant reported it to his superiors, who in turn reported it to the BNDD. Two men in Paris and another five in New York were arrested, and $50 million worth of herion was confiscated.

It was the beginning of the end for the French operation. Over the next year or so, six heroin labs in the suburbs of Marseilles were raided. The *Caprice de Temps*, a shrimp boat, was boarded as it put to sea bound for Miami with more than 400 kilos of heroin on board.

Crippling the French Connection was a major coup, but the federal drug effort was not running entirely smoothly. There were still certain rivalries and lack of coordination, especially between the BNDD and the U.S. Customs Service. And drugs continued to be available on an unprecedented scale.

For these and other reasons, it was decided to restructure the federal effort yet again. Consequently, in July of 1973, President Richard M. Nixon abolished the BNDD by executive order and created the Drug Enforcement Administration. Like its predecessor, the DEA was under the Department of Justice's umbrella. But the DEA was granted much more power and much more leeway.

President Nixon had declared an "all-out global war on the drug menace," and the DEA was to be America's enforcement arm in that war.

The drug trade itself was undergoing a change. The burgeoning drug culture fueled an insatiable appetite for drugs of all kinds, which in turn led to the formation of budding criminal organizations in South and Central America devoted to meeting the new demand.

Critics charged that the government was slow to respond. They castigated the government for not doing enough. The Chicken Littles among them warned that America would soon be awash in drugs from shore to shore, and that nothing the government could do would stop it.

Their claims were unfounded. The BNDD had done a fine job with the limited resources at its disposal. And it should be noted that only a few years elapsed between the height of what many dub "the hippie era"—the last half of the '60s—and 1973, when the government kicked its anti-drug campaign into high gear with the formation of the DEA.

Federal officials actually reacted swiftly, given how slowly the gears of government can sometimes grind. As soon as the problem's full magnitude became known, measures were implemented to counter the spread. The government did all it could do, short of sealing off America's borders and closing all her ports.

Critics carped that the government had no business enforcing drug laws; that what people did in the privacy of their own homes was none of the government's business. If adults wanted to use drugs, then they were entitled to do so without hindrance.

Those same critics turned a blind eye to the misery and deaths drugs caused. They conveniently ignored what was obvious to everyone else—namely, that drugs were unraveling the very fabric of American society. As only one example among many, America's high schools went from being clean-cut bastions of learning to drug-infested quagmires where metal detectors and armed guards became a daily part of the educational experience.

How did American get from "there" to "here"? What changes took place, internally and externally, to bring about the situation as it exists today? The answers are inextricably interwoven with the history of the Drug Enforcement Administration. The DEA's story is, in effect, the story of the drug culture as it has evolved over the years.

Sit back, then, and prepare for a tale of pathos and courage, of intrigue and deception, of heroism and denial.

A tale made all the more poignant because it is true.

1973–1974

Laying the Foundation

The DEA had a lot of work to do before it could be the effective tool that President Nixon hoped for.

A three-story former bank building was converted into a National Training Institute to train new agents in three divisions: special agent training, international training, and police training. It included a firing range on the second floor. While adequate, it did not offer facilities for real-life application of the techniques and procedures the new agents were learning, so training was often conducted on city streets.

The DEA also got its hands on a house in Maryland and a twenty-acre farm in Virginia in order to conduct training raids and general field exercises.

Training for Basic Agent status lasted ten weeks. The DEA was off and running with three classes of fifty-three agents each. A whole gamut of courses was taught, with the goal always in mind of turning out agents able to deal with the complexities of the worldwide drug trade.

Training alone was not enough. Early on, the DEA realized that technology would play an equally crucial role. But the agency had not inherited very much from its predecessor. The BNDD's budget for high-tech items had been less than one million dollars annually. Most of the money went for simple things like radios so the agents could keep in touch, and support for their teletype operation.

This was before the days of hand-held video cameras no bigger than a paperback novel. Early camera equipment was large, bulky, and expensive. The same with early sound equipment. The DEA did not have the money to buy much of either, and as a result, certain aspects of their investigations, such as wiretaps, were adversely affected.

A small improvement had been made in body recorders. The old models were large belts that were hard to conceal. Newer models were smaller, but they still contained a transmitting device and the batteries to power it. As if that did not make it hard enough for DEA undercover operatives, the belts had a tendency to run hot and would sometimes burn the backs of those wearing them. The problem was further compounded by an unfortunate tendency for the belts to malfunction.

The DEA implemented its own radio network, but technology was limited in those early days, and their capabilities suffered. Individual pagers were a thing of the future. (It was possible to institute a paging system in 1973, but each pager had to have its own frequency, and with hundreds of agents, this made the idea impractical.)

Cellular phones were also far off. The DEA did have a mobile telephone service, but the only person with a mobile phone was the DEA administrator. Needless to say, this further impaired their abilities.

With all this in mind, it should be stressed that at the time, the DEA had some of the best equipment on the market. All the incredible developments in technology that would immeasurably enhance modern law enforcement were yet to occur.

The DEA also had it own air wing. Started by the BNDD in 1971 with one plane and a budget of less than sixty thousand dollars, by 1973 the DEA had twenty-four aircraft and forty-one pilots to fly them.

Air surveillance was crucial. Suspects were always on the alert for tails on the ground and could take measures to elude them, but it wasn't as easy to elude a plane. Pilots could shadow suspects virtually undetected.

Another element, and the DEA's most important in some regards, was its labs. In order to make its cases stick in court, the DEA had to prove that the substances it seized were in fact illegal drugs, and it could not rely on outside laboratories to perform the elaborate testing and confirmation. Evidence had to be treated carefully or a court case could be thrown out.

At the time it was created, the DEA inherited six national labs from the BNDD. A seventh was added in 1974 to help cope with the dramatically increasing workload, but it would not prove to be enough.

The DEA had agents, equipment, and facilities—all of which would be useless unless DEA agents could penetrate the drug organizations they were to combat. Reliable intelligence was paramount. With that in mind, in July of 1973 the DEA's Office of Intelligence was created for the sole purpose of gathering drug intelligence.

The need for good intel could not be emphasized enough. The DEA *had* to uncover the makeup and operation of drug traffickers and their organizations, and the only way to do that, short of informants, was through intelligence.

A new DEA position was established: Intelligence Analysts. In 1974, eleven I/As graduated from the DEA training school. Decades later, their total number would push seven hundred.

It was during these early formative years that the DEA set up its first field intelligence unit in conjunction with New York City police and detectives. It reaped dividends almost immediately. The DEA uncovered a major heroin operation and information that led them to the Cali cocaine organization, which will be described in subsequent chapters.

One last step worthy of mention: DAWN was created in 1974. The acronym stands for the Drug Abuse Warning Network, an invaluable system designed to monitor drug abuse in the United States. One of the first steps that DAWN took was to have hospitals report patients who showed up in emergency rooms in need of treatment for the abuse of illegal drugs.

Finally the DEA was up and running, and about to launch a series of major investigations.

Then unexpected tragedy struck.

Shortly after 10 a.m. on the morning of August 5, 1974, the roof of the DEA's Miami office collapsed. Seven agents were killed, and many others were trapped amid concrete and rubble until they could be rescued.

At first, an explosion was thought to be to blame. But the cause was much more mundane and far less sinister.

Not long before the collapse, the parking lot on the roof had been resurfaced. Salt in the materials used had seeped down and eroded the steel supports. The extra weight proved too much for the weakened supports to bear. On that fateful morning, with the parking lot filled with vehicles, the roof came crashing down.

By now DEA agents were out doing what the DEA was created to do, and making scores of arrests.

Perhaps the highest-profile case during this period involved Dr. Timothy Leary. Leary was once on the faculty at Harvard, where he gave LSD to his students as part of an experiment to alter human consciousness. Leary and another professor were subsequently fired.

Undaunted, Leary moved to New York and installed himself in a mansion where he entertained the likes of Aldous Huxley, Jack Kerouac, and Abbie Hoffman, among other notables. Psychedelic drugs were freely used.

It was Leary who coined one of the most famous phrases of the counterculture. His "Turn on, tune in, drop out" became a '60s mantra for those who made drugs their way of life.

Eventually Leary was arrested for marijuana possession and sentenced to ten years in prison. That might have ended his claim to notoriety had he not escaped from the California Men's Penal Colony and fled overseas.

Leary and his wife skipped from country to country until they were arrested by DEA agents in Afghanistan and extradited to the United States. A photograph of Leary in custody, and being escorted by the agents, appeared in many American newspapers. It was a great publicity coup for the DEA, and it served notice that the long arm of United States drug enforcement was not limited to the country's borders.

Leary became a leading guru to the drug crowd. He was a "superstar" whose intellectual pretensions were endlessly quoted.

❊ ❊ ❊

As part of President Nixon's relentless new campaign against drugs, thirty DEA agents were sent to Thailand in a special op intended to staunch the flow of Southeast Asian heroin into the United States. Operating out of Bangkok, and working in conjunction with Thai police, the thirty agents seized huge quantities of United States-bound heroin. So effective were their efforts that Southeast Asian heroin dropped from 30 percent of the total United States market to only 8 percent.

As the DEA was soon to learn, however, putting an end to one source of supply invariably opened new avenues for drug traffickers elsewhere. There was always another drug lord or drug organization more than willing to fill the vacuum.

In the case of Southeast Asian heroin, as the market there dried up, new suppliers surfaced in Mexico. Within a few short years, Mexico went from supplying 40 percent of United States heroin to supplying almost 90 percent.

The worst, as they say, was yet to come.

1975–1980

The Durango Drive Shaft

The DEA was off and running.

Counter-drug ops were underway around the globe. Of particular concern were the developments in America's neighbor to the south.

Mexican traffickers had been involved in smuggling drugs into the United States for years. During World War II, the Allies found themselves cut off from various sources of needed medicinal drugs, and Mexico became a leading source of morphine. Mexico also supplied much of the hemp needed for rope. After the war, those involved in morphine production switched to producing heroin, and those growing hemp for rope simply sold their marijuana on the illicit market.

In 1969, President Nixon tried to end the influx by requiring every person and every vehicle crossing the border to be searched. Operation Intercept created huge traffic jams and raised the hackles of civil liberties groups and newspaper editors to a feverish degree, and there was a public clamor for the searches to stop. Intercept was terminated.

A lesson had been learned. The government decided to try a different approach in the form of increased support of Mexican attempts to eliminate cannabis and opium operations.

But with the shutting down of the French Connection and the sharp drop in Southeast Asian heroin, the aid came too late to prevent a dramatic jump in the Mexican heroin trade.

One of the leading Mexican traffickers was James Herrera-Nevares. He headed a family-run criminal empire that had been involved in heroin since the 1950s. Their operation was unique at the time in that the family was in total control of the operation, from the cultivation of the opium poppy plants to the processing and packaging, to smuggling the finished product into the United States.

Herrera-Nevares was an early, obvious target, and bit by bit the DEA made intel inroads.

They knew, for instance, that the family operated out of the village of Los Herreras, in Durango, Mexico. They knew that Herrera-Nevares oversaw a distribution network that stretched from Durango to Chicago. Once there, the heroin was distributed to other United States markets, making Chicago, in effect, the hub of the Herrera-Nevares operation in the United States.

The family was clever. To avoid having their heroin seized, they came up with a novel way of smuggling it. The "Durango drive shaft," as it became known, consisted of a specially constructed sleeve that fit around the drive shafts of various vehicles—a sleeve in which kilos of heroin were hidden.

The family was one of the first groups to rig vehicles with

gas tanks with special compartments for heroin, and they also resorted to a trick widely copied by other traffickers: hiding heroin in door panels.

The DEA believed the Herrera-Nevares family was importing close to eight hundred pounds of heroin into the United States every year. This translated into eight *tons* of cut heroin flooding American streets.

In Chicago, the family controlled an estimated 90 percent of the local heroin market. How much they controlled in other cities was hard to assess, but it was safe to say that their organization was responsible for a large percentage of the United States total.

In Mexico, there was no doubt that the family was the single largest heroin syndicate in the country. Mexican authorities estimated the annual profit from their illegal activities at more than one million dollars, but this might have been much too conservative a figure.

In the mid-'70s, the DEA was able to trace some of the family's financial exchanges amounting to two million dollars' worth, barely 1 percent of the total the family channeled back into Mexico from their United States operations.

In Chicago alone, the Herrera-Nevares group was making $60 million a year. They soon had set up shop in Miami, Los Angeles, Denver, and Pittsburgh. By 1980, they were branching into cocaine and had connections in South America.

The DEA's persistence paid off. In 1979, three key figures in the family's Chicago operation were arrested. But that was only the beginning. The DEA's investigation stretched well into the next decade, and in July of 1985, close to five hundred federal, state, and local law officers arrested 120 drug traffickers linked to the group.

Three years later, Mexican officials closed in south of the

border. Jamie Herrera-Nevares, Sr. and Jamie Herrera-Nevares Jr. were arrested and sent to prison.

Homeland Problems

Another major DEA investigation focused on the notorious Leroy "Nicky" Barnes. Barnes grew up in Harlem, and at an early age he was impressed by the money that drug dealers flashed around. He saw their fancy cars and fine clothes, saw the power they wielded, and he wanted a taste for himself.

The trick, though, was to stay out of jail. Barnes was sent to prison in 1965 for drug dealing. Most would consider prison a bad break, but for Nicky Barnes it was a stroke of luck. While there, he met Crazy Joe Gallo, a gangster who wanted to spread the tentacles of his own drug operation into Harlem. The problem? Gallo's organization was conspicuously short of African-Americans. So the wily Gallo recruited an eager Nicky Barnes.

Prison became Barnes' college. From Gallo he learned the ins and outs. And he learned his lessons well.

One of Gallo's lawyers succeeded in having Barnes' conviction overturned. Back on the streets of Harlem, Barnes did his mentor proud. He set to work establishing a drug network that became so successful, Barnes essentially controlled the heroin trade in the state of New York and spread his operation north into Canada and south into Pennsylvania.

His organization was formidable. At its peak, Barnes had seven lieutenants who oversaw more than a dozen distributors to forty street-level dealers. The money rolled in. Even better, by insulating himself with multiple layers of underlings, Barnes warded off legal prosecution. Time and again he was arrested, and time and again the government could not make the charges stick. Barnes became known as Mr. Untouchable, a nickname he relished.

With his newfound illicit prestige came notoriety. The *New York Times* ran a piece on Barnes and his extravagant lifestyle in 1977. He owned 300 suits, 100 leather coats, and fifty pairs of shoes. A whole fleet of cars could be found in the garages of his five homes. Cadillacs, Lincoln Continentals, Thunderbirds, and a Mercedes-Benz, to name just a few.

Nicky Barnes had it all. He wore the best clothes, ate the best food, rode in the best cars. Bodyguards protected him twenty-four hours a day. He was at the peak, but when you're at the top, the only way to go is down.

The DEA infiltrated the Barnes organization and a solid case was painstakingly built. In 1978 the Federal District Court in Manhattan sentenced Mr. Untouchable to life in prison.

Barnes was not the only high-profile trafficker the DEA was after. They also set their sights on the Black Tuna Gang. Based in Miami, the gang had smuggled an estimated 500 tons of marijuana into the United States.

About their name—"Black Tuna" was the code name for the Colombian who supplied the marijuana. When making radio contact, the Miami members always referred to him as "Black Tuna."

A DEA/FBI task force kicked into gear. They learned that Black Tuna was Raul Davila-Jimeno. Santa Marta, Colombia, was his base of operations. With the millions from the drugs he smuggled he had hired his own private army. He virtually ruled Santa Marta.

Raul Davila-Jimeno had a flair for organization. The gang kept in touch by radio, using code words, and bought equipment so they could listen in on frequencies used by police organizations, the Colombian military, and United States Customs. The trucks that the gang used to transport the marijuana to the coast were rigged electronically so the gang always knew their location.

For a short while in Miami, the Black Tuna Gang based its operations out of the Fountainbleau Hotel.

Money buys unexpected bedfellows, and the Black Tuna Gang was working money-in-fist with the vice president of an upscale Fort Lauderdale yacht brokerage. Through him, the Black Tuna Gang got its hands on a small fleet of very special boats, ingeniously designed so they would not sit low in the water even when they were loaded with marijuana, thus deflecting suspicion should a patrol boat happen by.

After the boats were moored and unloaded, the marijuana was distributed to a number of stash houses along the waterfront, houses invariably in ritzy neighborhoods where they were less likely to draw attention.

Drug traffickers like their cloak-and-dagger. They have resorted to a wide array of codes, hideouts, and special vehicles to keep the law at bay. But it is safe to say that in the entire history of drug dealing, no one ever used a more bizarre signal to start a delivery on its way than the one used by the Black Tuna Gang. When the Miami members needed more marijuana, they sent Raul Davila-Jimeno a box of disposable diapers. It was their way of saying, "the baby is ready, send the mother."

The DEA and FBI dug deeper. They needed to find out who headed the gang's Miami operation. As part of their probe, the agents initiated Operation Banco, delving into the records of Florida banks. They traced the Black Tuna Gang's profits through several financial institutions and discovered that there were two leaders, partners who ran a Miami car agency. The pair were indicted, and with them behind bars, the Black Tuna Gang fell apart.

This case is notable in that it was the first time that the DEA and the FBI combined forces on a drug profit probe.

Advances

While all this was happening, the DEA developed a new tool—the Heroin Signature Program. Heroin could now be analyzed and classified according to its chemical signature, enabling the DEA to have a running database of geographic origin points, which, in turn, helped them to pinpoint sources and identify traffickers.

But heroin was not their only worry. Marijuana smuggling into the United States was on the rise, and, as with heroin, much of it came from Mexico.

Together, the DEA and the Mexican government launched Operation Trizo. This poppy-eradication program centered on three states: Chihuahua, Sinaloa, and Durango. Helicopters sprayed herbicides over thousands of square acres, effectively crippling the poppy crop. Four thousand arrests were made. The Mexican share of the United States market plummeted.

But there were unforseen repercussions. The three states were thrown into economic chaos, and politicians in Mexico City were quick to take notice. In 1978, the Mexican government formally demanded that Operation Trizo come to an end. The DEA had no choice but to honor the request.

Marijuana had also been entering the country from Colombia. Now, with the Mexican output curtailed, the Colombians were happy to boost their production to fill the void. The DEA became aware of the magnitude of the new influx when a ship containing 113 tons of marijuana was seized off the coast of Florida.

"Colombian Gold," as it became widely known, was extremely potent—the marijuana of choice for discriminating users. Never ones to do anything on a small scale, the Colombian growers shipped their product to the United States in huge oceangoing vessels dubbed "mother ships." These vessels would anchor well off shore to elude detection and then were unloaded by well-organized fleets of smaller craft that included yachts, speedboats, and fishing boats.

It was a slick operation, but for every strategy there is a counter-tactic, and the DEA was soon flying air patrols along the Colombian coast. Operation Stopgap had been launched. DEA pilots reported suspicious vessels to the intelligence center in El Paso. From there the intel was relayed to the U.S. Coast Guard, and before long Coast Guard cutters were intercepting and boarding mother ships.

As another first, U.S. Navy satellites were used to track the vessels from Colombia to United States waters.

Operation Stopgap was an enormous success. More than one million pounds of marijuana was seized, an estimated one-third of the yearly influx. It drove the price up, so that by the time Stopgap was phased out, Colombian marijuana had gone from $20 a pound to $80 a pound.

The Medellín Cartel

The statistics were disturbing. By 1974, more than five million Americans had admitted to having used cocaine. By the end of the decade, that figure jumped to 22 million. Cocaine became so widely used because it was regarded as the ideal recreational drug. At first its users were mainly the wealthy, but as supply boomed and prices dropped, everyone got into the act.

Cocaine had an advantage over heroin, if it can be called that, in that it was not as physically addicting. Mental or emotional addiction was another matter, but this was yet to be recognized as a significant concern.

In 1979, cocaine use hit its peak in the United States. That year, it was estimated that 20 percent of the population had tried the drug at least once.

Colombian dealers could barely keep up with demand. But they had a problem. For years, cocaine distribution in the United States had been controlled by the Cubans. Friction developed when the Colombians started to move in on the Cubans' turf. The so-called Cocaine Wars erupted, and a new element became interwoven with the drug trade on a widespread scale: violence.

This was graphically illustrated by an incident at the Dadeland Mall in Florida in July of 1979. A panel truck pulled up in the parking lot of the state's largest shopping center and two men got out and walked into a liquor store. With no warning, and with no regard for bystanders, they gunned down two men inside who were later identified as a Colombian cocaine trafficker and his bodyguard. They also wounded the store clerk.

Headlines about the shooting were splashed across front pages throughout America. For many, it was their first acquaintance with what would later become a daily occurrence.

The Cubans tried to hold on to their share of the cocaine market, but they were outnumbered, outgunned, and outfinanced. As more and more bodies dropped, the two sides came to an agreement. The Cubans were allowed to continue their coke trade, but under conditions dictated by the Colombians.

The DEA only gradually became aware of the change. Agents began to see connections between shipment seizures and realized that what they had taken for isolated incidents were in fact interconnected. A pattern emerged that indicated a highly efficient organization at work.

More and more cocaine was showing up in New York City and other metro areas. Colombian-based traffickers were processing over 70 percent of the product and had an efficient operation running, the most efficient that the DEA had yet seen.

In fact, a trafficking alliance of unprecedented scope has been established by a Colombian named Carlos Enrique Lehder-Rivas. Like Leroy "Nicky" Barnes before him, Lehder's inspiration for his drug empire came from a prison stint. While there, he met a marijuana smuggler by the name of George Jung and learned how Jung had smuggled tons of marijuana in airplanes. When Lehder got out, he began using the same system for smuggling cocaine.

If that was all Lehder had done, he would hardly merit mention. He was just another drug trafficker among many. But then Lehder took the trade to a whole new level. He approached other Colombian drug lords, each ruler of his own drug domain, and soon had a cooperative system of manufacture, transport, and distribution organized.

The Medellín cartel had been born. Lehder, Pablo Escobar, Jorge Ochoa, Griselda Blanco, Jose Rodriguez-Gacha, Benjamin Herrara, and Gustavo were the kingpins of the most formidable drug operation the world had ever seen. Although they were only a handful of the hundreds of Colombian cocaine traffickers, they were the power elite. The city of Medellín, high in the Andes, became *their* city.

To give some idea of the increased breadth of their operation, before they formed the cartel, their total cocaine output was in the range of twenty-five tons a year. Soon after the cartel's formation, the output was 125 tons, and it was rapidly rising.

Increased supply saw an inevitable drop in prices. At one time a kilo of coke had gone for $800,000 on average. Thanks to the new cartel, the price of a kilo in New York City fell to only $30,000, and in Miami, a kilo could be had for the unbelievably paltry sum of $16,000.

Carlos Lehder, always one of the more flamboyant of the cartel members, bought an entire island in the Bahamas that was used as an air base for cocaine flights between Colombia and the United States.

Law enforcement agencies could not help but notice the surge. In 1970, U.S. Customs seized a total of 108 pounds of cocaine. In 1975, they seized more than 700 pounds. At the Miami airport, yearly seizures went from an average of about thirty-six pounds to hundreds. By 1979, the drug trade in south Florida was the state's biggest industry, reaping $10 billion annually, wholesale.

To give a better idea of just how much money was involved, when drug dealers had to total up large amounts of cash, they would weigh it instead of counting it to save time.

The DEA was trying to stop a flood with a thimble, but try they did. In 1979, in conjunction with the U.S. Customs Service, they descended on South Caicos island in the Bahamas. This was not Carlos Lehder's island, but another used as a refueling stop for smugglers from South America bound for the United States. Certain key government officials on South Caicos had been persuaded by the drug dealers to look the other way in exchange for having their pockets lined.

The DEA probe was three-pronged. While they went about investigating the scope of the South Caicos corruption, they put West Caicos, an uninhabited neighboring island, under covert surveillance. West Caicos was where many of the drug-laden planes landed. The third phase involved placing two DEA agents undercover. The pair took their lives in their hands by posing as airplane mechanics, but it paid off. After living in a DEA DC-3 plane for six weeks, they learned the identification numbers of various aircraft that the smugglers used and then passed on the intel so the planes could be intercepted.

The end result was spectacular. A total of twenty-seven aircraft were seized. Over eight tons of marijuana and 1,203 pounds of Quaaludes were confiscated. Seven hundred eighty-five pounds of cocaine was also intercepted. These were the largest such seizures up to that time—yet another indication of how much the flow from South America had increased.

Perhaps the most amazing development was the arrest and conviction of the prime minister of South Caicos. The head of the island nation had himself been bought off by the smugglers.

A Challenging Landscape

Closer to home, a troubling statistic emerged.

By 1979, the number of young American adults who admitted to trying marijuana leaped to 68 percent. It accounted for the estimated fifteen tons of marijuana that Americans were now using annually. Exactly how much of that was "home grown" was hard to determine. One estimate pegged the figure at 25 percent, another at 10 percent. But it was known that most of the American-harvested marijuana came from two states, California and Hawaii.

Accordingly, the DEA initiated a Domestic Cannabis Eradication and Suppression Program. Special agents worked with local authorities to gather intel and help with arrests. The DEA air wing lent support in the form of air searches, and by training local authorities in search techniques.

At first, only California and Hawaii were involved, but as the number of illicit growers climbed, more and more states joined the program, so that by the early 1980s, twenty-five states were included.

The problem was pervasive. To avoid discovery, many marijuana growers harvested their crops in national forests and parks. The pesticides they used to protect their marijuana proved harmful to other plant species. Some growers cut down trees and set up clandestine irrigation systems, thereby harming the ecosystem. Worse, the growers protected their patches with trip wires rigged to explosives, and other booby-traps designed to maim and kill.

Enter PCP

Cocaine use was on the rise. Marijuana use was on the rise. But they were not the only drugs, as the Quaalude seizure on Caicos showed.

In the mid-'70s, phencyclidine, or PCP, hit the drug scene with a vengeance. An animal tranquilizer known on the street as angel dust, PCP was particularly lethal. Of the three dozen deaths attributed to hallucinogenic drugs in 1977, all but one was linked to PCP.

In response, the DEA created a special action office to combat the problem. During the first year and a half, 23 PCP labs were raided and more than 5 million doses were confiscated.

Then, in December of 1978, the DEA made one of the largest PCP seizures in its history. Fifty DEA agents and deputies from the Los Angeles Sheriff's Department swooped down on a PCP lab in Los Angeles. Close to 900 pounds of the drug were found, roughly $300 million worth.

The DEA had made a major dent in the PCP trade.

Drug traffickers were becoming more sophisticated. To hold its own, the DEA had to do the same.

By the end of the decade, the air wing had been expanded. A new DEA lab was built in San Diego, the site dictated by a surge in the amount of heroin entering the southwestern United States from Mexico. The lab was notable for having four times the vault storage space of any other DEA lab in the country.

The DEA extended its basic agent training course from ten weeks to twelve. New agents were given more instruction in law and spent more hours in field training. They were also required to go through a three-day conspiracy school, a step mandated by the growing number of complicated conspiracy cases that the DEA handled.

Thanks to an increase in funding, the DEA was set to begin the 1980s with the best communications technology available. Communications centers were up and running in Dallas, New York City, Los Angeles, and Seattle. Operating 24/7, the centers provided tactical support to agents in the field.

In the late '70s, the DEA adopted the Policefax DD-14 system. Basically a forerunner of modern-day fax machines, the DD-14 transmitted high-quality fingerprints from the DEA's field offices to its central identification bureau. Now agents could learn in a relatively short time whether suspects had prior records.

"Relatively short" was the key phrase. Although the DD-14 was state-of-the-art, it took hours to transmit the data from one machine to another and then fourteen minutes per page to reproduce the fingerprints.

Still, it was an invaluable tool, and as the new decade loomed, the DEA would need all the high-tech tools it could find to deal with the challenges on the horizon.

If the DEA thought the last five years had been hectic, they hadn't seen anything yet.

1981–1985

High on Cocaine

As the 1980s dawned, international drug traffickers were operating on a scale never before witnessed. Their organizations were, in the main, well structured and efficient. They controlled all aspects of their illegal trade, from growing to processing to distribution.

Cocaine was everywhere. On average it was being sold for $100 a gram, at over 50 percent purity. The United States government tried every method it could devise to warn of the danger: radio and TV spots, newspaper advertisements, testimonials by those who had been swept up in the drug culture and come to their senses, passionate appeals by religious and political leaders. But was anyone listening?

The public still widely regarded cocaine as harmless. It didn't help that certain high-profile drug users, notably movie and TV stars along with certain writers, praised drug use as the be-all and end-all of existence. Timothy Leary and those of his ilk waxed eloquent about how drugs could expand human consciousness and take humankind to a whole new level of understanding and love. No surprise, then, that drugs and sex became inextricably linked, the one to enhance the other.

In 1981, *Time* magazine did a cover story entitled "High on Cocaine." Coke was running rampant through middle-class America, *Time* reported, and had become *the* drug for untold millions of what *Time* described as "conventional and often upwardly mobile citizens." The verbal picture *Time* painted was a rosy one.

But was the situation really so serene? No. Drug use was off the scale, as was drug-related violence. Rival traffickers were fighting for their share of the extremely lucrative market, and they did not care how many bystanders were hurt in their gun battles.

As drug use proliferated, so too did the number of labs that produced the drugs. South Florida, in particular, had become a Mecca of conversion labs, laboratories which turned cocaine base into HCl, the form in which coke was sold on the street. Florida was not the only state, though. By the mid-1980s, authorities had raided four labs in California, four in New York, and one each in Arizona and North Carolina, and the numbers kept climbing. The authorities raided nearly two dozen labs in 1986 alone.

All this was bad enough, but far worse was to come.

The cocaine glut brought on an unforeseen problem for the traffickers. There was so much of the drug that prices dropped to all-time lows. That impacted profits, and they couldn't have that. They were in the drug trade for one reason only: to make lots and lots of money.

Their solution was diabolically ruthless, and its aftermath caused social devastation on a staggering scale.

The drug trade came up with crack, a smokeable form of cocaine. It was easy to make and cheap to produce, and at first glance it might not seem much of an improvement from a marketing standpoint. But there was a major difference between ordinary cocaine and crack, a crucial difference that would wreak havoc with countless lives.

Crack was horribly addictive. Users were hooked in a very short time, and the habit was extremely hard to shake. Worse, in order to feed their need, crack users would do anything for money. They would rob, they would mug others, they would kill if they had to.

Within a few short years of crack's advent, hospitals saw a gigantic upsurge in the number of drug-related emergency-room treatments. By 1985, the total had jumped a whopping 12 percent. But that was nothing. The very next year, with the crack epidemic in full bloom, the figure skyrocketed a staggering 110 percent.

The DEA first became aware of the new threat in 1981. That was the year when they received reports of crack use in the Caribbean, Los Angeles, San Diego, and Houston. That was also the year when the first crack house was raided, in Miami.

But the full extent of the menace was not readily apparent. At first, most of the users were middle-class—white professionals and suburban teens. No one realized how quickly crack would permeate every strata of society, or how addicted and violent its users would become.

Crack first appeared in New York City in December of 1983. By 1986, it had spread like wildfire through the city's less affluent neighborhoods. New traffickers came on the scene, foremost among them violent dealers from the Dominican Republic.

The fire spread. By the end of 1986, crack use was documented in twenty-eight states and the District of Columbia. By the end of 1987, crack was available in all but four states.

In nineteen cities nationwide, crack use and the violence associated with it surged to epidemic levels. Miami, Los Angeles, and New York City were hardest hit. But cities like Detroit and Dallas, Portland and Minneapolis, Kansas City and Oklahoma City, America's heartland, became battlegrounds in the war on drugs.

Crack-related murders went through the statistical roof. In New York City alone, Bureau of Justice figures revealed that 32 percent of all murders were linked to crack, but the actual figure was much higher. When all factors were entered in, over 60 percent of *all* drug-related homicides were linked to crack use.

The violence spread throughout the country. Evening newscasts in major cities reported endless drive-by shootings by rival gang members and crimes committed by users to get their hands on badly needed money for their next fix.

The situation was grim.

Incredibly, it got worse.

Crack was so cheap to produce that the cost to the user was as little as $5 a rock. Because it was easy to use and did not involve needles or have the stigma of "bad" drugs like heroin, crack appealed to a whole new element of society, an element that had traditionally tended to shun drugs. That element was women. Soon, many thousands of women were hooked. That in itself was tragic. More so was the fact that many women became pregnant while addicted, resulting in a whole generation of what the media dubbed "crack babies." These babies were often developmentally traumatized and abandoned by their mothers, who couldn't afford to support both their infants and their habits, and were compelled by their addictions to choose to feed their habits.

By the end of the decade, it was believed that one out of every ten babies born in the United States had been exposed to crack or some other harmful drug while in the womb.

The government, rightfully, was alarmed. It was decided that the best and quickest way to stem the crack epidemic was to stem the flow of cocaine into the country.

Not an easy task. The Medellín cartel was at the height of its power, and cartel members would do anything to stay on top. Assassinations, intimidation, and bombings were common occurrences in Colombia. The country had the highest murder rate in the world. In Medellín, in 1985, the cartel allegedly killed 1,698 people. A year later, the blood of an additional 3,500 victims was believed to be on their hands. Judges, legislators, the military, the police—no one was immune.

The Medellín cartel had become the most feared criminal syndicate in all of South America.

In the United States, the Colombian rings were expanding their financial horizons. They began to invest in legitimate businesses, especially in the banking and import sectors. They still controlled a lion's share of the cocaine market, but they were not its undisputed masters. New gangs—from the Dominican Republic, Haiti, and elsewhere—who were not afraid of the Colombians, and not averse to spraying lead, all wanted a piece of the pie.

Another rival, the Cali mafia, had become entrenched in the Northeast. Unlike the Medellín cartel, Cali members tended to shun violence and keep a low profile, but they were every bit as adept at marketing their product.

The War on Drugs

At the start of the 1980s, the DEA was largely focused on the Colombians. Operation Swordfish was launched. Centered in Miami, it involved setting up a corporation for the sole purpose of laundering money for drug dealers. By 1982, when the op ended, about seventy people had been indicted and a large quantity of cocaine had been seized, along with tons of marijuana and a quarter of a million methaqualone pills.

The huge marijuana seizure was a sign that the Colombians were as active in that aspect of the trade as in cocaine.

In 1981, the DEA, cooperating with the U.S. Coast Guard and twenty-one federal, state, and local agencies, launched the largest op to date. DEA agents went undercover, some working with the smugglers themselves. It was learned that the Colombians were making deliveries as far away as Maine. Eventually, more than one billion dollars' worth of drugs were seized, and 122 suspects ended up behind bars.

The very next year, the DEA tried a similar op, again with sensational results. Nearly 500 people were arrested. Ninety-five vessels were seized. Over a million pounds of marijuana in the United States and nearly five million pounds in Colombia were permanently taken off the market.

Interdepartmental cooperation was paying big dividends. Consequently, the Justice Department reorganized its drug effort. The DEA and the FBI formally joined forces. They now had concurrent jurisdiction in drug cases. The upshot was that more manpower could be utilized, with enhanced tech support.

Meanwhile, the DEA was active on other fronts. Methaqualone use had risen dramatically—by 40 percent in one year alone. Amazingly, the proliferation of so-called stress clinics were to blame. In Florida, New York, and New Jersey, under the guise of dispensing legitimate medical treatment, dozens of clinics were dispensing Quaaludes like candy, many of the tablets counterfeit, from overseas.

DEA investigations resulted in thirty-eight indictments. The publicity convinced Florida and Georgia to drop methaqualone from their list of substances acceptable for medical use.

Running with the idea, the DEA got together with the U.S. Department of State. Diplomatic overtures were extended to countries in Asia and Europe that produced the drug. Five of those countries clamped down. In 1984, the U.S. Congress effectively curtailed domestic production. By 1985, methaqualone emergency room treatments were down by 83 percent.

It was a tremendous coup for the DEA and other agencies involved. For the first time ever, the trafficking and use of a given drug was nearly completely stamped out.

Inroads were also being made against heroin, or so the DEA thought. The number of overdose deaths had fallen by 80 percent. The number of heroin addicts had dropped from more than half a million to about 350,000. The amount of heroin entering the country was down by 40 percent.

Then the heroin hit the fan, so to speak. A tidal wave of "horse" poured into the United States from the Golden Crescent in Southwest Asia. Afghanistan, Pakistan, and Iran were the major suppliers.

As if that were not bad enough, the DEA learned that the infamous French Connection drug route, with many of the same smugglers from France, Italy, and West Germany, was once again in business.

The DEA had a U.S. Customs Service dog to thank. While

conducting a routine check of a furniture shipment out of Palermo, Italy, the dog responded positively. Small wonder. Close to fifty pounds of heroin was hidden in the furniture.

The DEA was called in. Agents posing as truck drivers delivered the furniture to its destinations in Detroit and New York City. One man in Detroit and three in the Big Apple were arrested.

But the real hotbed of drug activity continued to be South Florida. The numbers of drug-related murders and crimes went through the stratosphere. In Miami, in 1979, there were 349 murders, almost one per day. In 1981, the number of drug murders rocketed to 621. Local law agencies did their best, but they were overwhelmed.

President Reagan took notice. Hundreds of extra federal agents were assigned to a South Florida Task Force. Miami received twenty more DEA agents and forty-three more FBI agents. The U.S. Treasury Department sent in experienced analysts to track the drug money. And for the first time ever, the United States military became involved in domestic drug interdiction.

It was all part of an intensive national effort to combat the growing nightmare. Twelve more drug task forces were soon up and running across the country. A special panel was formed to keep tabs on organized crime's part in drug trafficking. A federal facility in Georgia became a training center for state and local law officers.

The DEA had its share of successes. But as before, success in one area invariably resulted in a new problem elsewhere.

When the United States and Mexican governments were able to severely limit the amount of drugs coming across the border, the smugglers quickly adapted. Once again, the Caribbean became a prime drug route, but with a difference. Where before the smugglers had relied on ordinary oceangoing vessels and conventional planes, their new wealth gave them access to powerful speedboats and faster aircraft fitted with the latest in high-tech hardware, including global positioning equipment and cellular communications.

As if that were not enough of a tactical hurdle for the DEA to overcome, the drugs were being funneled through an area comprising some 100,000 square miles of open water. The smugglers had their choice of 700 islands to use as intermediate bases. This added another 5,382 square miles. In short, it was akin to searching for the proverbial needle in a haystack.

The DEA could not do it alone. Thankfully, they didn't have to. The United States government enjoyed a fine rapport with the Government of the Caicos and Turks Island, and with the Commonwealth of the Bahamas. The Royal Police Forces of both joined the DEA, the U.S. Coast Guard, the U.S. Customs Service, and the Southern and Atlantic Military Commands in trying to bring the traffickers to justice.

Whether the impact they made had a bearing or not, the influx of drugs along the United States-Mexico border increased. New Mexico state troopers first became suspicious when they realized that a growing number of routine traffic stops and checks of vehicles were resulting in drug arrests and seizures. The obvious conclusion was that more drugs were being brought across.

Interestingly, at about the same time, New Jersey state troopers saw an increase in drug arrests along their highways.

The smugglers had developed a pipeline clear from Mexico into the Northeastern United States via the nation's highways. The DEA's response, fittingly enough, was called Operation Pipeline.

Early on, law officers had noticed that drug couriers fit a

certain profile. Interview techniques were perfected to elicit incriminating information. Knowing what to ask became as important as making the stop.

Operation Pipeline brought highway patrol and police officers from around the country together to learn from officers who were experts in highway interdiction.

The op was successful beyond anyone's wildest expectations. Between the mid-1980s and 1998, some 34,000 highway drug seizures took place. Among the drugs confiscated were over one hundred thousand kilos of cocaine, 350 kilograms of heroin, almost half a million kilos of methedrine, and over eight hundred thousand kilograms of marijuana.

South America

Down in South America, a startling situation was taking form.

It began when a DEA attaché in Bogotá stumbled on a crucial overlooked fact. The attaché requested that a study be done on chemical imports into Colombia, specifically ether and acetone, which were used in the manufacture of illegal drugs. To the DEA's consternation, they discovered that 98 percent of the ether imported into Colombia was being used to produce cocaine. Even more staggering, 90 percent of it came from West Germany—and the United States.

The DEA contacted United States chemical firms and asked them to send word whenever large orders were placed.

The attaché's discovery reaped amazing dividends. When a Colombian walked into a chemical company in New Jersey and placed an order for two metric tons of ether, offering to pay cash, company officials contacted the DEA.

The DEA quickly set up a sting operation. They created a front company called North Central Industrial Chemical and got in touch with the Colombian. They could fill his order, they said. Was he interested? He certainly was. He had seventy-six drums of ether shipped to New Orleans. From there the drums were shipped out of the United States.

What the Colombian didn't know was that the DEA had rigged two of the drums with tracking devices. Using satellites, the DEA tracked the drums to Colombia, to a little village in the remote jungle, a village with the quaint name of Tranquilandia.

The DEA and Colombian National Police thought they had uncovered a Medellín cartel lab. They carefully and quietly organized a raid. What they found stunned them. There wasn't a lab, there was an entire *factory*. A production line for cocaine, if you will, with living quarters for more than 100 people, storage areas, and workshops where cars, trucks and planes used to smuggle drugs could be maintained and repaired. This one facility was capable of synthesizing twenty tons of coke each month. In two years, it had put $12 billion into the bank accounts of cartel members.

Tranquilandia was not the only drug factory. As months passed, more were found. It placed the scope of the Medellín Cartel's operation on a whole new level.

Another indicator turned up elsewhere.

The DEA had a money-laundering op in place, called Operation Pisces. The intel revealed a direct money link between the Medellín cartel and street gangs in the United States. That was not surprising. What *was* surprising, though, was that the DEA learned that the drug lords were making $4 million *per month* in drug profits.

The Medellín cartel was rolling in money. With the purity level of their cocaine at 90 percent or higher, drug dealers were clamoring for their product. By the end of the decade, an estimated 10,000 gang members were involved in the drug trade in at least fifty United States cities from coast to coast.

In 1985, a chance occurrence revealed that not all the coke was being imported. In April of that year, the South Minden Fire Department of Minden, New York raced to a fire on a ten-acre farm. They quickly doused the flames, and that proved very fortuitous: if they hadn't, the fire would have caused an explosion powerful enough to leave a crater a quarter of a mile in diameter.

The farm was a drug lab. And what a lab! More than 200 fifty-gallon drums of ether and other drugs were discovered on the site. The lab facilities themselves consisted of high-tech equipment, vats for mixing, the works. All told, the lab could turn out $700 million in cocaine yearly. Subsequent arrests showed that this wasn't a Medellín operation; it was the brainchild of the Cali mafia.

Casualty

The Colombians were not the only major drug rings involved in illicit substances.

Down in Mexico, the Guadalajara mafia had been born. It had close links to the Colombians. Not satisfied with smuggling cocaine and marijuana into the United States, the Guadalajara ring began smuggling Mexican black tar, which was heroin in powder form.

They had thousands of airfields at their disposal, both registered and unregistered, from which drug flights could penetrate United States air space.

All this gives some idea of what the DEA was up against. An army of drug dealers on America's streets. Global cartels with unlimited financial resources. Crooked politicians taking money under the table. Judges and others in South and Central America who tried to nip the supply at its source were assassinated—or "mysteriously disappeared."

Make no mistake: those involved in the drug trade were savagely ruthless. They would kill anyone who got in their way. Men, women, children—it made no difference. That applied to DEA agents as well, and in 1985, one of those agents lost his life in an incident that made headlines around the world and hardened the DEA's resolve more than anything else could.

Special Agent Enrique Camarena was typical of the DEA's idealistic young bloods. He viewed drugs as a serious and grave threat, and he was doing his part to combat it.

Special Agent Camarena had been assigned to the DEA's resident office in Guadalajara. On February 7, 1985, he left the office to meet his wife for lunch. He never showed up. As he was walking down the street, a car pulled up and four men jumped out. Special Agent Camarena was shoved into the back seat and the car sped off.

A few hours later, a Mexican national, a pilot named Alfredo Zavala Avelar, who was working with authorities, was also snatched.

By then, Mrs. Camarena had reported to the DEA that her husband had not shown up. Resident Agent in Charge James Kuykendall contacted DEA headquarters.

The Mexican police were asked to lend a hand. DEA agents in Guadalajara got in touch with informants. The United States ambassador asked the Mexican attorney general for help. Every attaché in Latin America was notified and told to uncover what they could. The DEA sent twenty-five special agents to Guadalajara to help in the search.

It did not take long to identify the alleged ringleaders behind Special Agent Camarena's disappearance. They were Ernesto Fonseca-Carrillo, Miguel Felix-Gallardo, and Rafael Caro-Quintero, three Guadalajara drug traffickers.

On February 9, Mexican Federal Judicial Police stopped Quintero from taking off in his private jet. But incredibly, after a short standoff, Quintero was allowed to leave.

The DEA was braced for the worst. Their fears were realized. A farmworker came across two bodies in a field in Michoacan, Mexico. One proved to be that of Special Agent Camarena, the other that of Avelar, the pilot. The FBI took soil samples and determined that the pair had been buried elsewhere, then dug up and dumped in Michoacan. Autopsies revealed they had been tortured, and that death in both cases came from blows to the head.

Special Agena Camarena's body was returned to the United States—yet another federal officer killed in the line of duty. That might have been the end of it, but it wasn't. The case made headlines throughout the United States and the world. Public attention became focused on the DEA, and what the DEA was trying to do, as never before. Special Agent Camarena's death made the drug war more personal, more real, to untold millions of Americans who otherwise hadn't given it much thought.

The publicity had an astounding effect in Mexico. Mexican authorities had sometimes been accused of dragging their heels in criminal investigations, but there was no heel-dragging this time.

On March 14, the Mexican federal judicial police let the DEA know that the MFJP had taken five Jalisco state police officers into custody. The five were alleged to have taken part in Special Agent Camarena's abduction.

Strangely, the DEA was not brought into the loop in the

MFJP investigation. The MFJP did not ask the DEA for help or cooperation, nor would it allow the DEA to take part in subsequent interviews of the suspects.

One of the Jalisco state police officers died while being questioned. Statements made by all five implicated Rafael Caro-Quintero and Ernesto Fonseca-Carrillo as the masterminds behind Camarena's torture and murder.

By March 17, eleven other individuals believed to be involved had been arrested. Warrants were out for others.

But it was the DEA who learned that Caro-Quintero was hiding in Costa Rica. On April 4, DEA agents, working with Costa Rican authorities, took him into custody. Before anything further could be done, the MFJP convinced the Costa Rican government to extradite him to Mexico. On April 5, Caro-Quintero and those taken into custody with him winged their way out of Costa Rico on Mexican government jets.

If the DEA was worried that Caro-Quintero might elude arrest, they need not have been. He was flown straight to Mexico City and interrogated. He implicated himself and others in the abduction but claimed not to know who actually committed the murder.

On April 7, Mexican police arrested another Guadalajara drug lord, Ernesto Fonseca-Carrillo, in Puerto Vallarta. He was taken to Mexico City. As with Quintero, he admitted his part in the abduction but disavowed any knowledge of who was responsible for Special Agent Camarena's death.

Interestingly, both Quintero and Carrillo pointed the finger of blame at Miguel Felix-Gallardo.

So far, so good. Two of the reputed kingpins had been caught. Then came a shocker. Word reached the DEA that there was an audio tape of Camarena's last minutes on earth;

his torture had been recorded. The Mexican government had the tape in its possession but had not told the DEA.

Surprise piled on surprise. There wasn't one tape, there were five. Under tremendous pressure from the United States government, Mexican officials supplied copies.

The DEA established its own investigation. Called Operation Leyenda—"Leyenda" is Spanish for "lawman"—the DEA eventually brought a number of the perpetrators to trial.

But that wasn't the end of the Camarena saga. A high school friend of his, Henry Lozano, along with a congressman and others, started the Camarena Clubs campaign. Club members pledged to live drug-free lives. The program earned national attention when the Clubs presented a proclamation to First Lady Nancy Reagan. Parents in California, Virginia, and Illinois expanded the program, and soon one week in October was chosen for wearing red ribbons in honor of Special Agent Camarena's sacrifice. National Red Ribbon Week became a symbol of support for the DEA.

They would need it.

1986–1990

The World . . . and Everything in It

The second half of the decade saw new developments on the domestic front. Congress passed the Anti–Drug Abuse Act, allocating $6 billion over the next three years for drug interdiction. Criminal penalties were increased.

President Reagan issued an executive order that, among other things, required federal employees in sensitive positions to be tested for the use of illegal drugs.

In June of 1986, two drug-related incidents made the news. University of Maryland basketball star Len Bias, who had recently signed with the Boston Celtics, died of heart failure induced by cocaine. Then, just eight days later, Cleveland Browns football player Don Rodgers died of a cocaine overdose. Combined, these two brought renewed national attention to the drug problem and reinforced the DEA's contention that cocaine was not by any stretch of the imagination "benign."

The pro-drug crowd was still trying to convince the American public that drugs should be decriminalized. In the face of overwhelming evidence to the contrary, they maintained that what a person did in the privacy of his or her own home was not in any way harmful to anyone else. They completely ignored the staggering social costs and branded the war on drugs a waste of resources and funds.

The American public remained unconvinced. Americans could see the results of drug use on the nightly news; drive-by shootings, overdoses, addicted mothers abandoning their children. Americans saw their public schools turned into armed camps. They weren't about to be fooled.

It didn't help, though, that the entertainment industry, while giving the drug war verbal support, glorified drug use in songs, videos, and movies. This was nothing new. Movies like *Scarface*, while purporting to show the evils of the drug trade, tended to glamorize it. Yes, the movie ends with the death of the protagonists, but an underlying message is that big bucks are made selling drugs. So what if Al Pacino's character met his end in a bloodbath of Homeric proportions? Before he died, he had it all, or thought he did. To a poor kid on the streets, it wasn't Tony Montana's death that mattered. It was all that money, the mansion, the cars, the girls, the *power*.

In June of 1986, the DEA set Operation Blast Furnace into motion. Bolivia had become one of the world's major cocaine-producing nations, with hundreds of farmers growing coca leaf to be used in the making of coca paste. To nip the flow in the bud, the DEA and Bolivian Narcotics Strike Force troops conducted sweeping raids on eight labs.

United States Blackhawk helicopters, flown by Army pilots, ferried in the strike teams. They struck so swiftly that the traffickers were taken completely by surprise. There was hardly any resistance.

It was a major coup. The flow of cocaine out of Bolivia dried up. Traffickers not snared in the op fled the country. The coca leaf market in Bolivia collapsed. In fact, the market was so depressed, Bolivian farmers appealed to the U.S. Agency for International Development for aid so they could grow legal crops.

The very next year, the DEA scored another coup, but this time it was against the Medellín cartel.

Back in 1981, flamboyant Carlos Lehder had been indicted in Jacksonville, Florida, on federal charges. In 1983, the United States goverment formally requested that Lehder be extradited, but the Colombian government delayed any action.

Lehder's influence in his native country had continued to grow. Never one to do things in a small way, he formed his own political party. Part of his party's platform was a vehement opposition to extradition.

Lehder's political rhetoric centered on Colombian sovereignty. It was not right, he said, for the United States to meddle in internal Colombian affairs. He asserted that cocaine was an important tool in resisting United States dominance, and he claimed to be working closely with M-19, a popular Colombian guerrilla group.

Some Colombians listened. They resented the United States presence. They saw it as an encroachment, not a benefit. They wanted Colombia's problems solved by Colombians. What they definitely didn't want was to have Colombians sent to the United States to face trial on foreign soil.

Equally as many Colombians were for extradition. They saw through Lehder's deception.

In 1984, things came to a head. Lehder and his party were opposed by Colombia's popular justice minister, Rodrigo Lara-Bonilla. Rather than engage Lara-Bonilla in public debate, the cartel resorted to its old tactics. The justice minister was murdered.

Enough was enough. The Colombian government arrested Carlos Lehder, and in February of 1987 he was extradited to the United States. Convicted, Lehder was given 135 years in prison.

But the Medellín cartel was far from finished. Its other leaders were alive and thriving. Lehder's arrest had no effect on their operation or on the terrorist tactics they had adopted.

In 1988, the cartel had Colombia's attorney general assassinated. In 1989, presidential candidate Luis Carlos Galan, an outspoken critic, joined the long list of victims.

Then, in 1989, another cartel bigwig suffered a setback.

The Colombian government had traced the financial dealings of Jose Rodriguez-Gacha, right-hand man to Pablo Escobar, to secret bank accounts in Switzerland and other countries. The DEA, in cooperation with agencies in Europe and the Colombian National Police, froze $80 million of Rodriguez-Gacha's assets. Most of the money was later divided between the countries that took part.

Rodriguez-Gacha, though, was still at large. Like Lehder, he would prove to be nowhere near as formidable as another Medellín drug lord, one who would bring Colombia to the brink of total anarchy, one whose name the world would come to know: Pablo Escobar.

Back on the home front, the Office of National Drug Control Policy had been created as part of yet another anti-drug act passed by Congress. The media dubbed its director America's "Drug Czar."

The pro-drug lobby wasn't idle, either. Their efforts to have marijuana legalized resulted in a ruling from an administrative law judge that would have resulted in doctors being able to prescribe marijuana as a medical treatment.

It had long been claimed that marijuana served legitimate medicinal purposes. Many people sincerely believed that it could relieve the suffering of cancer patients undergoing various treatments. Studies indicated differently. Nor was marijuana found to help patients with glaucoma or multiple sclerosis. To the contrary, research found that it weakened the immune system, rather than strengthening it, and might actually speed up—not slow down—the loss of eyesight due to glaucoma.

Proponents insisted that Delta-9-Tetrahydrocannabinol, or THC, one of some 400 chemicals in marijuana, reduced vomiting and nausea. But THC was already available in capsule form.

For these reasons, and others, the DEA administrator overruled the judge. It did not enamor the agency to the pro-drug lobby, but then, this lobby had been intensely opposed to the DEA from the moment of its inception.

In 1989, the DEA took part in Operation Green Merchant. The op targeted marijuana cultivators in the Netherlands who were selling cannabis seeds through the mail. The seeds came from indoor marijuana grows, and in order to locate them, the DEA tried a new heat-seeking technology, thermal imaging. It proved to be spectacularly effective—so much so that within a few short years, the number of indoor operations the DEA uncovered jumped a whopping 175 percent. The DEA had stumbled onto an effective new tool.

The two biggest drug-related events of 1989, however, did not have anything to do with marijuana.

In February, former Panamanian strongman Manuel Noriega was indicted by a grand jury in Florida. The United States government alleged that Noriega had been in league with the Medellín cartel, and that under his regime, Panama not only served as a shipping point for cartel cocaine but as a sanctuary for cartel members. Noriega allegedly helped obtain chemicals for the cartel and helped launder cocaine money through several Panamanian banks.

In effect, the Medellín cartel had a whole country at its disposal. The same could be said of Colombia, but many Colombians were critics of the cartel, as the more than 1,000 murders a year demonstrated. In Panama, Noriega basically gave the cartel carte blanche, with official sanction.

For United States officials, this was an alarming development. The war on drugs had become a variation on the domino theory, with country after country gradually falling under the drug trade's sway. In Panama, thanks to Noriega's willing and overt cooperation, the Medellín cartel had taken the war to a whole new level.

It was a precedent that could not be allowed to go unchallenged. Other countries might be tempted to follow Noriega's lead. If the United States sat back and did nothing, the collective influence of the drug cartels in Central America would grow exponentially.

America simply had to do something, and America did.

On December 20, 1989, the United States invaded Panama. For weeks Manuel Noriega evaded capture, but as the net was tightening he gave himself up to the DEA. He was flown to Miami and held there. Over the next two years, the DEA conducted an extensive investigation, and with a mountain of evidence to bolster its case, Noriega was brought to trial in 1991.

The case made headlines everywhere. The American public was shocked by the revelations, which showed how pervasive drug operations could become and gave the public much food for thought.

Among the many witnesses for the prosecution was one that had cartel members in Colombia furious. Their old buddy and fellow cartel kingpin, Carlos Lehder, struck a deal with federal authorities. In exchange for having his sentence partially reduced, he told everything he knew about the cartel's dealings with Noriega.

Ultimately, Manuel Noriega was sentenced to forty years in prison. He appealed, claiming he had been framed. His case went all the way to the U.S. Supreme Court, but the high court would not overturn his conviction. He had received a fair trial and must take his punishment.

Cocaine to Spare

Americans were given a timely reminder of how much cocaine was entering their country when the DEA conducted a raid on a warehouse in Sylmar, California. Over twenty-one tons were seized.

Normally, the drug lords did not stockpile anywhere near that amount. They were prudently wary of exactly what happened in Sylmar, and they would not let that much of their product be stockpiled and thus vulnerable to seizure.

But a schism had developed between the overlords in Colombia and the Mexican networks they relied on to ship their drugs. Inexplicably, the Colombians hadn't been making timely payments to the Mexicans for services rendered. The Mexicans naturally resented it, and they refused to distribute the coke until the Colombians made good.

The Sylmar seizure spurred the Colombians into making a decision that was to have a profound impact on the drug trade. It was a decision based purely on greed.

The Colombians could easily have paid up. One thing not in short supply at their end was money. They could fill their swimming pools with it. But instead of forking over what they owed, they proposed something else.

There was one other thing the Colombians had in abundance: cocaine. They were producing so much that they reasoned they had cocaine to spare. Consequently, they offered the Mexican traffickers a deal. Instead of paying, they would let their Mexican allies keep up to half of each shipment to cover expenses.

The Colombians thought it was a smart move. They were saving money. In the long run, it would enrich their swollen coffers even more. But their decision was shortsighted. It failed to take into account the fact that their Mexican cohorts were motivated by the same overriding greed.

Suddenly the Mexican traffickers had more cocaine than they knew what to do with. They quickly turned their surplus into pesos by going into the coke business for themselves.

Now criminal syndicates south of the border were not merely traffickers; they were distributors and dealers as well.

The net effect was to make the Mexican drug picture drastically worse.

As the decade closed, the DEA was honing its resources. DEA headquarters was moved from Washington, D.C. to Virginia, a step mandated by the equivalent of growing pains. The house in D.C. had long since burst at the seams, and the DEA's 1,500 headquarters personnel were spread among a dozen other buildings. Their new facility in Arlington centralized their operation, and it also left room for expansion.

The DEA changed its training facility as well. They wanted one geared toward drug-law enforcement. A site was chosen adjacent to the FBI Training Academy at Quantico. Since the DEA and FBI often worked together, the new facility permitted the two agencies' personnel to take various training courses together. That would translate into smoother cooperation in the field.

In the tech department, the DEA had a computer network up and running by 1986. It was about time. Computerization increased efficiency. Over subsequent years there would be periodic upgrades to enable the DEA to effectively deal with increasingly complex drug organizations.

Finally, the DEA expanded its air wing. The number of aircraft had grown from thirty to more than sixty—so many that, at their old facility, aircraft were often left sitting out in the open where anyone could tamper with them because there wasn't enough hangar space.

A new site in Texas solved the problem. Forth Worth became the DEA's air hub. From there, planes could be dispatched to the East and West Coasts in about the same flying time. Even better, Fort Worth was close to Mexico, and that much closer to Central and South America, where so many of the DEA's air ops were conducted.

This, then, was the state of affairs between the DEA and its adversaries as the 1990s began. The DEA had some major successes to its credit, but its many enemies were firmly entrenched and determined to flood America with an endless torrent of illegal drugs.

Little did the DEA know that their ongoing battle with one of their oldest foes, the Medellín cartel, was about to come to a head. And when the dust settled, only one of them would still be standing.

1991–1994

The Fall of the Medellín Cartel

The leaders of the Medellín cartel did not realize it at the time, but the arrest of Carlos Lehder was a harbinger of things to come.

The cartel was fighting viciously for its life. Cartel members did not want to share Lehder's fate. Their campaign against extradition took on the form of a bloodthirsty frenzy. Dozens of government officials in favor of extradition were exterminated. Scores more were bribed into mouthing the cartel party line.

But perhaps "bribe" is the wrong word, considering that everyone knew refusal meant certain death. In effect, the cartel held out a wad of cash in one hand and a pistol in the other, then said, "Choose."

In July of 1991, the Medellín cartel scored an impressive political victory. The Colombian congress adopted a new constitution that expressly prohibited extradition of Colombian nationals.

Pablo Escobar and his cronies were elated. All their hard work—the many assassinations and bombings and bribes—had paid off handsomely. They had everything they wanted—but their triumph was short-lived. The sweet taste of victory soon turned into the bitter taste of defeat. In their arrogance and conceit, they failed to take into account the fact that many of their countrymen had had enough.

Most Colombians were not involved in the drug trade. Most were honest, hardworking people who had grown to resent having the cartel lord it over them as if Colombia were the cartel's private plaything.

Some cartel members saw the handwriting on the wall early. In December of 1990, cartel leader Fabio Ochoa turned himself over to authorities. In January, his brother, Jorge Luis, surrendered. A third brother, Juan David, soon followed suit.

Pablo Escobar was now top kingpin. But he soon experienced a severe setback when the assassin who routinely performed Escobar's many killings was himself killed in a gun battle with police.

The assassin's name was David Ricardo Prisco. He and his younger brother, Armando, were wanted for the murders of more than fifty Colombian police officers, as well as for nine assassinations that included a justice minister, and for assorted bombings.

The death of David Prisco shook Escobar. His strong right arm, his rabid wolf on a leash, was gone. He took a cue from the Ochoas: he turned himself in and was placed in Envigado prison.

Case closed. Or was it? The DEA soon learned that things were not as they seemed. During Escobar's negotiations with the Colombian government over the terms of his surrender, certain "concessions" were granted. Escobar was allowed to retain his bodyguards. No restrictions were placed on his movements within the prison or on his contacts with the outside world.

The wily Escobar had done the unthinkable. He had turned Envigado prison into his own private sanctuary and continued to run his drug empire from behind its walls. The sweetest aspect of the whole arrangement was that no one could touch him. Not the DEA, not his rivals, not diehards in the Colombian government who thought he had gotten off too lightly.

All went well until once again Pablo Escobar's arrogance got the better of him. He was convinced that certain of his cartel associates were out to topple him, so he gave orders to have twenty-two of them eliminated. Amazingly, he had two brought to Envigado prison, where he personally oversaw their torture and deaths.

Word leaked to Colombian authorities. They were outraged. Those Escobar had bribed could no longer protect him. It was decided to transfer Escobar to a Bogotá jail. But Escobar was warned, and newspapers the next day bore headlines proclaiming his escape.

In truth, Pablo Escobar had simply walked out, taking his entourage with him. Close to thirty members of the prison staff were later charged with aiding him.

Escobar was once again free, but freedom came at a high price. He became the focus of the largest manhunt in his country's history. For almost a year and a half he eluded capture. Then the Colombian national police traced him to a residence in Medellín. They closed in, and a firefight broke out. Escobar and his bodyguard tried to escape by fleeing across the rooftops. They were gunned down.

That is the official version in a nutshell.

The truth might be something else entirely. It is far too convoluted to present here, especially since it does not pertain directly to the DEA. The players in the drama include U.S. Delta Force members brought in to help the Colombians; *Los Pepes*, a mysterious vigilante group that waged ruthless war on anyone and everyone even remotely associated with Escobar; a special government unit set up to bring Escobar down; and a wound that suggested Escobar wasn't so much "shot in a gun battle" as executed.

Be that as it may, few mourned Escobar's passing. His death was also the death knell for the Medellín cartel. All its leaders were either behind bars or buried. The DEA's most formidable enemy had been neutered. But once again, there was another enemy ready and willing to fill the void.

The Cali Mafia

The Cali mafia had been around since the early 1970s. Unlike the Medellín syndicate, their chief rival, the Calis kept a low profile. They shunned violence except when it was absolutely necessary and devoted their proceeds to legitimate business interests. In short, they relied more on brains than on brawn, which would make them that much harder to topple.

Based in the Cali region of Colombia, they had tentacles in Bolivia, Peru, and other countries. Because they were less violent and put on a respectable facade, they avoided both public and official scrutiny.

Opportunists, the Cali mafia were quick to capitalize when the Soviet Union fell. They moved into Eastern Europe, and from there spread their operation throughout much of the continent.

The DEA believed the Calis were exporting up to 800 tons of cocaine per year from Colombia. The whole Cali operation was modeled along the lines of a multinational corporation, and even the DEA was impressed by their acumen. The Calis relied on the latest technology, hired the best financial experts, and consulted the best lawyers.

Intel was hard to come by, but the DEA established that two brothers, Gilberto and Miguel Rodriguez-Orejuela, were the Cali mafia's transport experts. The brothers oversaw the shipping of cocaine from Colombia to the United States and Europe. A third individual, Jose Santacruz-Londono, set up distribution cells within the United States borders, each of which was run by a Colombian who reported directly to the drug lords.

The operation ran like organizational clockwork. Shipment and money information was exchanged electronically. Shipments were monitored so that the drug lords knew the whereabouts of any given package at any given time. Just as in a business, production quotas were set, and then every facet of the operation was rigidly controlled. The Cali bosses left nothing to chance.

It was the DEA's worst nightmare. Intelligently run, supremely efficient, the Calia mafia was superior in every respect to the Medellín cartel.

The Front Lines

The cocaine front wasn't the only situation that had taken a turn for the worse.

Heroin was making a comeback. Illicit production of opium had doubled. Most came from Southeast Asia, and most of that from Burma, where a drug lord named Khun Sa had his own private army and was so powerful that he controlled the state of Shan and intimidated the Burmese government into adopting a hands-off policy toward him and his mini-empire.

Colombian drug lords, too, were now marketing heroin on an unforeseen scale. In fact, Colombia was now third in global heroin production, behind Burma and Laos. In February of 1992, the Colombian national police raided the first-ever heroin lab found on Colombian soil.

In the United States, heroin was cheaper and purer than ever. In 1980, the purity level had been 5 percent on average. By 1990, it was 66 percent. In some instances, seized heroin was 95 percent pure.

In 1991, the DEA struck back. Agents had learned of an inbound heroin shipment and were able to keep close tabs on its progress. This was white heroin from Southeast Asia. The drug was stashed in produce bags imported from Taiwan. The DEA swooped down on those involved and seized over 1,000 pounds of heroin with a street value of over one *billion* dollars.

Other countries became involved in the heroin trade. Traffickers in Nigeria became major players. So, too, interestingly enough, did traffickers in Communist China. The Chinese operation, like that of the Cali mafia, was extremely well organized.

The war on marijuana also saw changes. Marijuana was now the most widely used illegal substance in America, but many Americans refused to regard it as dangerous. It was considered relatively benign, as cocaine had once been.

Ironically, by 1990 the marijuana being sold on America's streets was radically different from the marijuana of the 1960s. It was much more potent. The THC content had risen to over 7 percent.

A National Household Survey found that close to 15 percent of young adults were now regular users. Four percent of those between the ages of twelve and seventeen and 10 percent of those between the ages of twenty-six and thirty-four fell under the same banner.

During the 1980s, growers had continued to cultivate their illegal crops in national forests and on national park land. By 1990, all fifty states had reported marijuana grows and were taking part in the Domestic Cannabis Eradication and Suppression Program.

The DEA added a new angle with Operation Wipe Out. They struck the growers at the source, with a herbicidal eradication program that was remarkably successful. In Hawaii, where the DEA first put it into effect, over 90 percent of the marijuana crop was destroyed.

So much pressure came to bear on the illegal growers that they took a logical step: they moved their outdoor operations indoors. As it turned out, indoor marijuana was of extremely high quality and of consistently high potency. Domestic-grown grass became the grass that users preferred.

But for every move the drug traffickers made, there was a counter-move. As the DEA had learned from its experience in the Netherlands, indoor operations could be detected by thermal imagery. What worked there would work here. The number of indoor crops seized jumped from about 900 a year in the mid-1980s to almost 4,000 by 1992.

In one instance, the DEA uncovered a marijuana operation in an old mine in Northern California. Back in the late 1800s the mine had produced gold. Now it was producing *sinsemilla* plants. There were five growing rooms and a high-tech irrigation system for supplying the nutrients the plants needed.

Close to nine million dollars' worth of plants were confiscated—the equivalent of five tons.

As if all this were not enough for the DEA to contend with, there was a new kid on the drug scene. Steroids had become big business. Young athletes in record numbers were using them. A Government Accounting Office survey revealed that up to 6 percent of high school seniors had succumbed to temptation. Another survey indicated that up to 20 percent of college-age athletes had done the same.

Illicit trafficking in steroids had become big business.

Congress responded with the Anabolic Steroid Enforcement Act, which placed steroids in a class of controlled substances.

The DEA went after the traffickers. Domestic sources were soon shut down, so the DEA went after foreign sources. They set up an international conference attended by representatives from source countries.

Cocaine, heroin, marijuana, steroids. Not to be outdone, LSD made a resurgence. A steadily increasing number of emergency-room mentions of LSD as a contributing factor alerted the DEA to the growing fascination with the drug among teenagers.

But the latest resurgence was different from the peace-and-love hippie days of the 1960s. Increasingly, violence played a part in LSD use.

In 1991, in Virginia, a high school student who had taken six hits of LSD shot a police officer. In San Marcos, Texas, a college student took several hits of LSD, then shot and killed two friends and wounded his girlfriend.

✶ ✶ ✶

DEA investigations and arrests continued apace. In 1992, an undercover op called Operation Green Ice, begun back in 1989, bore major fruit.

The DEA had set up its own bank, called Trans America Ventures Services (TARA). Their goal was to lure in drug traffickers with money to launder.

Hispanic Business Weekly listed TARA as one of the top 500 Hispanic corporations in America. Such an unwitting sterling endorsement had a spectacular effect. It completely deceived the Cali mafia.

Undercover DEA agents were contacted by drug-money brokers acting on behalf of the Cali syndicate. The agents offered to pick up Cali money anywhere and launder it as needed. The Cali brokers sent the agents to Los Angeles and San Diego, to Chicago, New York City, Miami, Houston, Fort Lauderdale.

Front shops that the agents set up soon had laundered some 20 million in Cali drug profits. The Calis were so impressed, they asked the undercover agents to do even more laundering for them. They wanted the agents to handle funds from Europe, Canada, and the Caribbean.

Operation Green Ice was expanded. International law agencies became involved. The Cali money brokers never suspected a thing. The DEA agents had earned their total trust—so much so that in September of 1992, the DEA had a dream come true. The money brokers agreed to set up a series of meetings with the Cali top echelon.

At last the DEA had a chance to snare top-ranking Calis. The drug lords showed up and were promptly arrested. All told, the DEA snared seven leading Cali kingpins, seized $50 million in Cali assets worldwide, and arrested 177 little fish.

This was not the only success the DEA had in their relentless war against the Calis. The syndicate's New York kingpin was targeted. Helmer "Pacho" Herrera-Buitrago supplied most of the coke for the New York market. In a unique move, the DEA simultaneously tapped into 100 cellular phones used by members of the Herrera organization. The end result; almost 100 arrests and 2.7 tons of cocaine seized. In addition, the DEA got its hands on Herrera's computerized records.

The Cali mafia relied heavily on computers. This increased their efficiency many times over, but it also left them vulnerable when those same computers were seized before they could erase or destroy the hard drives and discs.

This became all too apparent when the DEA and the Colombian national police conducted the first-ever raids on a Cali operation *in* Cali, Colombia.

The DEA got its hands on crucial financial records that identified important Cali bank dealings in Colombia, the United States, and London.

As a footnote, one of the Cali raids netted Ivan Urdinola, one of the top Cali drug lords.

The DEA investigation gained steam. By the end of 1991, 300 tons of Cali cocaine had been seized worldwide.

One of those seizures came about after the DEA learned of a devious tactic the Calis were using to smuggle coke into the United States. Fence posts filled with cocaine were being regularly shipped from Venezuela to Florida and Texas.

The DEA and the U.S. Customs Service shut the fence-post operation down, and in the process they learned of yet another. The ever-inventive Calis were smuggling cocaine into the country hidden in shipments of broccoli and okra. Ten more Cali members were taken into custody, including a top honcho.

Fence posts. Broccoli. What was next? The DEA found out when they raided a Cali warehouse in Panama. This time the cocaine was concealed in ceramic tiles.

Back in the United States, a task force of DEA agents, New York state troopers, and local police targeted the Jose Santacruz-Londono organization. Once again wiretaps were used, along with video surveillance of a suspected lab.

In subsequent raids, not one but two labs were shut down. Agents found more ceramic tiles with cocaine base inside. The Cali chemist who masterminded the tile method was arrested.

Equipment found in the labs explained how the Calis could operate a laboratory in a heavily populated area without having to worry about strong chemical odors giving them away. They had a device that condensed chemical vapors through the use of dry ice, so that little of the smell leaked from the building.

The arrests proved timely in another regard. One of those taken into custody was charged in a murder conspiracy. *El Diario*, a Spanish-language daily newspaper, had run articles blasting the Cali drug lords and their insidious organization, and the Calis had decided to eliminate the editor responsible.

Diplomatic Breakdown

In 1993, the Enrique Camarena case made news again and had a staggeringly adverse impact on the DEA.

United States officials believed that a Mexican gynecologist by the name of Humberto Alvarez Machain had played a part in Camarena's murder. They suspected him of injecting Camarena with stimulants to keep the DEA agent alive while Camarena was being brutally interrogated. Dr. Machain had been indicted in Los Angeles, but Mexican officials refused to arrest and extradite him.

Out of frustration, drastic measures were taken. American authorities hired four Mexican bounty hunters. They approached Dr. Machain, identified themselves as Mexican judicial police, and forced him to board a plane to El Paso, Texas, where he was arrested. A directed verdict of acquittal eventually freed Dr. Machain to return to Mexico, but the damage had been done.

Mexico was furious with the United States. The abduction was a top news item, made even more visible when the U.S. Supreme Court ruled that it did not violate United States law.

In 1992, the Mexican government came down hard on the agency they held most to blame: the DEA. Regulations were imposed on the DEA's activities, the first-ever anywhere in the world. They were severe restrictions the likes of which the DEA never imagined having to face.

For starters, Mexico announced that it would henceforth limit the number of DEA agents permitted to operate within its borders. The agents must live and operate within only six cities. They were not allowed to go anywhere else without express written approval. Perhaps the worst restriction of all was that they were denied diplomatic immunity.

But that wasn't all. The Mexican government now required that all drug intel that the DEA gleaned on Mexican soil must be immediately relayed to Mexican authorities. Then came the final bombshell: the DEA agents were not allowed to carry weapons.

To call Mexico's actions deplorable is to be too kind. Fueled by hurt pride, they were the worst sort of overreaction. The DEA had been effectively crippled. The United States protested, quietly. Amazingly, pressure was not brought to bear to convince the Mexican government of the enormity of their mistake.

That a presumed ally in the drug war should take such drastic measures hinted at darker motives. Even granting that a Mexican citizen had been denied his legal rights, there had been extenuating circumstances, and Mexico had not helped matters by once again dragging its heels.

As a result of the new regulations, to all intents and purposes Mexico now controlled DEA activities within its borders. The DEA's ability to combat the drug trade was severely limited. Some would say it had been deliberately neutralized.

It certainly is no coincidence that drug trafficking in Mexico saw a significant rise. A question never raised during the clampdown was how big a part, if any, corruption played in the new regulations. Was it possible that officials being paid under the table by the drug lords had a hand in formulating the restrictions?

Corruption in Mexico was no secret. It was more on the order of a running joke. It was so rampant that a former president of Mexico publicly singled out drug-related corruption as a threat to Mexican national security. It was so pervasive that the Mexican government replaced many civilian authorities with military officers in the belief that the military would be less corruptible.

But would the drastic step work?

1994–1998

The Mexican Funnel

The situation in Mexico worsened. Four large drug syndicates rose to violent prominence.

    1. The Arellano-Felix Brothers Organization. The most powerful and violent group in all of Mexico, if not the world, the AFO's influence spread tentacles throughout Mexico's judicial system and law enforcement agencies. They were exactly like Pablo Escobar and the Medellín cartel in that they could buy anyone, anytime, and those they couldn't buy, they would kill.

    Originally run by Miguel Angel Felix-Gallardo, the leadership passed to the Arellano family after Felix-

Gallardo was sent to prison for his part in Special Agent Camarena's murder. The family consisted of seven brothers and four sisters who aggressively rose to dominate the market. The new system set up, in which Mexican traffickers were paid in product rather than cash, meant that organizations like the AFO were no longer just transporters. They were drug lords in their own right. And, as always, more money translated into more power.

2. The Miguel Caro-Quintero Organization. Rafael Caro-Quintero, commonly known as the Mexican Rhinestone Cowboy, was its leader. When he was arrested and imprisoned for his part in the Camarena murder, his two brothers, Miguel Jorge and Genaro, took over. Mexican police took Miguel into custody, but once again corruption played a part, and the charges against him were dismissed by a federal judge.

3. The Amado Carillo-Fuentes Organization. It lost its leader, too, but not to arrest. Amado Carillo-Fuentes died while undergoing plastic surgery to give him a new face, the better to evade the law. The organization he had built up went on without him.

4. The Juan Garcia-Abrego Organization. Like the AFO, it had ties to the Calis. It was Garcia-Abrego who pioneered the practice of being paid in drugs rather than cash. Of all the traffickers, he was the most violent. The FBI added him to their Ten Most Wanted list, the first time a drug trafficker merited that dubious distinction. In 1996, he was extradited to the United States and sentenced to eleven life terms.

Each of the four big Mexican syndicates had ties either to the Cali mafia or the Medellín cartel. They were funneling so much cocaine that cargo and passenger jets as big as 727s were gutted and used to transport multi-ton loads.

The Kings of Cocaine

In Colombia itself, the DEA had gone on the offensive. In sharp contrast to the limits imposed in Mexico, they were given outstanding support by the Colombian national police. The results were better than they could have hoped. Cali drug lords began to fall like tenpins.

The first to be nabbed was Gilberto Rodriguez-Orejuela. The CNP found him hiding in a concealed compartment in the bathroom of a house they raided. Among other discoveries at the same house was a DEA report entitled "The Kings of Cocaine," which had been translated into Spanish.

Gilberto's brother, Miguel Rodriguez-Orejuela, like Gilberto, was found hiding in a secret compartment in his residence.

Ten days later, on June 19, 1995, Henry Loiaza-Ceballos surrendered. He was believed to have been involved in several massacres of Cali enemies in Colombia and to have many more kills to his credit.

Victor Julio Patino-Fomeque gave himself up five days after Ceballos.

The Calis knew the CNP and DEA were closing in, and by surrendering, they hoped to receive lighter sentences. But they weren't all willing to give up. Jose Santacruz-Londono, the number-three man, was dining at a steak house in Bogotá when the CNP spoiled his meal by arresting him. He later escaped from prison. When the CNP tried to take him back into custody, he resisted and was killed.

Two kingpins were still at large, but they did not remain so for long. In March of 1996, Juan Carlos "Chupeta" Ramirez-Abadia gave himself up and received twenty-one years in prison.

That left Helmer "Pacho" Herrera-Buitrago, one of the founding fathers of the Cali mafia. He, too, turned himself in. Disturbingly, he was only sentenced to six years behind bars.

Still, the arrests marked the decline of the Cali syndicate. Their power and influence waned.

As always, though, there were other groups ready and willing to take up their share of the drug trade, and then some.

With the Calis neutralized, the single gravest drug threat to the United States became the heroin being smuggled in from Southeast Asia. The Chinese-Nigerian connection had proven lucrative. Up to 60 percent of the "horse" entering the United States was theirs.

The Nigerians served mainly as middlemen for the Chinese. Or, in one important case, middlewomen. One of the largest Nigerian operations was run by a Nigerian female. Her organization alone brought in some $26 million in heroin per year.

In response, the DEA launched Operation Global Sea. A task force of DEA agents, Customs Service agents, FBI, and law officers from Great Britain, France, Switzerland, the Netherlands, Mexico, and Thailand brought forty-four defendants to trial and put a serious dent in the Southeast Asian connection.

Technology

More and more, drug traffickers were relying on the latest technology. Cellular phones had become commonplace. Dealers would buy ten to twenty at a time, use them for only a few days or a few weeks, then get new phones. This was done in an effort to avoid having their phones tapped.

Digital pagers posed a problem for the DEA, too. Traffickers could send messages, usually in code, dealing with deliveries and the like, with the utmost ease and convenience. For a while, the DEA was stymied. Intercepting digital transmissions was next to impossible. To do it, the DEA had to have access to information they could only get at the paging companies, and the companies often let their subscribers know if they were under investigation. Soon, though, new equipment was developed that enabled the DEA to monitor digital pagers.

But technical obstacles continued to arise. Many companies were jumping on the new digital bandwagon, offering services such as multiplexing, in which digital information was sent in pulses over fiber-optic cables. This enabled traffickers to send simultaneous voice and data transmissions to more than one recipient. It wasn't like the old days, when the DEA could tap into a single wire carrying a single conversation. The new digital transmissions could not be intercepted.

Congress came to the DEA's aid. The Digital Telephony and Communications Privacy Act was passed. It required digital companies to cooperate with the DEA and other agencies. But law enforcement wasn't given carte blanche. The companies could not just hand over information on everyone and anyone. There had to be a specific suspect, and the information had to pertain to that suspect.

Debit telephone cards became a popular trafficking tool. The cards had a great advantage: they were extremely hard to trace, since the calls weren't billed to a given person or number.

The most difficult challenge for the DEA to overcome was

the increasing reliance on encryption. Drug organizations could send messages with impunity. Interception was costly. Again Congress stepped in, with the Communications Assistance for Law Enforcement Act. It basically required companies to do all they could to help the DEA and other agencies intercept encrypted communications.

While the Cali mafia had been crippled, in Los Angeles a Cali mafia cell continued to conduct business pretty much as usual. Accordingly, the DEA initiated Operation Zorro.

The name had nothing to do with the legendary swashbuckler of book, movie, and TV fame. "Zorro" was the nickname of the cell's Los Angeles ringleader. His real name was Diego Fernando Salazar-Izquierdo. He and his second-in-command were known for their cunning. They relied heavily on the latest in high-tech, including cell phones and fax lines. They were also big on computers, and they used special software to steal the telephone numbers of scores of individuals, which were then used for illegal purposes.

Zorro and his assistant had a distribution network any drug lord would envy. From Los Angeles, the drugs were shipped to San Francisco, Chicago, and New York City. Those three cities, in turn, were relay points for drugs sent to dealers in places like Newark, St. Louis, New Orleans, and San Antonio. Zorro was well on his way to blanketing the country with his illicit wares.

Fifty-five federal, state, and local agencies prevented that from happening. The raids not only netted Zorro and his henchman, but 189 other suspects. Over six tons of cocaine was seized.

Wreckage

In 1994, an important conviction was won. Dandeny Muñoz-Mosquera was given ten life terms, two twenty-year terms, plus an extra five-year term for various crimes. If that seems a tad excessive bear in mind that Mosquera was the Medellín cartel's number-one assassin.

Mosquera had been arrested in Queens, New York. He was the mastermind behind the bombing of Avianca Flight 203. One hundred and seven people died in the crash, just so Mosquera could kill one informant. Two of the 107 were American citizens.

Mosquera was one of the most feared and deadly professional assassins on the continent. He was allegedly linked to hundreds of murders. In that context, his sentences were more than fitting.

That same year, another crash impacted the DEA, but in a different way. In August, a DEA aircraft with five special agents on board involved in routine reconnaissance lost contact with air traffic control. It was disappeared in the Andes Mountains of western Peru, in an area overrun with drug labs and secret airfields from which drug shipments were flown out.

The DEA, U.S. Special Forces, the Peruvian Air Force, and Peruvian police launched an immediate search. The wreckage of the twin-engine plane was spotted from the air, and a team was dispatched. Cutting through the jungle was slow, arduous work, compounded by heavy rains. The team reached the crash site, only to find all five agents dead.

1994 saw the culmination of another investigation, one unique in DEA annals and perhaps in the history of the drug trade.

It started with the tiny community of Charleston, in Boston,

Massachusetts. Over a period of about fifteen years, Charleston had experienced forty-nine murders. For a community its size, this was unprecedented—and even stranger when you consider that thirty-three of those murders had gone unsolved.

The authorities did know, though, that tiny little Charleston had become a cocaine and PCP distribution center for a drug gang known as the Irish Mob. This brought the DEA in. They joined forces with the Massachusetts state police, Boston police, and the Boston Housing Police Department.

The first thing the DEA had to do was get people to talk. A code of silence prevailed in Charleston. No one would tell what they knew. Part of the reason had to do with fear of reprisals. Another part had to do with the belief that Charleston should handle its own problems without outside interference.

Winning the residents over was not easy. Protection was offered to any and all witnesses who agreed to cooperate with the investigation, and eventually the DEA found a few informants.

It took three years, but forty members of the Irish Mob were indicted on murder, attempted murder, racketeering, conspiracy to distribute cocaine, and armed robbery charges.

The dam broke. Once the Mob was behind bars, the code of silence dissolved and hundreds of calls were placed to a DEA hotline.

Charleston became just another typical small American community where people could go about their daily routines without fear.

In Burma and Thailand there was fear to spare. Warlord Khun Sa and his private army in Shan State were a grave threat to stability in the region. Not only that, but the share of Southeast Asian heroin entering the United States had jumped from 7 to 58 percent, in large part due to Khun Sa.

Numerous Burmese government officials were in Khun Sa's back pocket. The government did make a token effort to contain him, but his army successfully held the Burmese army at bay.

Enter the DEA and Operation Tiger Trap. Working with the Royal Thai Police, the Royal Thai Army Special Forces, and Thai Office of Narcotics Control Board officers, the DEA set up a sting. Suspects in Burma were lured into Thailand, where handcuffs could then be slapped onto their wrists.

Thirteen top Shan United Army members were among those arrested. All were wanted on indictments out of New York, and the United States wanted them extradited.

The Royal Thai Army, meanwhile, working with Thai border police, closed the Thai border with Burma to goods entering the Shan State.

Khun Sa was still in business, but on a reduced scale.

The MET

A rare lighter moment in the DEA's unending war took place when, in conjunction with the IRS, they made an unusual seizure in 1994.

A few years earlier, the government had set up another phony financial institution and front businesses as part of their campaign against the Cali mafia. Completely duped, Cali members asked the undercover agents to do them a favor and sell three paintings the Cali mafia had acquired: a Rubens, a Picasso, and a Reynolds, valued at more than $15 million.

Instead, the DEA and the IRS confiscated them.

Back home, the DEA was determined to do something about the rising tide of drug-related violence. But what? The agency was already spread so thin; what strategy could possibly be adopted that would have an appreciable effect?

The DEA's adminstrator, Thomas A. Constantine, had an idea. In April of 1995, he implemented the Mobile Enforcement Team (MET) program. Special DEA teams were formed and deployed to hot spots as needed.

The simplest solutions are sometimes the hardest to come by. A problem can be examined from every angle by a host of people and the right answer still not be found. In this instance, Administrator Constantine had struck on the ideal solution, as the MET concept's early successes demonstrated.

In Galveston County, Texas, drug violence was rife. In one week in May of 1995, there were five drive-by shootings. The Galveston County sheriff asked the DEA for help, and a MET team was sent in. Within days, seven suspects in a local drug gang had been arrested.

In Opa-Locka, Florida, the problem was crack cocaine and the man who headed a local drug ring. Rickey Brownlee was his name, and since 1993 he had allegedly waged a vicious onslaught of killing and intimidation. He was believed to have been involved in at least thirteen murders. A MET unit brought him and his organization down, earning a formal letter of gratitude from Opa-Locka's mayor.

The MET teams had certain advantages over local law agencies. For one thing, the DEA's special agents were highly trained to deal specifically with drug-related scenarios. For another, most local law officers were well known in their respective communities. Undercover work for them was problematical at best. DEA agents, however, were literal unknowns, and they could blend into the local criminal community without arousing suspicion.

Success stories like the two mentioned here were repeated across the United States. By 1998, MET teams had arrested some 6,800 offenders—and not just "average" offenders. The MET teams concentrated on the most violent; on those most to blame for the quantum leap in bloodshed in American communities.

Oklahoma

On April 19, 1995, a massive explosion destroyed the Alfred E. Murrah Federal Building in Oklahoma City, Oklahoma. The toll was horrendous; 168 people killed, among them 19 children. The disaster shook the country.

The DEA had offices on the seventh and ninth floors. Together they comprised the Oklahoma City Resident Office. Its personnel included ten special agents, four investigators, three secretaries, and assorted task force members. Like everyone else in the building that day, they had no idea of the horror about to be unleashed.

When the bomb went off, DEA Special Agent David Schickedanz was in an elevator talking to ATF supervisor Alex McCauley. The blast caused the elevator to drop six floors, but Schickedanz survived the plunge and made it out through a trap door. Instead of escaping what was left of the building, he went back up to search for survivors.

Midwest City Police Officer Regina Bonny, on assignment with the DEA, was knocked unconscious by the explosion. When she came around, she helped an ATF officer, then went back up to the ninth floor to look for missing DEA staff.

Special Agent Schickedanz sustained a partial loss of hearing. Policewoman Bonny suffered nerve damage in addition to a head injury and shoulder wounds. Both were later honored with the prestigious Police Officer of the Year award.

Within an hour of the blast, DEA agents were on their way from Tulsa, Dallas, Lubbock, Los Angeles, and other points. The DEA, like other agencies, set up a command post at the scene and had a trauma team on hand. The counseling would be needed.

Two days after the bombing, the deaths of DEA employees Kenneth G. McCullough and Carrie Ann Lenz were confirmed. Mrs. Lenz was six months pregnant with her first child. Soon thereafter, rescue workers announced the deaths of two more on the DEA staff, Rona L. Chafey and Shelly Bland. Then, on April 24, the death of office worker Carol Field was confirmed.

All told, the DEA lost five of its own, with three severely injured.

Timothy McVeigh received the death penalty for the killing of the 168 innocents.

Filling the Void

The vacuums created by the fall of the Medellín cartel and the Cali mafia had been filled by other drug syndicates. Although not as powerful as their predecessors, they were rapidly growing.

Because of the pressure put on them by the Colombian national police and the DEA, the traffickers started to rely more and more on old smuggling routes through the Caribbean. Ever larger shipments of cocaine and heroin were being seized. In Puerto Rico and the Dominican Republic, seizures of up to 2,000 pounds became common. Soon Puerto Rico qualified as an official High Intensity Drug Trafficking Area.

To stem the flow, the DEA opened a Caribbean division in San Juan.

From the Caribbean, the drugs were smuggled into the United States at various spots along the East Coast. Gangs from the Dominican Republic came to dominate the shipping and distribution.

As an example, in New Haven, Connecticut, one such gang controlled 90 percent of all the heroin sold in New Haven.

Philadelphia became a hotbed of activity, as did the Washington, D.C., area.

The Dominican influence even spread to the Deep South. In July of 1997, Dominican Republican traffickers were arrested in Charlotte, North Carolina. It turned out they were transporting large amounts of heroin from New York City to Charlotte for rave parties.

In 1998, the DEA and the Hartford, Connecticut police department took forty Dominican Republican traffickers into custody.

Drug-inspired violence jumped throughout the Caribbean. Puerto Rico saw its annual homicide rate vault from about 480 in 1984 to almost 900 in 1996.

Methamphetamines

Another change had taken place on the Mexican smuggling scene.

Traffickers there had found something that rewarded them with even higher profits than heroin: methamphetamine. They began selling more of it than even domestic motorcycle gangs, the drug's traditional suppliers.

Thanks to their long experience in working with the Medellín cartel and the Cali mafia, the Mexican traffickers had a distribution network second to none. Soon they had saturated the West Coast. From there they spread eastward.

Prices for "speed" or "crank" as the drug was known, fell drastically as the supply increased. At the start of the decade, a pound was going for close to $6,000. By the mid-1990s, it had dropped to an average of $3,000.

Concomitantly, the number of emergency-room cases in which speed was a factor more than doubled.

Speed contributed to the constant rise in violence. In Tucson, Arizona, DEA Special Agent Richard Fass was slain by a methamphetamine trafficker.

All in all, it was a somber picture, made worse by the fact that the traffickers controlled the whole operation from beginning to end, from the making of the meth in Mexico to its sale on America's streets.

The question that the DEA wanted answered was this: Where were the Mexicans getting the chemicals, such as ephedrine or pseudoephedrine, needed to make the methamphetamine?

The DEA soon had the answer. Most came from four source countries: China, India, Switzerland, and the Czech Republic. At least 170 tons of it from mid-1993 to early 1995, according to figures the DEA uncovered, and that was probably nowhere near the total.

So many meth labs were being discovered domestically that a special conference was called in California to address the crisis. Hosted by the DEA, it brought in experts from all around the country. Suggestions on how to respond were then submitted to the Attorney General.

Before long, Congress acted. The Comprehensive Methamphetamine Control Act was passed. It restricted the availability of the chemicals the meth makers needed and allowed for the tracking of chemicals bought through the mail. It also set severe penalties for firms supplying the chemicals if those chemicals were used for illegal purposes, which had the net effect of forcing the firms to delve into the backgrounds of their buyers. The days when just anyone could waltz in off the street and order huge amounts of chemicals were over.

The Fallen

By the mid-'90s, a high number of DEA agents had been killed or wounded in the line of duty. (See Appendix A.) Combating the drug tide was an extremely dangerous occupation, and agents paid dearly for their devotion, some with the ultimate sacrifice.

An advisory committee suggested that the DEA honor them in some way. The military had long awarded Purple Hearts for those wounded in battle, and the DEA felt that what was good for the military was good enough for them. Thus, the DEA Purple Heart Award was implemented. The hearts were given to agents who were wounded or had died in the performance of their duties as the direct result of hostile action on the part of criminals.

Later on, another advisory committee recommended expanding the Purple Heart program to include state and local law officers who were attached to the DEA. The recommendation was adopted.

Smuggler's Remorse

About this time, the DEA's campaign to stop the influx of drugs from Mexico heated up.

A previous op, called Zorro II, had closed down a large ring engaged in the usual transport of South American drugs into the United States. But it was just one ring among many, and the problem was growing.

In Tyler, Texas, in October of 1996, two state troopers made a highway stop that netted more than two million dollars in hidden drug cash.

On December 13, again in Tyler, the same two state troopers pulled a tractor-trailer over. In a hidden compartment they found 2,700 pounds of marijuana.

Subsequent investigations showed that transportation cells were ferrying in large amounts of cocaine in big rigs. In one instance, the cocaine was concealed in stacks of plywood that appeared perfectly ordinary but had been hollowed out to hold drugs. The same trucks were then used to ferry money back across the border.

In April of 1997, the U.S. Customs Service discovered $5.6 million in cash hidden in a tractor-trailer.

Traffickers were continually coming up with new ways to smuggle their wares. In New York, over 1,600 kilos of cocaine were found hidden in a shipment of chopped up carrots intended for use as horse feed.

That gem of ingenuity was the handwork of a major transportation cell headed by Alberto Beltran, who was part of the Carillo-Fuentes organization out of Mexico. Each month, the cell smuggled in an estimated 1.5 tons of cocaine in crates of fruits and vegetables.

Operation Limelight was launched to bring Beltran to bay. It involved the DEA and several other agencies.

In the end, forty-eight people were arrested, including Gerardo Gonzales, the head of the Beltran ring in the United States. Over 4,000 kilos of coke and over 10,000 pounds of marijuana were confiscated.

Special Interests

Numbers like this were proof positive, as if any was needed, that America was awash in a sea of drugs. But that did not stop certain wealthy special-interest groups in California and Arizona from putting the issue of legalizing drugs on the ballot.

The pro-drug crowd, untiring in their efforts to legalize drug use, were now to blame for a new phase in the drug war: what might be deemed the "legalization war." And make no mistake: it *is* a war. Many of those who want drugs to be legal have ulterior motives.

In California and Arizona, slick ad campaigns blitzed the media. Again and again, the pro-drug lobby harped on how marijuana could help the terminally ill. Other provisions in the ballot initiatives were conveniently glossed over.

The DEA was staunchly against both initiatives. They had an ally in the International Association of Police Chiefs. The IACP came out publicly against the two measures. The Chiefs noted that marijuana is more carcinogenic than tobacco and that it makes diseases such as asthma, multiple sclerosis, and tuberculosis worse, and they pointed out that there was no proof that marijuana helped prevent blindness from glaucoma, as the pro-drug groups claimed.

Regardless of their efforts, both propositions passed.

The Arizona measure was more restrictive. It required that

any physician prescribing marijuana must cite a study confirming that the drug had a proven benefit. The patient then had to get a confirming opinion from another doctor. Other provisions of the measure had nothing to do with the prescribing of drugs. One mandated the release of convicted felons who had been sent to prison for possessing a controlled substance.

In California, Proposition 215 was all the pro-drug crowd could hope for. Written prescriptions weren't required. All someone had to do was to walk into a doctor's office and claim to have a medical condition, and if the doctor *verbally* okayed the use of marijuana as a treatment, the "patient" was good to go. Minors, prisoners, anyone could do it. Those who got a doctor's okay were then free to not only smoke but cultivate marijuana for their personal use.

Many of the people who voted for the two measures were unaware of the less publicized aspects. They had been duped.

The pro-drug groups were elated. They began to work for legalization of marijuana in other states.

But all the while, their underlying and fundamental goal wasn't merely to make marijuana acceptable; they were out to make drug use legal everywhere in the United States of America.

Although primarily an enforcement arm of the United States government, the DEA couldn't let the pro-drug lobby's efforts go unchallenged. Educating the public about the true nature of drugs was the key, and over the years the DEA has held innumerable conferences and engaged in other activities of a public relations nature to achieve that end.

For example, in 1996 the DEA and the Boys and Girls Clubs of America announced a partnership. The Clubs, located in all fifty states, had almost two and a half million members. The DEA cosponsored a joint publication that was passed out. Entitled *Getting It Straight*, it gave the young boys and girls the literal straight dope about the dangers of drugs.

To slow the spread of meth, the DEA and Wal-Mart joined forces. The corporate giant agreed to control its sales of chemicals used by meth makers. This might sound ridiculous, since Wal-Mart sold its products over the counter, not in bulk shipments. But at illegal labs across the country, DEA agents had found large bottles of pseudoephedrine sold at none other than Wal-Mart.

From then on, customers would be limited in how many bottles they could buy.

In 1997, a special heroin conference was sponsored by the DEA. It came about in response to the latest disturbing news out of South America and from the nation's hospitals.

Drug traffickers were now including *free* heroin in shipments of cocaine to make heroin more readily available. It worked. Annual total emergency-room treatments of heroin-related cases jumped from about 33,000 in 1990 to more than 76,000 by the middle of the decade. Heroin overdoses were on a steady upswing, in large part because the purity level had risen from 7 percent in 1985 to 90 percent ten years later.

Justice Served

1997 was also the year when the DEA finally caught up with a fugitive from justice who had been eluding authorities for fifteen years.

Back in 1982, two men, Jose Ivan Duarte and Rene Benitez, were hired by the Colombian cartel to kill a pair of DEA agents. Special Agents Charles Martinez and Kelly McCullough had becomes thorns in the cartel's side, and the cartel wanted them eliminated.

At gunpoint, the two agents were whisked from their hotel in Cartagena, Colombia, and driven fifteen miles to a secluded spot. Before they were even out of the city limits, Special Agent Martinez was shot. He was shot a second time when the car stopped. Agent McCullough broke away and bolted for the jungle. He was shot before he could reach it but kept going.

Incredibly, Agent Martinez was still alive. He fled, too. Duarte and Benitez tried to shoot him, but miraculously, the gun jammed.

Special Agents Martinez and McCullough made it to Cartagena. There, they contacted the U.S. Embassy and soon were whisked out of the country by a U.S. Air Force plane sent from Panama. Both agents eventually recovered from their wounds.

Warrants were issued for Duarte and Benitez. The latter was caught and extradited to Miami. Duarte, though, eluded capture until late 1997, when he was picked up by Ecuadoran police. Ecuador expelled him, and the United States was there to snatch him up.

The DEA was lucky. If the assassins had not been so inept, two more agents would have died.

In 1998, the DEA set up a Survivors' Benefit Fund to help the families of those lost in the line of duty.

The DEA was upgrading in other regards as well. Prior to that year, agents had been issued body armor—more commonly called "bulletproof vests"—able to blunt the impact of a 357 magnum round. In the old days, this was considered sufficient. But with the ever-more-formidable firepower being brought to bear by drug traffickers, the DEA decided to issue new body armor that could stop up to a 44 magnum slug.

Computerization was improved. The DEA's antique system was replaced with new Pentium-grade computers.

The air wing was given a budget boost. From its lowly beginnings, when it had an annual budget of $58,000, the DEA's air arm now merited $24 million. The DEA had a fleet of almost a hundred aircraft along with more than one hundred agents qualified as pilots.

All this was well and good, but a new century was looming. New challenges would arise, and new tactics had to be developed to deal with them.

1999–2000

Strategy

The DEA's multi-pronged strategy involved hitting the drug traffickers where they were most vulnerable. By restricting the flow of chemicals needed in the manufacture of certain drugs, the DEA had put a major crimp in their production.

Chemicals were at the processing end of the drug chain. At the other end were the profits the traffickers reaped from their illicit sales—profits that the traffickers needed to launder.

On several occasions, the DEA had set up dummy banks to trick traffickers into revealing the money end of their operations. But they couldn't rely on the same tactic all the time. So, for the first time, they set up an undercover stockbrokerage firm. They were going after drug profits flowing back into Colombia.

The op began after cocaine was found hidden in a shipment of frozen fish from Cartagena. The fish had been shipped by a company that was based in Atlanta. The DEA investigated and found that the owner of the Atlanta company was in league with remnants of the Cali mafia.

Strategy sessions resulted in the DEA going into the stockbroking business—ostensibly, at least, since they never actually engaged in stock trading. To all outward appearances, the firm appeared legitimate, and when it discreetly let it be known in certain black-market circles that it would gladly launder ill-gotten gains, the suspects took the bait. The DEA did such a convincing job that the traffickers told some of their friends, who in turn told some of their friends, and soon the stockbrokerage firm was being used to launder money by five separate drug-trafficking rings.

Drug kingpins were always looking for ways to clean up their money. They were making so much, and so fast, that they were in constant need of new laundering outlets.

Operation Juno involved dozens of pickups of cash crammed into duffel bags, boxes, gym bags, and luggage in cites spanning the globe: Miami, Chicago, Dallas, Houston, New York, Rome, Madrid. The money was transferred to Atlanta, and from there it was wired to bank accounts in the United States and abroad, as the traffickers required.

That was just the first step. The rest was more complicated.

Undercover agents were put in touch with a Colombian money exchanger who had a system worked out for converting United States dollars into Colombian pesos on the Colombian black market.

It worked basically like this: Colombian businessmen who wanted to avoid paying Colombia's tariffs and taxes on goods bought in the United States would contact the money exchanger. They would pay him in pesos for the dollars they needed to conduct business in the United States. The pesos were then deposited in Cali mafia accounts in Colombia. It was all done by wire transfers. Millions of dollars and millions of pesos changed hands without the money ever physically leaving the United States or Colombia.

To the drug lords, national boundaries meant little. In the monetary sphere, those boundaries meant even less. Global business ventures permitted them to operate on a global scale from the comfort of their luxurious estates without ever setting foot outside their guarded gates.

Technology had become their bedfellow. Computers, the Internet, advancements in telecommunications—all were boons to the trafficking trade. Money could be laundered with a sophistication never before seen, and it took increasingly more sophisticated methods for the DEA to cope.

Eventually, indictments were lodged against five Colombian kingpins. More than forty arrests were made in the United States. Even more important, the DEA had uncovered fifty-nine accounts in thirty-four United States banks and 282 accounts in fifty-two foreign banks that the traffickers were using to launder money. Over $26 million in drug money was seized.

Special K

The human capacity for finding new ways to chemically amuse and entertain never ceased to bewilder.

In July of 1991, a new drug was added to the DEA's list of controlled substances. It was nicknamed "Special K" but had absolutely nothing to do with breakfast cereal.

The "K" alluded to was ketamine, in use as a general anesthetic, principally by veterinary clinics. The effects that ketamine produced in humans were a lot like those of LSD and PCP. Chemically, ketamine shared similarities with the latter, although the high was not as intense and lasted thirty to sixty minutes instead of hours.

In the early '90s, the DEA began to notice and correlate some disturbing trends. More and more vet clinics were being burglarized, and the only thing being taken was ketamine. The Drug Abuse Warning Network reported a rising number of instances of emergency-room treatments for ketamine-related overdoses.

Special K had made the scene with a major splash. High school students were using it. It was being sold on college campuses. At nightclubs and raves it had become hugely popular and was often used along with marijuana, cocaine, and/or alcohol.

Users would feel a dreamy intoxication at first. That progressed to a delirium in which they couldn't move or feel pain. Worse, they couldn't remember what they did while under Special K's sway. It wasn't long before there was a documented case of a Special K–related rape.

Yet another drug to combat. Just what the DEA needed.

Business as Usual

As the Drug Enforcement Administration had learned in the case of Pablo Escobar, just because a drug lord was sent to prison didn't necessarily mean that his drug operation withered and died.

Take Alberto Orlandez-Gamboa. He was in prison in

Colombia on charges of kidnapping and murder, among other crimes. But although he was behind bars, the DEA believed he was still conducting business as usual.

"Business," for Orlandez-Gamboa, involved being the head of what was known as the Caracol organization. Based in Barranquilla, on Colombia's north coast, it funneled cocaine to North America and Europe.

When over 800 kilos of coke were seized, the DEA traced it back and an indictment was issued. The indictment alleged that the Caracol organization was smuggling drugs into the United States using a variety of transport methods, from speedboats to cargo ships to aircraft. The coke was hidden in cement, corn oil, engine parts, and an old standby, ceramic tiles.

The proceeds had been traced, and the indictment accused the Caracol organization of laundering millions of dollars through bank accounts across the world.

Orlandez-Gamboa, the DEA believed, oversaw it all from behind bars.

For a while, thanks to the efforts of the Medellín cartel, extradition of Colombian nationals had been forbidden. But with the demise of the cartel, common sense once again prevailed, and the Colombian constitution had been amended to allow for extradition of suspected criminals.

The DEA promptly requested extradition for Orlandez-Gamboa. If they succeeded, it would be the first instance since the ban was removed.

In late 1996, one of the leading members of the Medellín cartel, Fabio Ochoa, was released from prison. He immediately returned to his former trade—if, indeed, he had ever left it.

Ochoa became linked to Alejandro Bernal Madrigal, better

known as "Juvenal," reputedly one of the biggest drug traffickers in all of Colombia. His operation was believed to transport upwards of thirty tons of cocaine per month into the United States and Europe.

The DEA launched Operation Millennium to bring them down. After a formal request by the United States Colombian authorities set up extensive wiretaps. Hundreds of hours of intensive investigation reaped a gold mine of intel.

The result? In early morning raids, the CNP took fifteen suspects in Medellín into custody, another fourteen in Bogota, and one in Cali. Among them were Juvenal and Ochoa.

Back in the United States, the DEA was involved in a concerted effort to stamp out cells operated by the Amado Carillo-Fuentes organization. Fuentes himself was dead from his attempt to have his features altered by plastic surgery; he had been well known to the authorities on three continents and had hoped that by altering his appearance, he could better elude apprehension.

The ACF organization was smuggling hundreds of tons of Colombian cocaine through Mexico into the United States. They had distribution cells in New York, Atlanta, Chicago, and San Diego. From there the coke was relayed to cities like Nashville, Detroit, Philadelphia, and Houston, among others. The group relied on high-tech communications equipment to coordinate their activities.

Their smuggling route through Mexico was the province of Gilberto Salinas-Doria, who went under the name of Gilberto Garza-Garcia. Salinas-Doria, amazingly, was a former Texas police officer with a reputed homicidal bent.

The DEA had also learned the identities of three major cell heads. Jorge Ontiveros-Rodriguez purportedly ran the San

Diego cell. Jesse Quintanilla, who was Salinas-Doria's nephew, handled the Chicago end. Arturo Arredondo was in charge of all United States transportation and distribution. He had dual United States and Mexican citizenship. Arredondo personally oversaw the loading of tractor-trailers filled with produce—and cocaine. The trucking companies he ran were actually owned by his underlings, to add what he thought was an extra layer of insulation from arrest.

In cooperation with the FBI, the U.S. Customs Service, and more than a dozen other federal and state agencies, the DEA took part in Operation Impunity. The name was chosen to be symbolic of the fact that drug syndicates couldn't operate on United States soil with impunity. The idea was laughable to the traffickers, but not to the hundreds of dedicated agents and personnel who took part.

Arredondo, Quintanilla, and Rodriguez were all arrested. So was Doria/Garcia, by Mexican authorities. Eighty-nine others were taken into custody, and over 12,400 kilos of cocaine and 4,800 pounds of marijuana were seized.

These were impressive results, but they didn't put the ACF out of business. Other members were on the DEA's "wish list" of traffickers who they would like to see brought to justice.

Alcides Ramon-Magana, or "El Metro," coordinated cocaine traffic between Colombia and Mexico. His main pipeline stretched from Cancún to Reynosa, Mexico. Hand-picked by Fuentes himself, he had so far eluded arrest.

The next step of the smuggling route, from Reynosa to stash houses across the United States border, was overseen by Gilberto Salinas-Doria until his arrest.

Salinas-Doria saved the DEA the trouble of tracking down one of his top henchmen, Marco Flores. Flores was apparently killed under orders from Doria after a cocaine shipment was lost.

Another top henchman, Victor Ortega, aka Pelon, specialized in transportation routes to Chicago and various East Coast cities.

The warehouse end on the East Coast was under the care of Jose Luis Diaz, from the Dominican Republic. An Arredondo protégé, he and Julio Ramos, another Dominican, were arrested in August of 1999.

The head of the Los Angeles cell, Camilo Barraza, became a fugitive at large. So, too, did "Popeye," American Gary Lee Fox, who oversaw another cell.

Another American, Broderick Hurst, often referred to by his rather colorful nickname of King Kong, was the head of an Atlanta cell until his arrest by the DEA.

Nationally and internationally, the DEA had a long string of accomplishments to its credit. Trafficker after trafficker was being brought to trial. Cell after cell was eliminated. Entire criminal organizations were toppled. But always and again the DEA was confronted by the same problem. No matter how many arrests they made, no matter how many cells they destroyed, how many organizations they took apart from the roots up, there was always another trafficker, another cell, another syndicate, that would arise to take its place.

To say that it was frustrating is an understatement. The DEA was doing all it could to keep America's streets safe, but for every gain they made, a new source of drugs appeared. Or an entirely new kind of drug, as in the case of Special K.

Newspaper editors and broadcast reporters bewailed the drug crisis in America. By the start of the new century, the country's social fabric had been fundamentally changed. Drugs had become the status quo, not an aberration. They were available in every city and every town, from metropolitan centers like New York City to small farming communities like Cozad, Nebraska. Some pundits were saying that the counterculture of the 1960s had become the mainstream culture of the new millennium.

Exactly how pervasive the problem had become was illustrated in microcosm by a case out of Washington, D.C. The nation's capital was not immune. Far from it. D.C.'s streets were rife with drugs. In certain parts of the city at certain times of the day, dealers sold their wares on streetcorners. Various city parks were notorious for the drug dealing that went on. Whole neighborhoods were afflicted.

One such neighborhood was ruled with a violent fist by the Mahdi family. More commonly known as the 1-4 Mob, six members ruled its roost: Abdur Mahdi, or "Big Chief"; Rahammad Mahdi, or "Rock"; Malik Mahdi, or "Freek"; Nadir Mahdi, known as "Smokey"; Musa M. Mahdi; and Joseph Hooker, or "Little Joe," a close family friend. When "soldiers" were added in, the gang's membership totaled more than two dozen.

The 1-4 Mob gave a whole new meaning to the word "ruthless." The indictment against them listed seventeen violent crimes, including one murder, six counts of attempted murder, at least three armed robberies, armed kidnapping, and an assault on a police officer.

Some of the charges stemmed from the Mahdi family's intimidation of anyone in the neighborhood who dared speak out against them, others from an ongoing turf war that the Mahdis waged against another gang based on Delafield Street, the Delafield Mob.

The gang war started in January of 1999, when the leader of the Delafield Mob, Brion Arrington, shot a member of the I-4 Mob. The Mahdi brothers retaliated. Delafield member William Ray was shot and left paralyzed from the neck down.

One year later, Arrington and several other members of his gang killed Danny Webb, a Mahdi associate. Arrington would subsequently be tried and convicted for the crime.

The shootings escalated. Nadir Mahdi shot at Arrington and other members of the Delafield Mob. That very night, Arrington and his lieutenant, Harrell Hagans, tried to get revenge. The Delafield Mob stole two cars. Then, armed with assault rifles, shotguns, and pistols, they drove deep into Mahdi turf, to the Mahdis' home on the 3900 block of 14th Street.

They opened fire on the entire block. Eva Hernandez, an innocent bystander, had just come back from doing her laundry and was standing on her front porch with her four-year-old son when a round struck her. She died at the scene.

Another bystander, Gloria Flores-Bonilla, was struck when a slug smashed through her bedroom window and the headboard to the bed on which she was resting. Fortunately she was only grazed.

None of the 1-4 Mob was hit.

The Delafields sped off and ditched the stolen cars after wiping them clean of fingerprints—or so they thought. Harrell Hagans' prints were lifted from one of the vehicles.

As for the Mahdi brothers, they would be blamed for a long list of crimes. To cite a few examples:

On September 11, 1999, members of the Mahdi family assaulted some people who wouldn't vacate "their" alley fast enough to suit them.

On October 9, the Mahdis allegedly kidnapped a rival and threw him into the trunk of their vehicle.

On October 20, a member of the Delafield Mob and his girlfriend were standing next to the woman's vehicle, talking, when they were cut down in a hail of lead. Both survived.

Delafield Mob member Curtis Hattley wasn't as lucky. He was gunned down as he drove along in his car on November 17.

On May 26 and again on June 6, the Mahdi family tried to rub out their rivals. They failed both times.

The metropolitan police department was joined by the DEA, the ATF, and the United States Park Police in bringing charges.

Eventually, sixteen members of the 1-4 Mob were indicted. Fifteen pled guilty. Abdur Mahdi's case went to trial. "Big Chief" was found guilty on forty-nine counts of murder, assault, racketeering, and other charges, and given life in prison with no chance of parole.

One small neighborhood. One big drug problem. A scenario replicated in countless other neighborhoods across the land.

One of those neighborhoods was in Springfield, Massachusetts. The traffickers weren't a large gang like the 1-4 Mob or a slickly operated cell like those operated by syndicates in many major cities. It was just two men who sold crack and cocaine in an otherwise quiet and law-abiding town, and who didn't give a damn about the consequences or how much harm they caused. All that mattered was the money they made.

Usually the media tended to publicize the DEA's more spectacular cases. The big busts. The big arrests. But the DEA didn't limit its investigations to metropolitan areas or to large drug operations. Although cynics would claim otherwise, the DEA did care. The DEA did give a damn about innocent lives forever lost or warped by drugs.

What the cynics tended to overlook is that DEA agents were "people, too"—ordinary men and women who had dedicated their careers to making America a better, safer place in which to live. As an appendix as the back of this book shows, many lost their lives doing so.

Hollywood often portrays federal agents in the most unflattering of lights. The agents are either corrupt, or driven by a fanatical fever, or too dumb to tie their shoes. But Hollywood and the truth often part company, and the truth is that most DEA agents are responsible, capable people whose goal in life isn't to die in a cinematic blaze of glory, but to go about their jobs competently and maturely. If asked, few would say they want to make the ultimate sacrifice. The point is that they are aware of the potential cost, yet they do their job anyway, and they do it as well as they can.

In Springfield, more and more crack was showing up on neighborhood streets. A DEA task force sprang into action. An undercover agent insinuated himself into the local crime community, and after a ten-month investigation, two men were arrested and went on trial.

Ordinary thugs. An ordinary operation.

Not so ordinary was the op dubbed Operation Green Air. On this one, the DEA was working with the U.S. Customs Service, the U.S. Attorney's Office, and state and local agencies.

Ever inventive, traffickers never ceased to come up with novel means of transporting their illicit products. This case was unique in that the traffickers operated from within a highly respected corporation with branches around the world, a corporation that specialized in transporting mail and packages. That corporation was Federal Express.

It happened that one day at a FedEx facility in Los Angeles, a FedEx employee was sorting through packages and found one that contained marijuana. It was reported up through channels. Soon the DEA was involved, and Operation Green Air was up and running. What they uncovered amazed them. It was the first case of its kind, but it would not be the last.

Among the world's largest drug cartels is one based out of Tijuana, Mexico, known as the Arellano-Felix Brothers Organization, or AFO. They were smuggling large quantities of marijuana to Jamaican traffickers in Southern California. Once there, the Jamaicans distributed it throughout the United States.

It was one of the Jamaicans who came up with a brainstorm. Why go to all the work and effort of setting up their own distribution network when there was already an extremely efficient company in existence that could do the job faster and better than the Jamaicans could ever hope to do it? That company, of course, was Federal Express, and the Jamaican drug lord who came up with the idea was Mark Morant.

Over the course of a couple of years, Morant methodically bribed FedEx employees until he had dozens working for him and a system of delivery that stretched from his warehouse in Los Angeles to cities like New York, Newark, and Boston, as well as some in the South.

Morant's scheme was clever. His shipments were guaranteed to be delivered overnight, and there was little chance of interception by authorities. It was only a fluke that the Los Angeles employee found one of the packages and reported it.

The DEA estimated that Morant had shipped more than 4,000 boxes of drugs before the DEA closed in. Morant never paid a cent, since the system was set up so that he shipped the marijuana for free.

The FedEx employees who were bribed were paid $2,000 per week or more, even if there were no special packages to deliver that week. To earn their money, the bribed employees had to pack the marijuana into FedEx boxes, attach phony air bills, then hand the boxes over to drug dealers parked along various FedEx routes. Drivers, customer service reps, security personnel—all were involved.

Tons of marijuana was delivered this way. Tons more—seventeen tons, in fact—was seized when the Feds swooped down and arrested twenty-two of those involved in the ring.

Mark Morant was not one of them. He disappeared.

In an unrelated footnote, Mexican authorities arrested Ismael Higuerra-Guerrero, the chief of operations for the AFO.

Date Rape

In March of 2000, yet another substance was added to Schedule I of the Controlled Substances Act. This time it was gamma hydroxybutyric acid, or GHB.

Another drug-related problem had reared its head in the United States. It was an ugly problem, with ugly consequences for its victims; a problem that, like drug use itself, underscored the dark underbelly of a populace jaded by hedonistic indulgence. A problem that starkly highlighted the amoral quicksand into which America was sinking.

That problem was date rape.

The Federal government estimated that more than 300,000 females of all ages were raped each year. The government had to rely on estimates because many rapes went unreported. Many women were so traumatized and ashamed that they refused to tell anyone. Again, estimates varied, but anywhere from 30 to 60 percent of rape victims never came forward.

That a person, male or female, would resort to rape was despicable enough. They were the lowest of the low—sexual predators whose acts were devastating to their victims. Emotionally, psychologically, and physically, rape could leave permanent scars.

As repulsive as it sounds, sexual predators were now relying more and more on drugs to achieve their lecherous ends.

Certain drugs had become known as "date-rape drugs." The term was misleading, because many of those raped were not dating their rapists. The rapists slipped the drugs into their unsuspecting victims' drinks, and when the drugs took effect and the victims couldn't resist, the rapists had their way.

Victims were of all ages, from small children to the elderly. By far, though, most were young women of college age, although high school girls and women past college age were frequently targets.

Surveys indicated that 25 percent of all female college students were victims of rape or attempted rape. About 80 percent of the attacks were committed by people who the victims knew, which translates into 20 percent, or one-fifth, perpetrated by people the women didn't know. Alcohol played a factor in about 90 percent of all rapes. The percentage involving drugs was harder to estimate for a reason we will discuss shortly.

It should be observed that not all rape victims are female. The latest stats indicate that at least ten percent were male. And no, they were not all being raped by other men. A small but growing number of women fell under the sexual-predator banner, and their victims are often but not exclusively men.

GHB was now one of the more popular recreational drugs, and it was the drug that sexual predators most liked to use. Emergency-room statistics bore this out. In 1990, there were fifty-seven instances of overdose by GHB. In the year 2000, there were almost *five thousand*. The rise was staggering, and it showed no sign of declining any time soon.

So what is GHB? And where does it come from?

Initially it was used by bodybuilders to increase their muscle mass. It is synthesized from solvents used as paint stripper and for cleaning circuit boards, or from a chemical used in the production of plastics.

GHB is made in illegal labs in the United States. The quality varies. Since many of the illegal labs are makeshift affairs and their products' potency hard to calculate, overdoses are frighteningly common.

The effects of GHB are usually felt within ten to fifteen minutes of ingesting the drug. It metabolizes quickly, making it hard for hospitals and poison-control centers to detect its presence after the fact. This is why it is difficult to develop concrete stats related to drug use in date rape. In many cases, the drug is suspected but authorities can't conclusively prove that it was a factor.

The fact that it dissipates so quickly appeals to sexual predators. It helps them cover their tracks. So, too, does the fact that GHB can induce a state of temporary amnesia; victims have no idea what they did or what was done to them while they were under the drug's influence. A woman might suspect she was raped, but if she can't remember it, and if there is no trace of the drug in her system, she can't prove it.

More severe reactions included nausea, respiratory problems, and seizures. Seizures were more common when GHB was used in conjunction with methamphetamine. That is another thing about GHB: it is routinely taken with alcohol or other drugs to produce the desired effect.

Two undesired effects were coma and death. But both were increasingly common as GHB's use spread.

Another aspect that sexual predators liked was that GHB was odorless and colorless. It does have a slightly salty taste, but when it is mixed with alcohol, even that could not be detected.

GHB was usually sold in either liquid, powder, or capsule form. It was immensely popular at raves and night clubs, often contained in innocent-seeming water bottles. Some dealers and users mixed it with water in squirt guns, then either sold or used it "by the squirt."

Some of the more common street nicknames for GHB were self-explanatory: Easy Lay, Salty Water, Liquid G, Sleep, Fantasy, G-riffic, and Organic Quaalude.

As with heroin and other drugs, regular use resulted in chemical dependency, and shaking the habit was an ordeal in itself.

To some it might seem unwarranted for the Drug Enforcement Administration to become involved in the suppression of a drug used primarily for recreational purposes. But take another look at the emergency-room statistics and the number of date rapes each year. GHB, and other drugs like it, were not as spectacularly horrific as heroin or crack, but they still caused untold sorrow and suffering, and they were taking a growing toll in human lives.

New Mexico

In June of 2000, Operation Tar Pit ended in the arrest of almost 200 suspected heroin traffickers.

It was not widely known, and not something New Mexico liked to brag about, but the Land of Enchantment led the nation in heroin abuse. Odd, indeed, that there were more heroin-related deaths in New Mexico each year than there were in California or New York. Emergency-room treatments were common.

The DEA knew this, of course, and was eager for a lead on the major supplier. The little town of Chimayo, New Mexico, gave them that lead.

The DEA's interest in Chimayo was piqued when statistics revealed that between 1995 and 1998, eighty-five people had died of heroin-related causes there. Given that little Chimayo had a total population of less than 3,000, that stat stood out like a naked crackhead in the middle of Carnegie Hall. It was suggestive of an extremely active heroin cell.

The DEA was right. In October of 1991, an investigation brought about thirty-three arrests. They, in turn, led to seventeen more in Albuquerque, linked to the same cell.

But more were to follow. As more and more intel was gleaned, the full scope of the ring became evident.

Operation Tar Pit was launched. The op's target was the source of the heroin responsible for the deaths in Chimayo.

The state of Nayarit, Mexico, became the focal point. A gang specializing in the distribution and sale of black-tar heroin was based there. Best estimates had it that they were smuggling upward of a hundred pounds of heroin per month into two dozen United States cities.

Mexican officials would later dispute the categorization of the gang as "Mexican." They agreed that the heroin was Mexican and that most of the traffickers were Mexican, but they claimed that the actual base of operations was in Los Angeles, which, in their view, qualified the gang as "American."

Semantics aside, the gang was highly organized. They grew the opium in Nayarit, processed it there, then smuggled black-tar heroin across the borders of California and Arizona to stash houses in Los Angeles.

From there the heroin was distributed literally throughout the country. From Alaska to Hawaii, from Minnesota to New Mexico. Cells were active in twenty-two cities. In five states, the cells operated statewide and did not limit their activities to a single city. They were truly a coast-to-coast operation.

To distribute the heroin, they developed an ingenious method. They hired couriers—principally young girls and old men, on the theory that they were less likely to be suspected and searched. The girls hid the heroin in secret compartments in boom-boxes. The old men wore special belts around their waists.

The gang shipped some of its heroin by more conventional means: FedEx and the United Parcel Service.

Although not particularly violent, the gang had a nasty streak, as evinced by one means they hit on to boost sales. Developing new clients took time, so why not offer their product to people who were already addicts? Finding addicts wasn't a problem, thanks to a program intended to help them.

In response to the heroin epidemic, methadone clinics had sprung up across the nation. There, heroin addicts were given methadone to inhibit their craving for heroin. Critics asserted that it was a waste of time; that the government, in effect, was substituting one drug for another. Proponents argued that methadone was safer and that its use could be more easily controlled.

The black-tar gang saw the methadone clinics as a golden opportunity. They bribed clinic employees to send addicts to secret "shooting galleries," where the addicts could get all the real heroin they wanted, provided they had the money.

The addicts could hardly resist, especially since the purity level of the black-tar heroin had risen to where it equaled or exceeded that of Colombian heroin.

For years, the Colombians had dominated the market precisely because their purity levels averaged between 70 and 90 percent. Until this point, purity of Mexican heroin had been down around 30 to 40 percent.

Now that had changed. The Nayarit gang was selling heroin that ranged from 60 to 85 percent pure, and they were selling it for far less than the Colombians did. Routinely, Colombian heroin was going for an average of $125,000 per kilogram. The Nayarit gang sold theirs for as little as $13,000 a kilogram. At street level, half a gram was going for a measly $10.

The net effect was to glut the market with cheap, potent heroin. Cheap meant that more people could afford to buy it. Potent meant that users became addicted faster. It also meant more overdoses, and more deaths.

At those prices, it wasn't long before the Nayarit ring saw their product replace Colombian smack as the top-selling heroin in the United States—a dubious distinction turned sinister by official speculation that it was their intention all along. From the very beginning, the Mexicans were out to displace the Colombians at the top of the heroin supply chain, and their strategies paid off. They were now *numero uno*.

They were also *numero uno* on the list of gangs the DEA was after. The FBI, U.S. Customs, and other agencies were partners with the DEA in a Special Operations Division formed to deal with situations exactly like this one, and they went after the ring with a vengeance.

In June of 2000, the payoff was announced.

In raids across the country, 176 suspects were arrested and twenty-three pounds of heroin seized. This was in addition to previous seizures of over forty pounds.

The United States half of the Nayarit gang's smuggling empire had been neutralized, but the gang was still very much alive and well south of the border, and it would pose more problems down the road.

Pseudoepheorine

Heroin. Cocaine. GHB. Marijuana. The DEA was in constant battle on multiple fronts at once.

One of those fronts was methamphetamine. The sale of meth was flourishing. More and more meth labs were being uncovered in more and more states.

The DEA had tackled the problem logically and effectively by restricting access to pseudoephedrine, a chemical needed to make meth. But obviously, someone somewhere was getting their hands on pseudoephedrine in large enough quantities to create a new flood of meth. But who? And how?

The answer proved unsettling, and showed that in the devious world of drug manufacturing, the DEA could never take anything for granted. Sometimes the sources of illegal drugs were right under their noses.

Back in 1997, new federal controls had been imposed on pseudoephedrine production. Makers of the chemical were required to register with the DEA and to scrupulously monitor production. But in an investigation that was to take several incredible and unexpected turns, the DEA learned that not all makers were equally honest.

A national network was uncovered. Pseudoephedrine manufacturers in New York, Florida, Texas, Illinois, Ohio, Pennsylvania, Michigan, Colorado, Kentucky, and Arkansas were regularly sending huge shipments of pseudoephedrine tablets to California. From there, the tablets were sent to secret meth labs.

So far the situation seemed normal enough. Dishonest businessmen were trying to make a lot of dishonest bucks. Nothing new about that. But then the DEA found out who was behind it.

The manufacturers weren't the masterminds. A mysterious group calling itself "the Commission" had set up a system whereby they bought tablets from the manufacturers for four times the amount a customer would normally pay, and then, using front companies, resold the tablets to the meth labs for four times what they had paid for them.

The Commission was strange enough. Even stranger was what they did with the money: they sent it to the Middle East. Specifically, to Syria, Jordan, Saudi Arabia, and Israel. The DEA would not learn who was involved at the Middle Eastern end for a couple of years yet, and when they did, it would send shock waves through the international law-enforcement community.

In April of 2000, the DEA had built a solid enough case to arrest fourteen of the Commission's couriers, and to confiscate about 1,200 pounds of pseudoephedrine and millions in cash.

Through informants, the DEA learned that the Commission had called an emergency meeting in Florida. The arrests and seizures had panicked them, and they decided to take measures to make it harder for authorities to dismantle the rest of their operation.

The Commission decided to only use white Americans as couriers. They reasoned that white Americans were a lot less likely to incite suspicion than Mexican couriers or those of Middle Eastern descent. The Commission had been using unsuspecting commercial companies to funnel a large portion of the pseudoephedrine, but now they decided to change companies frequently in a variation on the old pea-under-the-thimble routine. And lastly, the Commission members agreed to be ready to make a quick getaway if they had to.

The DEA's evidence continued to grow, and in December, Operation Mountain Express was launched to shut down the network once and for all. Some investigators wanted to let the investigation run longer, but there were concerns that the Commission members would skip the country if they got wind of it. As it turned out, the concern was well founded.

Eight of the ten Commission members were arrested. Hassan Zaghmot, a Denver member, was all set to flee with $650,000 in cash that he had in his safe-deposit box. A federal grand juror had tipped Zaghmot off that a federal indictment had been handed down against him. That juror, identified as Mark Hinckley of Evergreen, Colorado, was also arrested.

Another Commission member did get away. The tenth happened to be out of the country.

The DEA seized ten tons of pseudoephedrine, eighty-three pounds of meth, 136 pounds of other chemicals, and $8 million in cash.

Operation Mountain Express was a sensational success. The DEA had shut down the network, effectively shutting off the flow of domestic pseudoephedrine.

As always, though, success was transitory. No sooner did the DEA plug the influx of drugs at one point than a new opening appeared. It was like trying to plug an old rusty bucket. Every time the DEA plugged one leak, a new one appeared.

No sooner did the domestic supply dry up than the meth makers and found a new source in Canada. Although the United States tightly regulated pseudoephedrine, its neighbor to the north did not. In fact, Canada had practically no restrictions at all.

Meth makers, particularly those based in Mexico who ran secret meth labs in various locations in the United States, had been smuggling pseudoephedrine out of Canada for some time. But now they turned the flow up to full volume.

Shipments of Canadian-originated pseudoephedrine began to be seized with increasing frequency. To mention just one example, a tractor-trailer was stopped crossing the border into Detroit, and inside, the U.S. Customs Service found 10,700 kilograms of pseudoephedrine.

Canadian authorities were as concerned as were their American counterparts. In a few more years they would impose regulations of their own, but in the meantime, the meth rings took advantage of their lapse and the meth crisis in America steadily worsened.

Caribbean Channels

Cocaine, meanwhile, continued to pour in through the Caribbean and the Gulf of Mexico at a rate of an estimated 500 metric tons per year. About 80 percent of that was brought in by speedboats. Souped to the max and rigged with electronic counter-surveillance devices, the speedboats were hard to detect and harder to catch. Nine out of every ten got through. The ones that were caught either broke down or were stopped by neighboring nations who were not quite as mindful of the degree and type of force they used to stop them.

The use of commercial cargo vessels was also on the rise. The Colombians were at it again, using huge ships to transport cocaine to some twelve countries in North America and in Europe. But cargo vessels had two drawbacks: they were impossible to hide on the open seas, and they were a lot easier to catch.

That didn't stop Colombian Ivan De La Vega from setting up a transportation organization that relied heavily on cargo ships.

Operation Journey was designed to dismantle it. The DEA was working with various other agencies, including many from overseas. France, Spain, Great Britain, Greece, Italy, the Netherlands, Albania, Belgium, Panama, Venezuela, and of course Colombia were all involved. There were so many taking part, each with its own laws and systems of jurisprudence, that prosecutors from the Narcotic and Dangerous Drug Section of the U.S. Justice Department's criminal division were called in for crucial legal guidance.

The investigation took two years.

It turned out that Ivan De La Vega was running the cargo-vessel equivalent of FedEx. He wasn't shipping cocaine for just one cartel. He had set himself up as a one-stop shipping service for any cartel that wanted to avail itself of his services.

Operating out of Colombia and Venezuela, De La Vega had a fleet of eight- to ten-ton vessels at his disposal. Some he owned outright. Others he owned through companies he had set up in Greece and elsewhere.

It wasn't a small operation, by any stretch. The cocaine was conveyed from Colombia either over land or by air to the Orinoco River Delta region on the northeast coast of Venezuela.

It was kept at hidden jungle camps until the time came to ferry it by speedboat to cargo ships offshore. The ships were fitted with secret compartments that held thousands of kilograms of cocaine at a time.

Off the ships went, to ports around the world. The cocaine was usually offloaded to waiting speedboats before the cargo vessels docked.

To confuse the law, De La Vega randomly chose when a ship carried cocaine and when it carried nothing but legitimate cargo. He set up codes for his people to use, and switched his cell phones often to make it harder for his conversations to be overheard.

It didn't help. In the end, the DEA and the other agencies uncovered the full scope of his operation.

One by one, De La Vega began losing his ships. A British naval vessel with U.S. authorities on board stopped the freighter *China Breeze* near Puerto Rico. Hidden in the *China Breeze*'s sewage tanks were 3,880 kilograms of cocaine bound for the Netherlands. The British navy escorted her to Texas, where the captain and four crew members were arrested. It was subsequently determined that De La Vega has used the *China Breeze* to carry some ten tons of cocaine to the United States and Europe.

Next, the Dutch seized the *Pearl II* when she docked in Amsterdam. In a secret compartment that measured five feet by five feet by sixty feet, they found over 2,000 kilograms of cocaine. By questioning those arrested, the Dutch established that the *Pearl II* had conveyed some eleven tons of cocaine to the U.S. alone.

In August, the U.S. Navy stopped the *Suerte 1* near Grenada. They thought they had a sure thing. A few days earlier, Venezuelan authorities had intercepted two speedboats loaded with cocaine bound for the *Suerte 1*. But when the boarding party searched her, no cocaine was found. The Navy escorted her to Houston, where she was seized by the U.S. Customs Service.

At the same time, Venezuelan authorities arrested Ivan De La Vega and turned him over to the United States. In conjunction with the arrest, in a joint United States/Venezuelan op, raids were launched against cocaine-storage sites in the heavy jungles of the Orinoco River Delta. At the first camp, five speedboats and communications equipment were found, but no cocaine. At the second storage site they were luckier; they discovered about 4,000 kilograms of cocaine. At a third and yet a fourth camp, they collected 2,000 kilograms each.

The cocaine at the last two sites was believed to have been intended for the *Suerte 1*, but the smugglers had changed their minds when the first two speedboats were intercepted.

While all this was going on, arrests were being made in Greece, France, and Italy.

The one-stop shipping service for the Colombian cartels was out of business.

Ecstasy

One of the last big ops to be conducted in 2000 was Red Tide. This time the target was a syndicate dealing MDMA, or "ecstasy," as it is more commonly known.

Like GHB, ecstasy was popular at raves and nightclubs. Raves got their start in Los Angeles and San Francisco in the late 1980s, but by 2000, they had spread to every metro area in the country.

Why were they so popular? In a word—drugs.

Participants paid high fees to get in. Once through the door, they were literally in ecstasy. They could party hearty all night. Dancing and sex were secondary attractions.

Rave-club owners liked to advertise their raves as alcohol-free. To parents, that sounded ideally innocent, but the truth was that many club owners actively promoted the sale of club drugs, mainly ecstasy. In addition, they would sell overpriced bottles of water so users could stave off the dehydration that inevitably resulted from sustained ecstasy use. They also sold pacifiers to deal with teeth-clenching, an involuntary effect of the drug, and neon glow sticks to heighten the effects.

Ecstasy users were under the same delusion as GHB users: namely, that the drug was basically harmless. But data provided by the Drug Abuse Warning Network proved otherwise. Between 1998 and 2000, there was a 58 percent jump in emergency-room treatments of ecstasy-related cases, from 2,850 to 4,511.

Ecstasy doesn't always produce the desired euphoria. Too often, it causes paranoia, hallucinations, and amnesia, and those are just the temporary side effects.

There is considerable evidence to show that chronic use of ecstasy results in sustained brain damage. Chronic use also brings about a drop in the serotonin in the brain, and when that happens, severe depression can result. Research in Britain has established that the temporary amnesia some users report can become a permanent state of mental disruption. Heavy users reach the point where they can't conduct a conversation without losing their train of thought.

As if that were not enough to discourage its use, the teeth-clenching alluded to earlier was a boon to dentists. Regular users routinely suffered worn teeth, cracked enamel, and jaw problems.

It should be noted that ecstasy abuse wasn't restricted to the

United States. The drug had gone global in a big way. Britain, Australia, and Ireland led the world in the percentage of their populations using the drug.

Profit was the motivator behind syndicate interest. When you consider that an ecstasy tablet that cost well under a dollar to manufacture could be sold for $25, you begin to see why the illegal trade in ecstasy boomed.

The Netherlands and Belgium were responsible for 80 percent of all the ecstasy produced. Russian and Israeli crime syndicates specialized in smuggling the drug into the United States.

To give a fuller idea of the burgeoning problem: in 1993, the DEA had seized 196 ecstasy tablets. By 1998, that figure had risen to 174,278 tablets. In 1999, it was one million. In 2000, the DEA seized *three million* tablets.

Part of that total was from Operation Red Tide. A task force that included the DEA, the FBI, the U.S. Customs Service, and other federal, state, and local agencies was out to put a transnational ecstasy syndicate out of operation. They were ably aided by the Dutch national police as well as by authorities in Mexico, Israel, Germany, Italy, and France.

The head of the syndicate was an Israeli. Tamer Adel Ibrahim might be appropriately described as an ecstasy kingpin, although he was involved in cocaine trafficking, too.

More than twenty suspects in the United States and in four European countries were arrested. Acting on intel unearthed by the DEA and the FBI, the U.S. Customs Service boarded a commercial airliner that had recently arrived in Los Angeles from Paris. The largest single ecstasy seizure in United States history resulted: 2.1 million ecstasy tablets.

Tamer Adel Ibrahim was in the United States when the crackdown occurred. Before he could be apprehended, he heard about the seizure and fled to Mexico. But a team of special agents from the DEA and FBI were hot on his trail. They discovered that he was setting up another ecstasy shipment from the Netherlands to Los Angeles. This one would involve 1.2 million tablets.

In September, Ibrahim flew from Mexico to Amsterdam to oversee the shipment. Others members of his syndicate flew in to help. They were all promptly arrested by the Dutch national police, and the 1.2 million tablets were seized.

In November, thanks to intel garnered by the DEA/FBI team, the DNP arrested seven more co-conspirators.

Scratch one ecstasy syndicate.

The Friend-Killer

Along the United States border with Mexico, cocaine and marijuana smuggling continued to thrive.

The DEA had made a sizeable dent with Operation Impunity, which crippled the Amado Carillo-Fuentes and Juan Garcia-Abrego gangs. But then along came Osiel Cardenas-Guillen. The enterprising Guillen took over the remnants of the two gangs and forged them into his own.

Based in Matamoros and Reynosa, Mexico, Guillen soon had his drug-trafficking empire up and running. Notoriously violent, his nickname was "the Friend-Killer"; he had a habit of whacking his friends if they slipped up.

Guillen was blamed for an assault in June of 1999 on an undercover investigator from the Cameron County (Texas) sheriff's office who was working with the U.S. Customs Service. He was also wanted in connection with an assault on DEA and FBI agents in Matamoros in November.

Guillen had strong links to the Colombians. His gang would

smuggle Colombian cocaine into the United States hidden in tractor-trailer loads of lettuce, carrots, and jalapeño peppers. Most of the coke ended up in New York, but other cities were involved: Chicago, Houston, Louisville, Columbus and others.

Operation Impunity II hit his organization hard. The DEA, the FBI, and U.S. Customs made 132 arrests. Over 5,200 kilograms of cocaine was seized, as well as over 9,000 pounds of marijuana and ten million in United States cash.

Osiel Cardenas-Guillen, however, was not one of those taken into custody. He had slipped through the net.

Enter the State Department. Federal officials take a jaundiced view of federal agents being assaulted. A $2 million reward was offered for the capture of Guillen or either of his top two lieutenants.

The Friend-Killer now had even more cause to distrust his friends.

A new millennium had dawned, but for the DEA it was the same old, same old, only worse. The illegal drug trade was flourishing.

If it had been so inclined, the DEA had a lot of successes to boast about. But like unchecked weeds, each time a drug lord or syndicate was taken down, another sprang up. What the DEA needed was a "weed killer" for all contingencies, but there was none. Hard work and perseverance were called for. Untiring efforts were needed on many fronts at once.

The DEA believed that it was up to the challenge.

But was it?

2001–2002

Drug Syndication

The original Colombian cartels were gone. Most of the old-school Colombian drug lords were behind bars or dead. In their place had sprung up slightly smaller but equally if not more efficient drug syndicates that preferred to keep a low profile to avoid arousing the ire of politicians and the attention of law enforcement.

Gone, too, were the days when Colombian traffickers only smuggled cocaine. They still dominated the cocaine market, but they were now active in the heroin trade, and doing just as well at it. Best estimates: upwards of 60 percent of all heroin entering the United States could be traced to the Colombians.

They were using the best tech money could buy: computers, faxes, the Internet, radar-controlled aircraft, automatic weaponry.

Each syndicate had small armies at their disposal, to work and kill at the whim of their leaders.

Several other interesting developments had taken place.

The traffickers now had highly efficient laboratories hidden throughout Colombia. They were no longer dependent on Peru for their cocaine base; they made it themselves. Coca-leaf cultivation in Colombia had gone through the jungle canopy, as it were.

The most troubling development was that certain traffickers had forged an alliance with rebel groups out to overthrow the government. In return for money and weapons, insurgents like FARC would protect trafficker assets and guarantee the safety of drug shipments within areas under their control.

All this made combating the Colombian trade that much harder, and much more dangerous. Thus it was that with a justly deserved feeling of accomplishment, the DEA announced the success of Operation White Horse.

The op centered on a heroin ring. Three kingpins in Colombia were arrested. They were ferrying large amounts of heroin into the northeastern United States, but in relatively small amounts at a time, thanks to the method they employed: fleshbags.

There have always been people willing to make a buck no matter what they had to do to earn it. The Colombians had no shortage of prospects they could hire as "swallowers."

They didn't invent the practice. Other drug rings had already tried it with considerable success. It involved placing drugs in balloons or other "wraps." Couriers then swallowed them, and could waltz through airport security and customs with no one the wiser. Once the wraps were expelled from the body, the drugs were recovered and sold.

Individuals who hired on as fleshbags ran a great risk.

Sometimes the wraps leaked or broke, flooding the body with drugs and resulting in coma or death.

Still, as smuggling tactics went, it got the job done. The defendants used swallowers to transport heroin into New York City and Philadelphia. In addition to the bigwigs in Colombia, more than fifty other suspects were taken into custody. One, the head of the New York end of the operation, was arrested in Aruba, where he had gone to arrange to smuggle in more heroin.

In June, the DEA announced another successful op. Working with the FBI and the U.S. Customs Service, they scored a coup against a formidable network of Mexican transporters who served as middlemen for the South Americans.

For "formidable," think "violent." The situation along America's border with her southern neighbor had deteriorated drastically, from bad to worse to reprehensible. Mexican traffickers had no qualms of conscience about squeezing the trigger, and they did so with alarming frequency.

The most sensational incident was the murder of the Matamoros state police chief in broad daylight on a city street.

Jamie Yanez Cantu was the kind of officer others looked up to. He had risen through the ranks with an impeccable record. Hundreds of arrests were chalked to his credit. He was a great detective, famous for solving difficult homicides. He was also relentless in his opposition to the drug rings and their hired gunmen. He helped take down three prominent Gulf drug lords. His nickname was "the Assassin Hunter."

Some would say it was inevitable that Cantu would fall victim to some of those assassins. He and his assistant were killed with shots to the head and dumped in a car a few blocks from state police headquarters.

Money was found in the car—a suitcase containing $20,000. The implication was that Cantu was a good cop gone bad; that he was accepting drug money. It didn't jibe. Mexican authorities believed the money was planted to besmirch the memory of an honest crusader.

There were many other violent incidents, both below and above the border. In Laredo, Texas, the bodies of a young couple were unearthed in the backyard of a suspected drug dealer. Not long afterward, two more bodies were found at a ranch owned by the family of a man believed to be a drug assassin.

Ironically, the DEA's earlier success in smashing several major Mexican drug rings was partly, and indirectly, to blame for the rise in bloodshed. Several smaller and much more violent drug syndicates were fighting for control of the market previously ruled by the likes of Amado Carillo-Fuentes and Juan Garcia-Abrego.

One of the more violent rings was known as the Marquis organization. Made mainly of some remnants of the Fuentes ring and others, it was based in Nuevo Laredo, Mexico. Drugs from Colombia were brought to Nuevo Laredo and smuggled from there across the border into Texas, where they were stored in warehouses before being sent to cells across the United States.

Most of the drugs were brought across in tractor-trailers filled with produce. Sizeable amounts were also smuggled through checkpoints in cars and small trucks with concealed compartments.

The Marquis would use any means to stamp out rivals, three of whom were shot to death in San Antonio by an alleged Marquis assassin.

The DEA, the FBI, U.S. Customs, and Mexican authorities teamed up to bring the Marquis ring down. Simultaneous raids were conducted in Texas, New York, Philadelphia, Baltimore, and Memphis. Warrants for fourteen Marquis members in Mexico were given to Mexican authorities. The raids capped an eighteen-month investigation that saw 268 arrests, over 19,000 pounds of cocaine confiscated, and over 27,000 pounds of marijuana intercepted.

Another problem the DEA had to contend with was corruption. Many public officials and law-enforcement personnel were secretly on the payroll of various kingpins and syndicates. Colombia and Mexico were notorious examples, but they were not the only countries where corruption ran rampant, as we have seen.

Money, a lot of money, had a way of turning the head of even the most scrupulous public servant and defender of the law. People are only human, as the old saw has it, and public servants generally didn't earn the superstar salaries of professional sports figures. Far from it: many struggled to make ends meet and feed their families. So it was perhaps inevitable that when drug rings secretly approached judges or politicians and offered to fill their pockets with more money than they ever dreamed of having, many succumbed.

No one was immune. Not customs agents, not the military, not congressmen or senators or prime ministers. Certainly not policemen.

It was particularly unsettling, though, when the police gave in to temptation. They are society's protectors, the guardians of the law. When they turn bad, the dismay the public feels cuts a bit deeper. The psychological impact is a shade more profound.

With that in mind, we turn to Puerto Rico, which has a police force of some 20,000. Most are honest and hardworking.

Most go about their daily jobs as they are required to do, diligently and professionally. But every barrel of apples has a few rotten ones, and in August of 2001, the DEA announced that six Puerto Rican police officers had been arrested on drug-related charges.

The DEA worked with the Bureau of Alcohol, Tobacco and Firearms (BATF) and the Superintendent of the Police of Puerto Rico to uncover the extent of the corruption and bring those accountable to justice.

The six officers and their associates hadn't been bribed by a local drug gang; they had set up their own. They went into the cocaine and heroin business. And the way they went about it was unbelievable.

Maybe they thought they were invulnerable. Maybe they believed their badges and their uniforms lent them so much power that no one could touch them. Or maybe they were just plain stupid. Because in an act of monumental audacity, they took to selling the drugs *from their patrol cars while they were on duty*.

Did they think no one would notice?

The DEA, BATF, and Puerto Rican authorities set up an undercover sting. DEA agents bought 250 grams of heroin from the cops gone wrong. The cops also took thousands of dollars from the undercover agents to safeguard make-believe shipments of illegal drugs.

Both male and female police officers were involved, ranging in age from twenty-one to forty-three. Several were veterans with over a decade on the Puerto Rican police force.

Puerto Ricans have a figure of speech they use to describe police gone bad: "honor perdido," or "lost honor." The FBI adopted the name for an op of its own that resulted in more arrests in November—arrests unrelated to the DEA case, but which further illustrate the extent of the corruption. Federal indictments were returned against forty suspects, among them police, politicians, and prominent citizens.

In yet another case, one of those indicted was the Speaker of the Puerto Rican house, who was charged with conspiracy, money laundering, and extortion.

In August, the DEA received a tidbit of encouraging news: Colombia would soon extradite Fabio Ochoa to the United States to stand trial. Ochoa, it will be recalled, was Pablo Escobar's right-hand man.

Another fugitive that the DEA was after, Osiel Cardenas-Guillen, was still on the loose, still a player on the drug scene, and still had a $2 million reward on his head. Several times, authorities thought they had him, but he always stayed one step ahead of the dragnet.

Back to Puerto Rico, where the DEA made yet more arrests. This time it was a heroin and cocaine ring operating out of Mayagüez.

Heroin was easy to come by in Puerto Rico. Most came from South America, although Mexican black tar and Southeast Asian heroin were not unknown.

To give some idea of the burgeoning problem: in 1999, federal officers seized 16.8 kilograms of heroin; in 2000, it was 43.5; in 2001, the figure catapulted to 114 kilograms. The amounts seized were never anywhere near the total. More drugs slip through than are intercepted. Estimates varied, with some saying that seizures barely stemmed 10 percent of the illicit flow.

Another statistic that bore out the degree to which heroin infested Puerto Rican society was that nearly 20 percent of all federal cases that involved drugs were heroin-related. Compare that to the national average of only 7 percent.

Part of the problem was that Puerto Rico had become a transhipment point for drugs being smuggled into the U.S. The usual methods were used, including concealing the drugs in cargo vessels and commercial aircraft, as well as employing "swallowers."

Every arrest and conviction was a triumph of law over chaos. So when the head of the DEA's Caribbean field division announced the apprehension of thirteen members of an alleged drug network, there was reason to smile.

More reason than one might imagine, given that a major scandal had rocked the Drug Enforcement Administration.

Five current and former DEA agents came forward to allege that the DEA's San Juan office regularly and routinely falsified arrest reports and seizure figures. The five asserted that other agents repeatedly claimed credit for arrests made by local police. Up to 70 percent of *all* the arrests the Caribbean office made between 1998 and 2000 were bogus, according to a former DEA supervisor.

If true, how had it been done? Easily, said the supervisor. DEA agents read local newspapers to learn about the latest drug arrests, then made out DEA arrest cards and submitted them, making it appear as if the DEA agents had a hand in the arrests when they did not.

But why would DEA agents do such a thing? An obvious answer was to boost their careers, but there was more to it.

The DEA assigned resources based on arrest stats. The more arrests a DEA field office made, the more resources they were allocated. Was it coincidence, then, that the San Juan office saw its arrest figures treble, and as a result, its staff size double?

The integrity of the DEA was at stake. Were the allegations true? Was it only the San Juan office that practiced the deception, or was the practice widespread throughout the DEA? The General Accounting Office, Congress's investigative arm, was asked to find out.

Before going public with their accusations, the five agents had tried to go through channels. Several contacted the Office of Professional Responsibility, the DEA's equivalent of Internal Affairs. They were told to put their complaints in writing. A supervisor involved in inflating figures was reprimanded, but others not only escaped punishment, but were promoted.

As for the five, they were either demoted, transferred, or reprimanded.

It was not the DEA's finest hour. A case could be made that the agents who inflated their reports were influenced by their supervisors, who constantly pushed for more arrests. But that does a disservice to the overwhelming majority of DEA agents, who perform their duties honestly and competently. As the five who came forward demonstrate, not all agents are willing to sacrifice their integrity for the sake of their careers.

Brand X

Back in the States, ecstasy was in the news again, involved in an incident that made national headlines.

The DEA was involved in Operation Green Clover, an effort to dismantle a drug ring that specialized in club drugs.

The DEA first became aware of the ring's existence when a state trooper in Colorado made an arrest and found ecstasy pills on the suspect. That, in turn, led to the arrest of six cadets at the Air Force Academy and airmen at the Cheyenne Mountain Air Station and at Schriever and Peterson Air Force bases.

But these were small potatoes. The DEA was after the supplier. The ring was supplying ecstasy, Special K, and LSD to clubs in Colorado and California.

A word about the name of this op, "Green Clover."

In order for traffickers to differentiate their ecstasy pills from those made by other suppliers, they were in the habit of imprinting their "brand name" or "logo" on their pills. The imprints might be anything from popular cartoon characters to names like "Rolls Royce."

This way, when certain kinds became popular, users would look for tablets with that particular imprint. It was the ecstasy trade's way of enticing repeat customers.

A good idea, except that drug dealers are not famed for their high morals and ethics. Whenever a brand became popular, other dealers would mimic the logo to increase the sales of their own pills. Quite often, the pills the mimickers manufactured were not nearly as stable as the popular brands.

The drug ring in Colorado and California was imprinting their pills with a four-leaf clover, hence the DEA's name for the op. In the end, it culminated in the arrest of fifty-five defendants from both states and the seizures of some 85,000 ecstasy tablets, 320 pounds of marijuana, 2.5 kilograms of cocaine, five pounds of meth, and 40,000 hits of LSD.

John Sposit, of Lakewood, Colorado, was considered a ringleader. He and two others were not only brought up on drug charges, they were also charged in connection with the death of a Colorado girl.

Brittney Chambers was celebrating her sixteenth birthday. Friends got together at her house for a party. Brittney decided to try ecstasy. But instead of reaching a state of euphoria, she felt ill. Drinking water seemed to help, and Brittney drank a lot. Too much, as it turned out, because the coroner later ruled that she died of "water intoxication," stemming from her hit of ecstasy.

Six of Brittney's acquaintances were arrested. Four were juveniles. Two others allegedly sold the ecstasy that Brittney used, on school property. The tablets were the clover brand made by the club ring.

The ringleader, Sposit, eventually pled guilty and was sentenced to twelve years in prison.

Caribbean Connections

Puerto Rico had been designated a high-intensity drug traffic area. During the latter half of 2001, the DEA tackled one drug ring after another, making arrest after arrest.

In August, a pre-dawn raid netted Luis Fornia Castillo, alias El Viejo, and fourteen others. They were accused of distributing heroin, cocaine, and marijuana in San Juan and Arecibo.

In September, Operation Sanctuary resulted in thirty-five arrests and the seizure of thousands of pounds of cocaine by the U.S. Coast Guard. The defendants were part of an international cocaine ring heavily involved in money laundering. Their organization stretched from Puerto Rico to the Dominican Republic to Venezuela and the United States. The cocaine arrived in ships and was transferred to speedboats offshore.

In an unusual twist, a Lebanese connection was unearthed at the money-laundering end. The DEA had noticed that more and more Middle Easterners were becoming involved in drugs, with more and more money funneled back to the Middle East. Exactly who was using the money, and to what purpose, would soon become all too clear, and would add the most disturbing element of all to the drug war.

In September, Operation S.O.S. saw the arrests of eighty-five people in a broad sweep through Puerto Rico. Most were from four cities; Ponce, Juana Diaz, Villalba, and Guanica. Arrests were also made in New Haven and Waterbury, Connecticut; and in Tampa, Florida; and Allentown, Pennsylvania.

Drug seizures at two stateside airports brought about Operation Face Off. At John F. Kennedy International Airport in New York, eleven kilograms of cocaine were confiscated. At Newark International Airport in New Jersey, fifteen kilograms. By tracing the drugs back, the DEA uncovered a cocaine ring centered in San Juan.

Extradition

On September 7, the Colombian government announced that they would extradite Fabio Ochoa to the United States to stand trial.

Ochoa had a long and checkered history. He had been a leading member of the Medellín cartel. In 1990 he turned himself in to Colombian authorities after they granted him partial amnesty. He was sent to prison, but he evidently continued to run his drug business from behind prison walls. In 1997, he got out and became linked to the Juvenal trafficking ring.

The DEA had been after Ochoa for more than a decade, and it pushed for his arrest. In a flamboyant gesture of defiance, Ochoa put up billboards in Colombia trumpeting his innocence. It didn't stop him from being extradited.

The trial was held in Miami. The defense claimed that Ochoa had not returned to his old ways. They said he was only socializing with drug traffickers and not actually involved in drugs himself. They claimed that government wiretaps failed to conclusively prove his guilt.

The jury felt otherwise.

When the verdict was announced—thirty years in prison—Ochoa made the sign of the cross and dropped to his knees.

The War Goes On . . .

On the home front, the DEA's efforts were having an impact.

On September 8, in the Hunts Point section of the Bronx, agents of the Drug Enforcement Task Force surrounded a tractor-trailer. Inside the trailer, in a false compartment, were some 700 pounds of cocaine, 680 pounds of marijuana, and twenty-five pounds of meth.

It was just one of many seizures. Users complained that the crimp in supply had raised drug prices. Bags of marijuana were costing up to ten dollars more. Special K was a lot harder to come by, and a lot more expensive.

On September 11, the day of the World Trade Center attacks, a firefighter gave police a tip that ecstasy was being sold from an apartment in Battery Park City. Over $100,000 worth was seized.

A journalist reported that one ecstasy dealer, after his arrest, grumbled that he thought the authorities "had better things to do," what with the terrorists and all.

In Los Angeles, the DEA and other agencies, working with Mexican authorities, took apart a large family-run heroin syndicate. The family's operation extended from Nayarit, Mexico, to Los Angeles, with cells in Portland, Las Vegas, St. Louis, and Fort Worth.

About 2 percent of the world's supply of opium poppies was being cultivated in Mexico. That doesn't sound like much, but most of the heroin derived from the poppies was bound for the United States market.

Until the 1980s, the majority of heroin coming out of Mexico was in the form of brown powder. Then the traffickers discovered that they could increase their profits if they changed to the black-tar variety, a hard gummy form cheaper to produce. It could be smoked as well as injected. Best of all, average purity levels for black-tar heroin were consistently higher than for brown-powder heroin, and for heroin addicts, purity was an important selling point.

In recent years, a type of white heroin has appeared, a costlier combination of Mexican opium gum and a Colombian processing method. Like brown-powder heroin, its popularity had paled compared to black tar except in the affluent northeast United States.

For the longest while, Mexican traffickers had mostly confined their trafficking to west of the Mississippi. But that had changed. They had pushed east and were selling their illicit wares along the Gulf and up the Eastern Seaboard.

And where before the Mexican traffickers had concentrated on transporting drugs manufactured by the Colombians, they were now making their own in secret, sophisticated laboratories. Two such labs were raided by Mexican police in Durango.

Despite the best efforts of United States and Mexican authorities, despite all the seizures and the arrests and the closing down of labs, the level of heroin coming out of Mexico stayed steady. Try as they might, law-enforcement agencies had no hope of putting an end to it.

On September 26, a multi-agency task force conducted a sweep in California, Missouri, and Texas. At the same time, Mexican police went after Mexican members of a ring with cells in St. Louis and Los Angeles. One hundred search and arrest warrants were carried out.

It was a routine op, but it was to have unforeseen repercussions that involved the DEA in another scandal.

Like all law-enforcement agencies, the DEA relied heavily on tips from informants. Intel gleaned in this manner often proved crucial to prosecuting cases against drug rings.

To encourage informants to come forward, the DEA and other agencies offered rewards. The financial incentive was justified by the fact that those involved in criminal enterprise were often too scared to come forward. The life expectancy of snitches was notoriously short. Their greed, though, was just as notoriously ingrained. Some were willing to take their lives in their hands and tell the authorities all they knew if they were paid enough.

Critics of the reward system warned of its drawbacks. For one thing, there was no guarantee that the information supplied by the informants was reliable. For another, there was a danger of "professional informants" springing up, people who lied under oath for the money.

Enter Andrew Chambers. He was a DEA informant for sixteen years. The information he gave resulted in the arrests of some 400 people.

Over those sixteen years, Chambers was paid a reputed $1.8 million.

Then came the bombshell. During his time as a snitch, Chambers had been arrested more than once on charges ranging from fraud to forgery. In each instance, either the charges were dropped or he was bailed out—by the DEA.

Worse, it turned out that Chambers had lied under oath. When asked in court if he had ever been arrested or convicted, he said no. He made claims about his background which were unsubstantiated.

The DEA maintained that while Chambers was not always honest about his past, the information he gave about drug ops was invariably accurate, as the evidence they collected proved.

Some in the media, though, saw it as another abuse of official power. They charged that informants like Chambers were using the system to line their pockets. There was a minor clamor for the government to stop paying informants, but if that were done, informants would stop coming forward. Some proposed that the authorities stop using informants entirely, but that was even more drastic.

And there matters stood.

Another high-intensity drug area sprang up in the homeland.

The ten counties that comprised San Francisco and its environs were now hotbeds of drug production and distribution. Foremost was meth.

Three states accounted for most of the meth labs in the country—California, Washington, and Missouri—but the Sunshine State was king.

To give some idea of the magnitude: in 1990, 286 California drug labs were shut down. In 2001, the total was a staggering 1,862.

Until about the turn of the century, most labs produced meth in relatively small amounts. In California, the DEA began to see a rising number of "super labs" that churned out meth in high volume.

In the San Francisco area alone, seventy-one meth labs were raided between January and October. Fifteen were super labs. Intel indicated that up to 80 percent of all the meth sold in the country came from the drug rings operating these labs.

The traffickers always had new labs up and running in no time. To illustrate: in April of 2001, a task force raided a lab in

Watsonville. Five suspects were arrested. They were believed to be responsible for meth distribution to a three-county area. And, indeed, analysis showed that after the arrests, the meth supply in those three counties dried up—but only for a month or so, and soon meth was once again flowing at its former levels.

Northern California was still a prime source of high-potency marijuana, too. Growers had thousands of square miles of national forest and other wilderness in which to cultivate their crops. Indoor operations were increasing.

Nor was there any shortage of heroin or cocaine. Mexican traffickers had spread north into the San Francisco area. The East Bay, and Monterey County, had become relay centers for drugs bound elsewhere.

In October, a major ecstasy ring bore the brunt of an investigation by the DEA's San Diego division. More than twenty people were taken into custody over a two-day period as part of a raid on the most sophisticated lab found to date in the United States. The timing of the raid could not have been better; the DEA pounced just as the ring was gearing up to begin distribution.

The op was called Triple X—not after the popular movie, but because the ecstasy ring imprinted three X's on the tablets they manufactured.

Close to 50,000 tablets were seized, along with a pound of meth. But the really important prize consisted of precursor chemicals that could be used to make even more tablets. A *lot* more. These included forty-eight kilos of 3,4-Propene, which could produce approximately half a million tablets; 700 pounds of camphor oil, which could be used to make a million tablets; and forty-five gallons of gamma butyrolactone, or GBL, which was used in manufacturing GHB.

As we have learned by now, unusual developments arise continually in the drug war, and in the ecstasy raid, the most unusual was the discovery that one of the suspects had reputed links to the Kosovo underworld.

During the course of the investigation, agents were surprised, while conducting a wiretap, to overhear the man mention alleged ties to a country more than 7,000 miles away, and which, until that moment, they had no idea was a factor. Reference was made to a mysterious "general," about which nothing else was learned.

The DEA believed that the suspect had referred to a former general in what was known as the Kosovo Liberation Army, a rebel force fighting for independence until 1999. After the KLA was disbanded, some of its members became involved in the drug trade. In fact, Kosovo acquired a reputation as a drug pipeline.

At the time, it was largely under United Nations control, with some 4,500 U.N. police keeping a lid on things. Six hundred of them hailed from the United States.

As for ecstasy itself, statistics revealed that close to six and a half million young people had used the drug at least once. Of those between the ages of twelve to seventeen, 2.6 percent went on to use it regularly. For those eighteen to twenty-five, the total was much more alarming: 10 percent who tried ecstasy liked it enough to continue using it.

This was reflected in emergency-room figures. The year before, there had been 4,511 emergency-room mentions of ecstasy as the reason treatment was sought.

The bulk of the ecstasy was still being made in laboratories in Europe, but a growing number of United States labs were being found.

In one month alone, the DEA concluded two ops against

ecstasy rings. The first netted twenty-eight suspects and about 85,000 tablets, along with some 40,000 units of LSD, 2.5 kilograms of coke, five pounds of meth, and marijuana and marijuana plants. The second ended with the arrest of 247 people and the seizure of 7.5 million tablets, an indication of the size of the ecstasy market.

With stats like these, it could be said with some justification that the public-education campaign was a failure. Ten percent of a given demographic is an unduly large number. But put conversely, it meant that 90 percent of those in the same age bracket *weren't* using ecstasy. That was impressive by any standard.

There will always be those who refuse to take warnings to heart, whether about drugs or alcohol or smoking. They think they know better.

Admittedly, among the young, peer pressure exerts an influence out of all proportion to what it should. When a high school student believes that "everyone" is doing something, the lemming syndrome kicks in, and he or she just has to do it, too. Peer pressure is recognized by some experts as *the* leading influence when it comes to young people making up their minds whether to do drugs or not. Premeditation doesn't enter into it. They go to a party or they are hanging at a friend's house, and suddenly someone offers them drugs. In order to avoid being ridiculed or offending their friends, they give in, and once the pattern is established, it's easy to repeat. By then, with certain drugs, addiction sets in, and they can't stop even if they want to.

Toppling drug kingpins was all well and good, but the DEA did not always go after the guys at the top. The DEA regularly targeted street-level cells, too. It was the cells, after all, who were pushing drugs in countless neighborhoods across America. Whenever one was taken down, it sometimes took weeks or even months before a new one appeared.

In November, the DEA and other agencies brought the legal boom crashing down on several Boston cells that specialized in cocaine. Coke was easy to come by in Massachusetts. New York was the source of most of it, but some was smuggled in from Florida and the desert Southwest. The usual means were relied on; namely, commercial aircraft, tractor-trailers, and cars with hidden compartments.

One Boston man tried a different approach. He ordered his drugs over the Internet, from a physician in Mexico and another source in Spain. The DEA teamed up with postal inspectors, the Massachusetts state police, and the Food and Drug Administration to put him out of business.

We have seen how enterprising drug rings got FedEx and the United Parcel Service to unwittingly—and in a case of a few rogue employees, wittingly—transport drugs. The U.S. Postal Service wasn't immune, either.

In 2001, postal inspectors made 1,662 arrests of individuals suspected of using the mail for drug trafficking or money laundering. They also seized more than 8,000 pounds of illegal drugs and an incredible amount of steroids.

Sometimes the DEA worked in concert with postal inspectors. In Morristown, Tennessee, two men were arrested after one signed for an Express Mail package that contained fourteen pounds of marijuana. It turned out that one of the men was the leader of a coke-and-grass ring that almost exclusively used the U.S. mail, FedEx, and UPS for shipping. They had a network of eight mailing addresses at different commercial mail-receiving businesses. On average, they were sending out about eighty pounds of marijuana each week. The coke, be it noted, was always sent Express.

Sometimes the culprits were postal workers themselves. In Detroit, a mail handler was taken into custody for selling marijuana to other employees while on the job. In Michigan, another mail handler was sentenced for the same crime. In Chicago, a letter carrier was arrested after he bought crack from a known crack dealer.

In Cambridge, Massachusetts, a man working at the local post office was arrested, while at work, for selling marijuana.

One of the more sensational cases came out of Boston. The DEA arrested a letter carrier for allegedly selling marijuana out of his U.S. Postal Service truck *while he was making his daily rounds*. Worse, he was selling it near school grounds.

The man had been with the postal service for almost twenty years. He was regarded as a dependable worker and never gave his superiors cause for suspicion. Then a customer of his was arrested and offered to tell all in exchange for a reduced sentence.

The letter carrier had a neat little system. He would ride around in his truck performing his usual pickups until a customer rang him on his pager. He would then meet with the customer, make the sale, and go on about his work as if nothing out of the ordinary had occurred.

The DEA got it on video. One of the sales took place in the West Side Social Club's parking lot, which adjoined the playground of a local school.

In November, the DEA, working with the Massachusetts state police and other agencies, went after a cocaine, heroin, and ecstasy ring with tentacles that stretched from South America to

Boston. It was the culmination of a four-month undercover op that relied heavily on wiretaps and surveillance.

The ring was what might be described as a "middleman cell." It obtained drugs from sources in Costa Rica and Colombia and smuggled them into New York City. From there, the drugs were taken to Boston, where they were sold to drug dealers, who in turn resold them at street level. Shipments were made weekly.

In Massachusetts, a DEA task force and Massachusetts state police stopped one of the ring's vans on the Massachusetts Turnpike at Hopkinton. Inside, in a special compartment, were eighteen kilograms of cocaine.

In Sturbridge, Massachusetts, the state police stopped another vehicle and found coke.

In New York, a swallower was arrested. He had ingested 700 grams of heroin.

Down in Costa Rica, acting on a tip from the United States, authorities stopped a man as he was about to board a plane for the United States. He had swallowed more than eighty packages containing a total of almost a thousand grams of heroin. The police were able to determine exactly how much once the packages "showed themselves."

In 1999, the National Highway Traffic Safety Association had issued grants to five states—grants that were eventually to benefit the DEA, as well.

The five states were Pennsylvania, Texas, Tennessee, Louisiana, and Georgia. Each was given a million dollars as part of a campaign against drunk drivers. The program involved setting up checkpoints and saturation patrols with an eye to getting drunk drivers off the road.

It was highly effective, and it had a collateral benefit. In

Georgia, for instance, sobriety checkpoints were set up statewide. Over a thousand DUI arrests were made. Almost 2,000 people were arrested for driving with suspended or revoked licenses. Almost 300 fugitives wanted on various warrants were snared.

But the statistic that concerns us was the 756 drugs arrests made. Intel gleaned from drug-related traffic stops is often relayed to the DEA as a matter of course. Sometimes, the information leads to bigger investigations resulting in the dismantling of whole syndicates and networks.

In Lithonia, Georgia, police received a report of suspicious goings-on at a local residence. They stopped four vehicles that had left the scene. In one, they found eighty-eight pounds of cocaine.

The DEA was notifed, and a federal search warrant was issued. Inside the residence were another 132 pounds of cocaine and evidence that led to two more locations and, ultimately, the arrests of six individuals.

Over in South Carolina, it was a speeding car that brought in the DEA after it was stopped by a Highway Patrol ACE Team and a K-9 search uncovered five kilograms of cocaine in the trunk. A follow-up by the DEA revealed links to Lithonia and another drug operation. Two Lithonia men were arrested and thirty-eight kilograms of cocaine seized.

Another highway stop by the South Carolina ACE team resulted in an arrest and the confiscation of two pounds of cocaine and twenty pounds of marijuana. This case, too, was handed over to the DEA.

These are only a few examples out of many that highlight not only the effectiveness of something as ordinary as a routine traffic stop but the pervasiveness of drugs in general. Consider that at the Georgia checkpoints mentioned above, there were almost half as many drug arrests as there were DUI's. Now multiply that figure by fifty states. Granted, it's imprecise, but it hints at the magnitude of the challenge that law enforcement faces.

Speaking of challenges, the heroin situation along the United States–Mexico border had continued to deteriorate.

Larger and larger shipments were being seized, which told the DEA several things. First, Mexican traffickers were producing heroin at record levels. Second, more must be getting across. Third, and this carried potential for trouble down the road, the Mexican heroin traffickers were now strong enough to challenge other heroin organizations, including the Colombians.

This was a case of a bad decision coming back to bite the Colombians where it would hurt. If you will recall, at one point the Colombians started paying Mexican traffickers in product, including heroin. It whetted the Mexicans' appetite for selling more of the same, and before the Colombians caught on to their blunder, Mexican traffickers were involved in heroin in a huge way.

Several routine seizures at the border brought about Operation Landslide. An organized-crime drug-enforcement task force that included the DEA kicked into high gear.

Black-tar heroin, as well as cocaine and meth, were being smuggled into the United States and stored in stash houses run by cells in Los Angeles, San Francisco, and San Jose. From there, the drugs were sent nationwide. Eleven states were involved: California, Washington, Oregon, Missouri, Illinois, Colorado, Texas, Arizona, Georgia, North Carolina, and Florida. More than thirty more cells and their members were identified.

Working with Mexican authorities, the task force struck. Thirty-eight people were arrested north of the border, five below it. Close to 800 pounds of heroin was seized.

The DEA had been in existence for three decades. It had many accomplishments of which it could be proud. It had made thousands of arrests and seized huge amounts of various drugs. But one thing it could not do, try as it might, was put a permanent end to the drug scourge.

This is why the DEA has resorted to educating the public as part of its anti-drug efforts. The more informed people become about the dangers of drugs, the fewer might be tempted to use them.

The media, and particulary the pro-drug lobby, had a field day when Nancy Reagan advocated her "Just say no!" campaign. They laughed her to scorn, calling the campaign juvenile. But as simplistic as it was, it did the invaluable service of stressing that drug use was an individual *choice*. People *could* say no, if they wanted to. That alone was a revelation to social lemmings who always went along with the crowd.

Still, even with their efforts to achieve prevention through education, the best the DEA could do was hold its own. By the turn of the century, drug use across the board, by and large, had peaked. The number of users was holding steady.

But if the DEA had learned anything from three decades of waging war on the front lines, it was the volatile and unstable nature of that war in which it was embroiled. There was no status quo, per se. New situations constantly arose. New enemies constantly appeared.

September 11, 2001, will forever be remembered as one of the most deeply disturbing days in American history. That was the day many Americans awoke to the realization that they could no longer afford to take terrorism lightly. The repercussions are still being felt.

For years the DEA had noticed that a growing amount of drug dollars were being funneled to Europe and Asia, not to line the coffers of ordinary drug syndicates, but to nurture organizations that were much more sinister; that had ties to fanatics of the worst sort.

The Colombian cartels. The Dominicans. The Mexican syndicates. These and others had become major players in the drug trade. Now, new players were on the scene. Players who weren't in it to get rich, and who didn't care about fancy mansions and fancy cars. These people wanted drug money for one reason only: so they could kill.

The day of the terrorists had arrived.

DRUGS AND TERRORISM

The DEA had gone up against a variety of adversaries over the years. The cartels, syndicates, and street gangs all had one thing in common to a lesser or greater degree—their willingness, in some cases their *eagerness*, to commit violent acts. Violence and the drug trade went hand in hand, but the violence was always an undercurrent to the trade, not the trade itself.

Terrorists were a whole new animal. Violence was their lifeblood. The drugs were secondary. They sold drugs so they could buy more guns or make better bombs. They sold drugs in order to be better at what they did, and what they did was take human life.

Terrorism had always existed; always had a small but persistent presence in the shadows of humanity. But in the last half of the nineteenth century, the scope of global terrorism had swelled, like a festering sore that couldn't be cured.

Much of it was in the Middle East. Israel has had to deal

with terrorism since her foundation. Europe, Africa, Asia, all saw their share.

America, by contrast, had been spared. Few terrorist acts were committed on her shores. Perhaps the first acquaintance many Americans had with the idea of terrorism was when Patty Hearst and the Symbionese Liberation Army made headlines.

Other terrorist acts were to further mold the national consciousness. Arab terrorists killed Israeli athletes and took others hostage at the Munich Olympics in 1972. Police snipers shot the terrorists but didn't kill them, and one of the terrorists was able to pull a hand grenade and kill the rest of the hostages.

In 1980, six Islamic terrorists took control of the Iranian embassy in London. They threatened to kill a hostage every half hour unless their demands were met. Two hostages died before the SAS went into action and killed five of the terrorists.

Americans overseas started falling victim. Citizens of the Great Satan, as the United States was branded, became a prime target for Islamic fundamentalists, and others.

In 1983, a suicide car-bomber in Beirut, Lebanon, crashed into the United States embassy. Sixty-three people died, seventeen of them Americans.

In October of that same year, terrorists bombed a barracks in Beirut where U.S. Marines and French paratroopers were billeted, and 299 perished. Of those, 241 were United States Marines. It is important to mention that the man believed to have masterminded the bombing was Imad Mugniyah, Osama bin Laden's mentor.

In December, another suicide bomber crashed into the United States embassy in Kuwait. This attack, long with two others, were carried out by terrorist groups with links to Iran.

In 1988, Pan American Flight 103 blew up over Lockerbie,

Scotland. Two hundred and seventy people died, including eleven on the ground and a group of Syracuse University students returning home after a semester abroad.

A truck bomb exploded at the Khobar Towers in Saudi Arabia in 1996. The towers were a domicile for the United States military. Nineteen died.

In August of 1998, the United States embassies in Kenya and Tanzania were hit on the same day. More than 200 died and some 5,000 were injured. It was a miracle that the death toll wasn't higher. The suspects belonged to a terrorist group few Americans had heard of—al-Qaeda.

These are just a few examples among scores that could be cited. The ones that made a big splash in the headlines. The ones everyone heard about.

Many others did not make the news domestically, or if they did, hardly anyone noticed. And some hit very close to home.

The *Sunset Limited*, an Amtrak train on its way from New Orleans to Los Angeles, was derailed in Arizona. Someone had deliberately tampered with the tracks. Letters were found that mentioned Ruby Ridge and Waco. The letters were signed "Sons of the Gestapo." To date, the suspects have not been apprehended.

Members of the El Rukens street gang, out of Chicago, were convicted of plotting terrorist acts on behalf of Libya.

Two men from Minnesota were sent to prison for intending to use ricin as a biological weapon. They were members of a group that advocated the violent overthrow of the United States government.

In 1993, a car bomb went off in the parking basement of New York's World Trade Center. Seven died, hundreds were hurt. This was the first terrorist attempt to bring the WTC down. The perpetrators saw it as a symbol of everything the

Great Satan stood for, and everything they hated. Few people are aware that the terrorists had rigged a cyanide-gas device to go off when the emergency crew arrived. Fortunately, the device was destroyed.

No more needs to be said about the Oklahoma City bombing or the second assault on the World Trade Towers. All Americans are aware that they were terrorist-related.

But what does all of this have to do with the DEA, whose prime mission, after all, is to combat drugs? We have seen hints throughout this book of links between various terrorist organizations and the drug trade; links that blossomed, upon investigation, into full-scale drug operations being run by terrorists for the express purpose of raising money so they could commit more terrorist acts.

A whole new term had been coined to describe the relationship between terrorists and drugs: narco-terrorism.

Before 9/11, most Americans, and many in law enforcement, tended to regard drugs and terrorists as separate problems. But that's not the case. More than half of the dozens of terrorist groups recognized by the U.S. Department of State are involved to varying degrees with drugs.

One of the earliest narco-terrorists was Pablo Escobar, the poster boy for the Medellín cartel. His drug money not only funded hundreds of murders and bombings, but also allied him with Communist insurgents out to overthrow the Colombian government, the FARC. The Revolutionary Armed Forces of Colombia initially ran a protection racket for drug lords and later branched out into dealing in drugs themselves.

The United Self-Defense Force of Colombia, or AUC, a "people's army" opposed to the FARC but every bit as violent, has made no secret of its ties to the drug trade. Their leader has publicly stated that about three-fourths of their funds come from processing and selling coke.

In Peru, a terrorist group called the Shining Path started partially funding its activities by "taxing" cocaine traffickers in the areas in which it operated.

On the other side of the world, Afghanistan fell to the Taliban, who hanged the previous ruler, closed the only university the country had, and announced that henceforth males, and only males, would be allowed a high-school education. Females could attend school up to the age of twelve, but after that, they were to stay home and concentrate on housework.

Afghanistan had long been a leading producer of opium poppies and heroin. Now all that income was the Taliban's to do with as it pleased. Some of that money was being channeled to terrorist organizations. Shortly after the Taliban took over, they permitted terrorist training camps to be established within Afghanistan.

Osama bin Laden was allowed to set up a camp of his own near the city of Jalalabad. A year later, he announced to the world that he had declared a *jihad*, or holy war, against the United States. For those who didn't get the message, his declaration in 1998 left no doubt as to his purpose: "To kill Americans and their allies, civilians and military, is an individual duty for every Muslim who can do it, in any country in which it is possible to do."

In 2000, the Taliban made a surprising announcement. Opium-poppy cultivation was banned—supposedly. About 70 percent of the world's opium supply came from Afghanistan, and if poppy cultivation had truly stopped, there should have been a corresponding drop in the amount of heroin available globally. But there was no drop. Some experts saw the ban as a ruse. They suspected that the Taliban had stockpiled opium and had imposed the ban to artificially drive up prices.

All this was rendered moot by the United States invasion. Or was it? The new government continued the ban on opium cultivation, but many growers ignored it. Latest estimates indicate that Afghanistan will produce 2,700 tons of opium this year.

Over in Uzbekistan, the IMU, an Islamic movement, was also financing its operation through heroin.

Hezbollah, a Muslim extremist group based in Lebanon, set up a network to smuggle cocaine out of South America and into the Middle East and Europe. In recent years, more and more of their money has come from the sale of drugs.

The Kurdestan Worker's Party, a Kurdish group in Turkey also known as the PKK, has long been known to traffic in heroin.

In Southeast Asia, the United Wa State Army (UWSA) controlled wide areas of Burma and was focusing more on drugs than terrorism since the Burmese government granted them the right to do almost whatever they pleased. Recent intel suggests that the UWSA has become active in the trafficking of synthetic drugs.

These are just a few of the terrorist organizations deriving money from drugs. As it is plain to see, a new interface has developed.

Narco-terrorism greatly complicates the overall picture for the DEA in several crucial ways. For starters, as was seen with the Taliban in Afghanistan and the UWSA in Burma, some terrorist groups are government-sponsored or government-sanctioned. It is difficult enough for the DEA to persuade friendly governments to cooperate in bringing down a drug ring; when the ring is an unofficial arm of an unfriendly government, it is next to impossible.

Terrorist groups are closely knit organizations. That makes them much harder to penetrate. Whereas the DEA can often buy information from drug-ring informants, terrorists can rarely be bought. They tend to be either political or religious idealists, or both, and as a rule refuse to compromise their fanatical beliefs for money.

Infiltration is equally impractical. While the DEA can use undercover agents of Hispanic descent to infiltrate, say, a Mexican trafficking ring, the number of DEA agents who can believably pose as Islamic extremists can be counted on one hand.

Then there is that violence quotient. Drug rings are dangerous enough. Many traffickers will kill if pressed. Some even like to kill. But killing is what terrorists are all about. Their entire mindset is geared toward it. They have no qualms about eliminating anyone who stands in their way, and that includes DEA agents.

The activities of the FARC in Colombia vividily illustrate what the DEA is up against.

Since 1980, the FARC has kidnapped more than 100 United States citizens and killed at least a dozen more. Three were missionaries who were executed simply because they were from the United States. The FARC harbors a special hatred for Americans. Their leadership has specifically targeted United States citizens.

The U.S. State Department Annual Report on Global Patterns of Terrorism in 2001 states that 55 percent of *all* terrorist acts in the world were committed by the FARC. To narrow it down even more, 85 percent of all terrorist attacks against United States citizens worldwide took place in Colombia and were sponsored by the FARC.

✲ ✲ ✲

At the turn of the century, a new pattern in weapons buying emerged. Previously, groups like the FARC paid cash. But now the FARC was swapping cocaine for firepower. Arms dealers from Russia, Nicaragua, and Venezuela, to mention just three, accepted drugs in exchange for machine guns, surface-to-air missiles, grenades, and AK-47 assault rifles.

The FARC's more active drug stance resulted in Colombia's coca cultivation jumping from about 50,000 hectares in 1995 to 169,800 hectares in 2001. Seventy-six percent of the world's total cocaine base came from Colombia—a total of 230 metric tons.

Gone were the old days when Colombian traffickers had to rely on Bolivia and Peru. Bolivia's cocaine output fell dramatically, from 240 metric tons in 1995 to eighty metric tons in 2000. Peru's also dropped, from 460 metric tons to 145. As in Bolivia, decreased demand by Colombian traffickers had a lot to do with it.

Interestingly enough, while the Colombian share climbed, their purity levels dipped an average of 10 percent. A contributing factor had to do with profits. The protection money that the drug rings were paying to the FARC cut into their profit margin, so the traffickers began to dilute their cocaine.

A third factor was unforeseen. The South American drug syndicates were so successful that they had branched out into Europe and Asia. But they weren't producing enough coke to meet the increased demand. This was even more reason for them to dilute it. Street prices in the United States and elsewhere stayed the same, but users were getting less cocaine for their money.

The DEA could also claim part of the credit. Their ongoing

campaign to restrict the chemicals that drug traffickers needed was having an effect. To illustrate: twenty-eight countries took part in Operation Purple, which reduced the supply of potassium permanganate used in making cocaine base.

Another encouraging statistic emerged after all the stats were correlated at the turn of the century: between 1996 and 1999, the total amount of cocaine smuggled into the United States dropped by 200 metric tons. From 1999 to 2001, the total climbed again, but not to former levels. It held steady at about 100 metric tons less than "normal."

If coke was on a downturn, horse was not. Heroin was coming out of Colombia in record amounts, and once again, the FARC had a hand in the pot. Approximately 59 percent of all heroin seized in the United States could be traced back to the former cocaine capital. Commercials airlines and cargo vessels were the conduits.

The DEA's Operation Plataforma put a dent in the pipeline when eighty-five people in Colombia, Peru, Chile, Ecuador, and Venezuela were arrested.

Another positive development was the formation of a heroin task force consisting of the Colombian national police, the Bogotá Country Office, and DEA offices.

In December, the DEA announced the results of Operation Seis Fronteras (six frontiers), which focused on the chemical end of the processing equation. Working with authorities in South America, the DEA confiscated large quantities of chemicals and shut down ninety-four labs.

The DEA ended the year on an upbeat note. Despite the rise in narco-terrorism, despite the proliferation of trafficking rings in general around the globe, the DEA closed out 2001 with some major hits.

But was it a trend or an aberration? Who was really winning the war on drugs? The DEA? Or those who waged relentless assaults on civilized societies everywhere? And what part would terrorism play in influencing the final outcome?

The answers remained to be seen.

2002

State of the Union

Drug use had peaked. That in itself was encouraging, although the number of drug arrests each year was still staggeringly high. More were made at the local and state level than by federal agents, and four-fifths of the arrests were for possession.

Drugs arrests comprised about 11 percent of all arrests made. How many was that? Roughly thirteen million. One and a half million were on drug charges, about the same number as for driving under the influence. More than a million physical assaults were committed, many either drug- or alcohol-related.

Overall, alcohol was still king. When all alcohol-related crimes were totaled, including public drunkenness and other violations of liquor laws, the total far exceeded those for drugs.

From 1987 to 1995, more arrests were made that involved cocaine or heroin than any other illegal drug. But then something interesting happened. Apparently, the public's fascination with hard drugs waned: after 1996, marijuana became the leading substance in drug arrests.

In 2001, 1,490 drug labs were raided. Of that total, 97 percent were meth labs. Synthetic drugs were still popular, but nowhere near as much so as coke, horse, and weed. More than three million marijuana plants had been destroyed the previous year, and close to 38,000 growing plots were no longer being used for that purpose.

Pause to consider this tidbit. At the federal level, there were some 93,000 agents legally empowered to make arrests, but only 4,020 of those were DEA agents. By comparison, the FBI employed more than 11,000 personnel.

In 2002, a national survey on drug use and health that focused on female substance abuse was completed. The results were intriguing.

It was already common knowledge that fewer females than males used drugs. This applied at all age levels. Slightly over one-third of all high school girls dabbled in illegal substances. For boys the total was more than half.

Even though fewer girls were users, statistics indicated that when girls did try drugs, they became hooked faster than boys did. A higher percentage became chronic abusers. Why? Were females psychologically and physically weaker? Of course not. But as the survey made clear, females tended to use drugs for different reasons than males did; reasons that compelled them to keep using drugs once they started.

One of the oldest stereotypes around is that girls mature quicker than boys. Socially, this is certainly true. Girls are more eager to fit in, more anxious to be accepted. Generally, they're not quite as impatient or as impulsive. Thus, while boys would often try drugs for the first time for the hell of it, girls were more inclined to do so in order to please their peers. For that same reason, girls would go on using drugs, while for boys the novelty would lose its luster.

The survey found that slightly over 3 percent of pregnant women used drugs. Not a large percentage, but disturbing in that when hard drugs were involved, prenatal development was often adversely effected.

Of the 21,683 people who died of drug-related causes in the year 2001, many of them overdoses, only 7.439 percent were females. But when it came to emergency-room visits, almost half were females.

The good news was that although the general figures showed fluctuation in the use of various drugs, drug use had reached its saturation level. Enforcement and education *were* making a difference.

Another survey bestowed a dubious honor on Seattle, Washington. Of the twenty-one metropolitan areas canvassed, including larger cities like Philadelphia and San Francisco, Seattle had the highest number of emergency-room visits for drug treatment.

Marijuana treatments there had soared 75 percent from 2000 to 2001. Cocaine treatments had jumped 32 percent. Meth treatments skyrocketed.

Had Seattle suddenly become the new drug capital of the United States? No. Other cities reported increases in emergency-room treatments, as well. A lot of the visits were due to club drugs. Young people continued to think that ecstasy and Special K were safe and harmless, when they were neither.

Northern Exposure

Canada still hadn't regulated pseudoephedrine. It was estimated that over fifty tons was being imported into Canada annually, with most intended for the illicit market. Of that total, about sixteen tons was stopped at checkpoints. That left an awful lot to slip through.

Canada had become the main source for pseudoephedrine entering the United States. Most was brought in by tractor-trailers. Customs checked as many big rigs as they could, but they couldn't check them all, and detection methods weren't infallible.

Pseudoephedrine was found hidden in shipments of everything from furniture to glassware—even in a shipment of bubble gum.

Sometimes there wasn't anything in the trailers. Or there wasn't supposed to be. On one occasion, a truck arrived at the customs station into Detroit with a manifest stating that the trailer was empty. The Customs Inspector had a look anyway. Inside were forty-three *million* pseudoephedrine tablets.

The Port of Detroit was the primary entry point for most of the smuggled pseudoephedrine, which was why the DEA, U.S. Customs, and the Royal Canadian Mounted Police chose it for the next phase of Operation Mountain Express. An unqualified success, it resulted in the seizure of thirty tons of pseudoephedrine and 300 arrests. In addition, nine labs were raided, and 180 pounds of meth were taken out of circulation.

Those arrested were part of a trafficking network that extended from Canada to California. Some of their trucks were seized at the border. Others, driven by undercover agents, were allowed to go on to labs in California, and arrests and seizures were made there.

All the arrests made were on the south side of the border. By Canadian law, the network members in Canada weren't doing anything illegal. It wasn't until they crossed the border that they committed a crime.

Many of those arrested were of Middle Eastern extraction. The first thought was that the profits were being funneled to a terrorist organization. It was established that the money trail led back to the Middle East, but beyond that, the government wasn't commenting.

They did comment on one aspect of the investigation—namely how, working with Canadian authorities, they had determined which Canadian companies were supplying pseudoephedrine to the ring. It must be remembered that in Canada this was perfectly legal. And besides, the companies had no idea what the purchasers were going to do with the pseudoephedrine. Or so they said.

Of the seizures made at the border, most were of the tablet form of the drug, in huge 32,000-tablet bottles.

Tractor-trailers weren't the only vehicles used. The ring had a United States Postal Service trailer that it had stolen. They also put the post-office logo and the FedEx logo on other trailers to lend the impression that they were legitimate.

As a corollary to the op involving the Canadian manufacturers, DEA agents converged on a United States company.

Neil Laboratories was properly registered to make and export pharmaceuticals and other chemicals. But when the DEA discovered that pseudoephedrine seizures in eleven states involved tablets made at Neil Labs, alarm bells went off. It couldn't be coincidence.

Warning letters were sent, and when Neil Lab tablets continued to show up on the illicit market, an audit was conducted. It was found that some of the company's distributors were diverting pseudoephedrine to places like head shops, liquor stores, and tobacco stores.

More warnings were issued. Finally, the DEA served a federal criminal search warrant. Records were seized. Tons of pseudoephedrine and ephedrine were confiscated. The production manager was arrested. The company president was served with a suspension order. Thirteen Neil Labs distributors were no longer allowed to deal in chemicals.

Los Greenes

In Puerto Rico, a tip led the DEA to a family-run ring that dealt in cocaine and crack. Operating out of Aibonito, the "Los Greenes," as they were known, were active in several Puerto Rican cities and were making inroads in cities in the continental United States, notably Chicago and Newark.

Authorities were concerned by a rise in ecstasy seizures in the Caribbean as a whole. In Aruba, almost 60,000 ecstasy tablets had been found on airline passengers. Use alone could not be a factor. At the time, an ecstasy tablet in the United States went for about $25. In Aruba, tablets only cost $15.

Ecstasy was also seized in Curaçao, Jamaica, and Puerto Rico. Some was destined for raves and clubs on the islands. Some was intended for the United States.

There was evidence that Aruba, in particular, had become a midway point for ecstasy.

Concern was further fueled when ecstasy labs were uncovered in Colombia. The Colombians were already major players in the cocaine and heroin trades, and they showed no inclination to become as big in the MDMA market, but the mere existence of the ecstasy labs suggested a strong probability the Caribbean would soon witness a greater influx.

The Colombians were always open to new markets and new avenues for distributing their drugs. For a while now, they had been using the ports of Manta and Guayaquil in Ecuador. A DEA investigation led authorities to two vessels, the *Forever My Friend* and the *Svedsa Maru*. In the former, eight metric tons of cocaine were found. In the latter, there were twelve tons.

In February of 2002, drug dogs with the canine unit of the Ecuadorian national police were sniffing a shipment of flowers at Quito International Airport when they reacted. The shipment was bound for Miami. Inside many of the hundreds of boxes were plastic pellets filled with heroin—all told, nineteen kilograms.

Intel led the DEA and the Ecuadorian national police to more suspects and the seizure of another thirty-one kilograms of heroin that was to be shipped to the United States.

Overturned

February was also the month when the DEA became embroiled in a firestorm of controversy. The pro-drug crowd and sympathizers in the media were stirred up as never before.

A Supreme Court ruling was the catalyst. By a unanimous decision, the nation's highest court ruled that marijuana was an illegal substance as defined by the Controlled Substances Act, effectively rendering state laws that permitted marijuana use for medical purposes invalid. California's Proposition 215 and laws in Alaska, Oregon, Washington, Hawaii, Maine, Nevada, and Arizona were nullified.

The case came to the Supreme Court by way of a September, 2000 ruling by a federal judge who issued an injunction barring the DEA or any other agency from investigating doctors who prescribed marijuana for medical treatment. Under that ruling, medical marijuana clubs could flourish.

The Justice Department had appealed. Now, with the issue legally decided, the DEA adopted a new policy toward hemp in general and marijuana in particular. That policy can be summed up in two words: zero tolerance.

First, though, the DEA issued warnings. Letters were sent to various individuals and groups growing marijuana for alleged medical use, letting them know that they would be arrested if they did not cease and desist.

Many in the pro-drug lobby consider the Drug Enforcement Administration a heartless gestapo. They quite literally hate the DEA, and they spew endless invective. But the fact that the DEA bothered to issue any warnings at all before launching its zero-tolerance campaign shows how fanatical the pro-drug crowd has become.

The DEA was under no legal obligation to do so. It was not being forced by the court to issue the warnings, but did so on its own initiative, giving those who suddenly found themselves in violation of the law because of the Supreme Court ruling time to comply. It is illuminating that so few did.

Even with the ruling and the letters, many believed that the DEA wouldn't really do anything. This, even after health-food stores had to discard any and all products that contained any trace of hemp. When the boom was lowered, the drug lobby was that much more outraged. They likened the DEA's sweep of California's growers to an invasion, and they blasted the DEA for what they perceived as underhanded tactics.

It didn't help their case that the DEA had evidence implicating certain growers who apparently weren't growing marijuana solely for medical use. To put it bluntly, some were doing it for the money.

Informants had come forward. It was alleged that some of the "marijuana medical clubs" were in truth fronts for drug dealers.

To test whether the allegation was true, the DEA sent in an undercover operative to make a buy at one of the clubs. The DEA's man asked to buy an ounce of pot. A club member told him it couldn't be done there, but that if the undercover operative would follow him home, the club member could sell him whatever he needed. Other DEA agents shadowed the pair to the house, where the buy was made.

In a related undercover op, the DEA sent a man to a physician, to whom he claimed to need marijuana to treat chronic migraines. The doctor asked for medical proof of the condition, and when the agent admitted he didn't have any, the doctor sold him an authorization for $200.

February 12 was the day of first big DEA sweep. The DEA focused on marijuana clubs and grows in and around San Francisco. Eight sites were raided and more than 8,000 marijuana plants were seized. The Harm Reduction Center, a well-known club on 6th Street, was one of the targets. Its director, who was in Canada, was arrested by the Canadian Mounties.

A prominent activist was taken into custody. In a raid on an indoor grow, about 3,500 plants were seized. The grower, a sixty-year old man with Hepatitis C, pled guilty and offered to testify against others.

The pro-drug crowd was incensed. Their allies in the press viciously attacked the DEA and portrayed those arrested as innocent victims.

That emotions ran high is understandable. Despite the

dearth of scientific evidence, many of those who used marijuana to alleviate a medical condition did so in the sincere belief that marijuana helped. To their way of thinking, the United States government, and by extension its drug-enforcement arm, the DEA, were acting like stormtroopers. They wanted the government to butt out, and they didn't care if what they were doing was against the law.

From the DEA's perspective, the exact opposite held true. Breaking the law is breaking the law. There are no shades of gray. Either a substance is legal to use or it is not legal to use. Either an act is legal to perform or it is not legal to perfom. And if the substance and the act are not legal, and if they pertain to drugs, then they fall under the DEA's purview and must be dealt with accordingly.

To suggest, as some have done, that the DEA simply "had it in" for medicinal marijuana users misses the essential point: the users were breaking laws that the DEA was sworn to uphold.

Some in the drug community exhibited behavior that bordered on paranoia. In their skewed view, the DEA was part of a greater government conspiracy to suppress all use of hemp so that the synthetic industry could prosper. But then, they tended to regard almost everything the government did as part and parcel of an attempt at global domination by a secret elite.

Many of the pro-drug crowd would like to see drug use made legal across the board—not just marijuana for medical purposes, but cocaine, heroin, you name it. Whatever people wanted to use, they should be free to use.

The pro-drug lobby argues that the tax money used to suppress drugs could be better spent on things like schools and hospitals. But just think of how emergency-room numbers would swell if this wish were to be granted. Think of the cost in lives ruined, families broken apart, babies born to addicts.

We have already seen the staggering social costs that drugs inflict. The toll in violence alone is enough to give any sane person pause. The pro-drug lobby claims that if all drugs were legalized, there wouldn't be any violence. Evidently they have never taken a look at the number of alcohol-related violent incidents that take place each year. The total is in the hundreds of thousands. Now imagine how high the total would be, and how much worse the situation would be compounded, if drugs, like alcohol, were legalized.

All this was moot as far as the DEA was concerned. Philosophical arguments were of no consequence. "It's the law, stupid!" might well be their official bumper sticker.

One would think, after the raids in San Francisco, that those involved in marijuana clubs and related activities elsewhere would get the message, close their operations down, and try legal avenues of redress. But that was not the case.

In June, in Mendocino County, California, two people were charged with growing marijuana on public land.

In July, a man was arrested in El Dorado County after he was found to be growing almost one thousand marijuana plants.

Three people were arrested in San Francisco in July for a 3,000-square-foot indoor grow.

In July, in Chico, a man was convicted of growing more than 450 plants.

The Woman's Alliance for Medical Marijuana in Santa Cruz was raided in September, and 167 plants were destroyed.

The Los Angeles Cannabis Resource Center in West Hollywood was raided in October and shut down. Supporters claimed that it was providing marijuana for more than 900 seriously ill people.

In October a prominent San Diego activist was arrested. Steve McWilliams had helped get Shelter From the Storm, a medical marijuana dispensary, up and running. Shortly after he had led a marijuana giveaway protest of the raid on the Women's Alliance for Medical Marijuana, DEA agents gave him a letter warning that he was in violation of the law and would be arrested if he did not stop growing marijuana. He failed to heed the warning and was taken into custody days later.

In the span of about a year, the DEA shut down some three dozen alleged medical marijuana grows. Each raid only angered the pro-drug lobby more. After the McWilliams incident, the DEA was accused of singling him out for prosecution. One glance at the long list of arrests disabuses that notion. As one DEA staffer aptly put it, "We're just enforcing the law."

Arrests of individuals supposedly growing marijuana for medical purposes has continued to this day. As recently as June of 2004, five people were arrested by the DEA after the California Highway Patrol raided a warehouse where about 4,000 plants were being cultivated.

Make no mistake: the activists know that what they are doing is illegal. But they do not believe that it should be. They think it heinous that the Supreme Court disregarded the will of the people of California as expressed in Proposition 215.

All sorts of protests were organized. Even some local entities got into the act. The Santa Cruz city council, for instance, decided to pass out medical marijuana at City Hall.

South of the Border

On the international front, in March of 2002, federal indictments were lodged against three members of the FARC in Colombia. The case was handled by the DEA's Bogotá and Brasilia offices, and it marked the first time that indictments were filed against members of a terrorist organization for alleged drug trafficking.

The commander of the 16th FARC front, Tomás Molina Caracas, otherwise known as Negro Acacio, and others, were accused of selling cocaine processed in labs along the Guaviare River. They operated out of the small village of Barranco Minas, situated in eastern Colombia close to the border with Venezuela. The village and the surrounding region were completely under FARC's control. They were free to do whatever they wanted.

The cocaine network that they had set up was funneling coke to the United States, Spain, Brazil, and other countries.

In Suriname, the DEA and Surinamese police tracked down and arrested a FARC member who stood accused of conspiracy to smuggle cocaine into the United States. Since he was in the country illegally, the Surinamese expelled him, and he was immediately flown to the United States in a DEA plane.

In Colombia, the CNP, working with the DEA, raided three labs run by the FARC. All three labs were near San Jose del Guaviare. Seven tons of cocaine base and HCI were seized.

In a separate investigation, the DEA and CNP conducted Operation Juliet. The target was an international drug ring headed by Jose Jairo Garcia-Giraldo. The ring was responsible for bringing heroin and cocaine into the United States. Sixteen members, including the kingpin, were arrested, and a heroin-packing house in Colombia was raided.

Over in Brazil, the DEA's Sao Paulo Office, allied with the Brazilian federal police, learned that a cocaine cell was active in Sao Paulo. A raid netted 1,238 kilograms of cocaine and resulted in twenty-eight arrests. More important, among the other evidence seized were documents that would prove invaluable to the DEA in the course of subsequent investigations.

That was often the case. Evidence found at one scene led the DEA to other suspects, other rings, other labs or stashes.

By now, the Colombians were dominating the heroin market. They had taken control from the Southeast Asian rings. Close to 60 percent of the heroin seized in the United States could be traced back to Colombia. Only about 24 percent came out of Asia.

As mentioned, encouraging news came from Bolivia and Peru: Bolivia's cocaine output had fallen by an estimated 67 percent, down from a whopping 240 metric tons to "only" sixty. Coca-eradication efforts had a lot to do with it, along with restrictions on chemicals.

Peru's decline, from 460 metric tons to 145, was helped by crop eradication, but also by a widespread fungus that attacked the coca plant.

In both Bolivia and Peru, another factor contributing to the decline was that the Colombians were not buying nearly as much coca as in previous years. They were growing their own, or had switched to heroin and other drugs.

In Peru, in June, another drug lord was brought down. Nelson Paredes-Ortiz headed a ring made up of Peruvians, Colombians, Mexicans, and Guatemalans. A conversion lab that could churn out 600 kilograms of cocaine per week was put out of operation.

The increased effectiveness of law enforcement in the region had to do with two new developments.

A special task force had been created in Colombia. The DEA was involved. So were the Colombian national police and agencies from other South American countries. By pooling their respective efforts, they were better able to unearth and apprehend rings operating on a regional basis.

Of equal significance were the new Sensitive Investigative Units (SIU) that the DEA had formed. Begun in Colombia, the program was soon being used in other countries because it was so remarkably effective. The units were especially trained to strike at the heart of the largest drug rings.

The program achieved such remarkable success that soon SIU units were established in Peru, Bolivia, Brazil, and Ecuador. Close to 600 law officers from those countries were trained by the DEA to take part.

The SIU's were an offshoot of the DEA's new Priority Targeting System, which was used to determine which trafficking organizations were having the most deleterious impact on the United States. Those rated the worst were put at the top of the list, and resources were channeled into taking them down.

To phrase it more simply, the DEA was going after the big fish in a big way. Arresting street-level dealers was well and good but they were at the bottom of the drug-trade pecking order, and their apprehension did not markedly affect the flow of drugs. Taking down major traffickers did.

That is exactly what took place in Mexico, when Benjamin Arellano-Felix was captured by Mexican authorities in Puebla. He and his siblings oversaw the AFO, one of the largest drug rings in all of Mexico. It also had the notorious distinction of being one of the most savage ever.

The DEA had been trying to end the blood-spattered reign of the Tijuana cartel, as it was called, for years.

Benjamin Arellano-Felix had become the head of the organization in 1989 after the arrest of his uncle, Miguel Angel Felix-Gallardo, who, it will be recalled, was implicated for his part in the death of DEA agent Enrique Camarena. Back in 1982, Benjamin had been arrested on drug-smuggling charges in Downey, California, but he posted bail and skipped.

Benjamin's younger brother, Ramon, headed the cartel's security apparatus. He saw to it that AFO enforcers were well armed and well trained in paramilitary tactics. Ramon personally oversaw the elimination of rival drug lords. He also directed the killings of law enforcement officers and snitches. His propensity for violence was exceptional. It landed him, in 1997, on the FBI's ten Most Wanted List. A $2 million reward was placed on his head by the U.S. State Department.

Third in the cartel's hierarchy was another brother, Francisco Javier. He managed the financial end. Along with Benjamin and Ramon, he had the dubious distinction of having a $1 million reward offered by the Mexican government for his capture.

A fourth brother, and the oldest, Francisco Rafael, had oversight of the narcotics selling, but he had landed in prison early on.

Yet another brother, Eduardo, handled cocaine shipments into the United States. He, too, had been arrested in Downey, California. He, too, skipped bail.

Carlo, a sixth brother, coordinated smuggling operations. Luís, a seventh, ran legitimate businesses through which drug proceeds were laundered.

In 2000, the AFO suffered setbacks. One was the arrest of

Higuerra-Guerrero, a highly placed member whose violent tendencies were almost as notorious as Ramon's. Mexican authorities linked him to the murder of Tijuana's federal police commander, as well as to the murder of a police officer and the deaths of three federal agents.

On May 4, Guerrero was relaxing in his beachfront home with eight associates when the Mexican military and police surrounded the house. He surrendered without a fight.

Another AFO lieutenant, Jesus Labra Aviles, was watching his son play soccer when Mexican soldiers closed in, automatic weapons at the ready.

The scope of the AFO's operation was like something out of the DEA's worst nightmare. The brothers were responsible for about one-third of all the cocaine being smuggled into the United States. Their power had grown to such an extent that for thirteen years they had been able to hold the Mexican and United States governments at bay.

How could they manage to do that for so long? Bribery. It was estimated that the AFO paid out approximately $1 million *every week* to government officials and others on their secret payroll.

Fear also contributed to their longevity—fear of being killed. Exactly how many victims the AFO racked up is hard to assess. Figures vary from a low of 300 to a high of more than a thousand.

The list of known victims is staggering. It includes two police chiefs and more than a dozen policemen, at least one federal police commander, countless witnesses who might have testified against the AFD, and innocent bystanders caught in hails of lead. Politicians, judges—no one was safe.

The AFO even killed a Roman Catholic cardinal. Cardinal

Juan Jesus Posadas Ocampo was mistakenly slain at the Guadalajara airport when AFO assassins opened fire on his car in the belief that a rival drug lord was inside.

The assassination barely received notice north of the border, but in Mexico it caused outrage and a severe backlash against the AFO. The brothers laid low until the uproar quieted.

Ramon became a Tijuana legend. Despite the rewards on his head, despite being sought by Mexican and United States authorities, he would deck himself out in a mink jacket and enough gold jewelry to make Mr. T jealous and cruise around Tijuana in a flashy red Porsche.

Many of Ramon's enforcers were recruited from some of the more violent street gangs. Others, incredibly, were bored rich kids who didn't have anything better to do, and who idolized Ramon.

An informant told Mexican police that Ramon would kill for the fun of it; that he would have acquaintances randomly point at people in passing cars, and have the people killed. It should come as no surprise that the informant was later snatched off the street and was never seen again.

The AFO killed anyone who wouldn't cooperate with them, anyone who refused to be bribed. They killed their competitors. They killed anyone in their organization suspected of the slightest disloyalty.

To give some idea of exactly how vicious they could be: in 1998, a spectacularly gory bloodbath made Mexican headlines. It seemed that an AFO underling by the name of Fermin Castro overstepped himself. Castro essentially ruled a small fishing village, El Sauzal. In return for the right to do so, he had to pay regular dues to the AFO. Somewhere along the line, he did something to anger the brothers. Ramon's enforcers were sent in. In the dead of night they surrounded the village, lined up every man, woman and child, and executed them.

Jose Patino Moreno, a Mexican prosecutor who couldn't be bought off, provided another outlet for Ramon's tyranny when he and two of his aides vanished. Later Patino's vehicle was found, smashed, all three bodies lying beside it. Their heads had been crushed, and virtually every bone in their bodies had been broken. The local police passed their deaths off as a traffic accident. Eventually, two police commanders allegedly on the AFO payroll were accused of the killings.

The amount of coke that flowed through the AFO pipeline was prodigious. The group used every method known, and then some. In February of 2002, acting on a tip from an informant, police raided a farm on the United States border. Hidden under a set of stairs was a large safe. They broke it open, but nothing was inside. That was when one of the officers noticed that the floor under the safe didn't seem right. They ripped up the floorboards. Underneath was a shaft connected to a tunnel. Rigged with electricity and rails, the tunnel ran some 1,200 feet *under the border*. It was a detection-proof means for the AFO to funnel drugs.

But all things, good *and* bad, come to an end, and for the AFO the beginning of their decline was marked by the death of their flashiest member.

On February 10, 2002, Ramon Arellano-Felix and one of his assassins headed for the resort city of Mazatlán. They weren't going there for a vacation. Ramon was out to eliminate a rival drug lord, Ismael Zambada Garcia, who reportedly had started to muscle in on Arellano territory. Ramon had heard that Zambada Garcia planned to attend Mazatlán's carnival and saw it as an ideal chance to strike.

Ramon left his red Porsche in Tijuana. To be less conspicuous, he was driving a white Volkswagen. Shortly before 10:30 that morning, police waved the Volkswagen over. Accounts vary as to why. One report has it that the police had spotted weapons in the Volkswagen, another that Ramon inadvertently drove the wrong way down a one-way street. Whatever the case, Ramon sped from the scene and the police gave chase.

The Volkswagen was brought to a stop in front of the Las Gaviotas Hotel. Ramon and his companion fought it out and died in a hail of gunfire, taking a policeman with them.

Initially, however, the police had no idea who they had killed. Ramon was carrying a fake ID under the name of Jorge Perez Lopez. Shortly after his death, reputed relatives of Jorge Perez Lopez showed up at the undertaker's and laid claim to the body.

The other assassin had papers identifying him as Hector Solarzano Jiminez. Fingerprints showed that he was really Efrain Quintero Carrizoza, a known AFO assassin wanted for his part in the deaths of twelve people in 2001.

Ramon's fingerprints were not on file.

Federal police were stunned when they examined the crime-scene photos in an attempt to figure out who the dead driver had been and someone noticed the resemblance to Ramon.

It wasn't until Ramon's brother Benjamin was later arrested and confirmed that it had, in fact, been Ramon, that the file on Mexico's most feared killer could be closed.

United States and Mexican authorities were elated.

But the question needs to be asked: Had anything been accomplished? One brother was behind bars and another was dead, but the AFO never broke stride. They continued pumping drugs into the United States.

Benjamin phrased it succinctly in an interview with reporters from the *Washington Post*. "I'm here, and nothing has changed."

It would.

In Puerto Rico, an epidemic of violence was spreading like a wind-whipped forest fire. Or, to be more accurate, a drug-spawned nightmare. Or, to be even more accurate, the lack of drugs.

Thanks to the efforts of the DEA, the FBI, U.S. Customs, and local agencies, the flow of drugs into Puerto Rico had slowed dramatically. As previously noted, Puerto Rico had long been a midway point. But on an island, there are only so many ways on and off, and interdiction strategies were proving effective.

One would think that this was a good thing. But once again, success produced an unforeseen outcome.

The homicide rate in the United States had been declining for several years, but not in Puerto Rico. Its homicide rate was three times the United States national average, at eighteen per 100,000 residents. San Juan and the other large cites were the focal points of the bloodshed. Caguas, Carolina, Bayamón, and Ponce were also affected.

Turf wars were to blame. With fewer drugs available, the competition for a customer base was more fierce than ever. Drug gangs were waging relentless war for control of their turf.

The problem was aggravated by other illegal items being smuggled in—guns. Not revolvers or shotguns, but nine-millimeter pistols and auto-rifles like the AR-15 and the ever-popular AK-47.

Naturally, the killings made headlines. Sad to say, however, because many occurred in poorer sections of their respective cities—in housing projects and other areas blighted by poverty—neither the general public nor many politicians rose up in indignant fury to demand an end to the bloodletting.

No one could rightly fault the DEA. They were doing their job, and doing it extremely well.

In March, the DEA and other federal and local law-enforcement officers descended on San Juan, Ponce, and Bayamón, and on the towns of Toa Alta, Toa Baja, and Catano. They were serving warrants on members of a drug ring that had been selling cocaine for up to $18,000 a kilogram and heroin in one-eighth-of-a-kilogram amounts for as much as $10,000.

The ring had tried the usual tricks. They relied heavily on cell phones and pagers to communicate. They had worked out a system of code and other clandestine techniques, but it all proved unavailing.

Most of the heroin that found its way into Puerto Rico came from Colombia, some from Asia.

The DEA uncovered one ring that was smuggling in large amounts from the former Soviet Republics of Kazakhstan and Kyrgyzstan. The drugs were sent by mail. The ring paid for them through wire transfers to Romania. The whole thing was computerized, so the ring could keep efficient track of the transfers. They also used cell phones and codes, but once again, that didn't prevent the inevitable.

Seventeen members of the ring were indicted, which effectively shut it down, and the result was even fewer drugs available on Puerto Rico's streets.

That gave the drug gangs even more cause to spill each other's blood.

The AFO wasn't the only big cartel operating out of Mexico. Another was known as the Southeast cartel. They brought cocaine in to Quintana Roo and Belize from Colombia by speedboat, and from there the coke was conveyed into the United States.

In July, indictments were handed down, but not against the traffickers themselves. The charges were issued against the former governor of Quintana Roo. Allegedly, he was on the ring's payroll. They paid him when each shipment came in, and paid him quite handsomely, to see to it that they were not interfered with. By DEA accounts, the total amount of cocaine he helped smuggle was upwards of 200 tons, and the total amount the ring paid him was somewhere in the range of $30 million.

Thirty million is a lot of money. The governor couldn't simply deposit it in his local bank. He needed help. He needed someone with financial expertise to launder his ill-gotten fortune.

The governor turned to a female acquaintance who at the time was working at Serfin Securities, a Mexican investment firm with an office in New York City. She later left Serfin for Lehman Brothers, one of the most prestigious investment firms in the United States, and continued her laundering activities there.

Mexican authorities worked closely with the DEA in building the intricate case. So did Lehman Brothers, sparing the firm a hefty fine. (Banco Popular de Puerto Rico, on the other hand, was fined $21.6 million in an unrelated case for failing to file suspicious activity reports on time. Many people are unaware that financial institutions are required, by law, to report any dealings by their employees or customers that might in any way be construed as potentially illegal.)

Close cooperation between the United States and Mexico had done the miraculous. It had slowed the amount of drugs flowing across the border. One indicator was that the purity level of cocaine in the United States had taken another 10 percent drop, a sure sign that less coke was available.

The DEA passed much of the credit to Mexico. A new administration was making all the difference. Far too many previous administrations had either aided and abetted the drug traffickers, or else simply disregarded United States requests.

Mexico's new leader, Vicente Fox, was serious about drugs. He saw them as a blight on his country's future and he had vowed to do all he could to stamp them out. If anyone had any doubts about his sincerity, they were quickly disabused when President Fox sent federal troops and federal police into Tijuana, the stronghold of the AFO.

The feds took more than 100 Tijuana police officers into custody for alleged links to the AFO.

More was to follow.

During President Fox's first two years in office, more than 11,000 traffickers were arrested. Major rings were shut down. Drug lords were put in prison. Hundreds of ring members, including money men and scores of assassins, were clamped in handcuffs.

Besides Benjamin Arellano-Felix, two other kingpins of note were taken into custody. One was Jesus Albino Quintero-Meraz, who was involved with a cocaine ring responsible for close to 10 percent of the cocaine entering the United States. Another was Adan Medrano-Rodriguez, a bigwig with the Gulf cartel that operated out of Matamoros.

Yet again, success had an unexpected outcome. Until now, Colombian suppliers had been willing to supply drugs on credit. Mexican traffickers would pay on receipt or after the drugs were passed on. But so many traffickers were being arrested, and so many shipments seized, that the Colombians were being hurt where they least liked to be hurt—in their wallets.

The Colombian cartels started to ask for their money up front. That, needless to say, did not go over well with the Mexican traffickers.

Another unexpected result was similar to the situation in Puerto Rico, but instead of street gangs battling for control of a few city blocks, in Mexico trafficking syndicates were pitted against one another in a battle for dominance.

The AFO, weakened by the loss of Benjamin and Ramon, was involved in a shooting war with the man Ramon had gone to Mazatlán to kill, Ismael Zambada Garcia. The prize was California, where most of the AFO drugs were smuggled.

Authorities were seeing a repeat of what had happened in Colombia a decade earlier when the Medellín cartel and Cali mafia were broken up, but in Mexico, the new syndicates were a lot less discreet.

The Saudi Connection

The war on drugs had taken many surprising twists and turns. None was more surprising than the next scenario to play itself out.

Through informants, the DEA learned of a new player on the international drug scene. This was a kind of player that they had not seen before: a Saudi Arabian prince.

In July of 2002, four noteworthy indictments were handed down. One of the four was of Prince Nayef bin Fawwaz al-Shaalan. He and his twin brother, Prince Saud, were sons-in-law of the brother of Saudi Arabia's king. Their older brother was married to a daughter of the crown prince.

To say that Prince Nayef was wealthy should not be necessary, but it is a pertinent point to keep in mind in light of what was to come. Why would anyone so fabulously wealthy become involved in drug dealing?

Prince Nayef was educated in the United States. He was fluent in eight languages. Reportedly, he neither drank nor smoked. He was prominent in OPEC talks. He also owned oil investments in Colombia and Venezuela, and he visited both countries now and again.

It all apparently started with an attractive real-estate agent in Miami. Whether the prince looked her up or their meeting was a coincidence is irrelevant at this point, although the former is certainly suggested. What matters is that the real-estate agent had ties to a drug cartel in Medellín. She contacted them, and it wasn't long before Prince Nayef had made the personal acquaintance of Oscar Eduardo Campuzano Zapata, otherwise known among the drug underworld as "El Flaco" (the Thin Man).

Zapata had been one of Pablo Escobar's a top lieutenants, and after Escobar's death, he had formed his own ring. He was one of the new breed: the kind who liked to stay under the radar and rely more on his gray matter than his armory.

Intel suggests that the pair held several face-to-face meetings before a final confab in Saudi Arabia. There, the prince outlined a grand scheme to begin smuggling five- to ten-ton shipments of cocaine on a regular basis.

The year before, the prince had started up a bank in Switzerland. Rumors floated around that the bank wasn't entirely legit; that the prince formed it for the express purpose of laundering ill-gotten gains. Which brings us back to our first question: Why did he want to deal in drugs, as wealthy as he was? To suggest that it was greed is ludicrous. In certain circles, there were whispers of ties to terrorism.

In any event, the conspirators arranged a trial cocaine run. Two tons of cocaine were involved. If all went well, larger runs would follow—and it would have gone well if not for the diligence of the DEA.

The plan called for the coke to be smuggled from Venezuela to France. Once there, it would distributed throughout Europe.

On a mild May evening, a Boeing 727 registered to a company owned by the Saudi royal family, Skyways International, landed at Le Bourget airport, not far from Paris. Prince Nayef, his twin brother, and other Saudi royalty were on board.

No one thought much of it when the 727 was met by a fleet of vehicles, including a pair of vans. Diplomatic immunity gave Prince Nayef the right to unload whatever he wanted without having it inspected by customs.

Hidden among the baggage, in special suitcases, was the cocaine, all two tons of it.

The Saudi vehicles filed from the airport. Halfway to Paris, the two vans discreetly left the caravan. They ended up in the suburb of Noissy-le-Sec, where the cocaine was to be stashed for a few days.

Unknown to Prince Nayef, the DEA had been keeping an eye on Zapata. They had intercepted a fax pertaining to the prince and the shipment. The intel was duly relayed to French authorities. But by the time the French figured out exactly where the cocaine was being stashed, a ton of it had gone on down the European pipeline. The remaining coke was confiscated.

Still, it wasn't a total loss as far as Prince Nayef was concerned. He reportedly earned $10 million for his share of the cocaine that slipped through.

Up to this point, the prince had no idea that he himself had been implicated. The French wanted to keep it quiet until he was in custody, an iffy proposition given his special status.

The DEA preferred to do things in a more straightforward manner. Zapata and some of his associates were taken into custody. In exchange for reduced sentences, they agreed to tell all they knew about Prince Nayef's drug dealings. Soon the DEA and the United States Attorney for the Southern District of Florida announced that an indictment had been sought.

The French were seething. They accused the DEA of botching the investigation by alerting the prince that he was under scrutiny.

A book written by Fabrice Monti, who was attached to the French Ministry of the Interior during the whole affair, alleges that the Saudi government brought pressure to bear on France to have the charges against the prince dropped, or else conveniently ignored.

Prince Nayef, meanwhile, under his invincible shroud of diplomatic immunity, was free to travel wherever his whims took him.

A sidelight to this farce was an incident that garnered almost as much media attention as the indictment itself. Two famous paintings entered into the transaction. *El Atraco a la Diligencia* by Francisco de Goya, and *Buste de Juene Femme* by Tsuguharu Foujita, were seized by the DEA. Worth millions, the paintings were to be part of the prince's payment to the Colombians.

At first glance, the whole scenario seems incredible. But when the DEA dug deeper, it was found that back in 1984, a federal drug charge had been leveled against the prince in Mississippi. He skipped out on his bond and hadn't been seen back in the U.S. since.

High Tech

From the underworld of high finance, we turn our attention to a seemingly mundane event that had taken place in Colombia some years before.

The CNP had raided a condo being used by the Cali mafia. They were out of luck in one respect: no drugs. But in another they made the find of that year or any other.

The first floor of the condo had been converted to a sophisticated computer center the likes of which IBM would envy. In fact, the main computer was an IBM AS400 mainframe, which retailed for about one and a half million dollars.

Since the condo was a front for Cali drug kingpin José Santacruz-Londono, the computer became known as the Santacruz computer. And since the Colombians did not have the expertise to examine it as thoroughly as their American counterparts could, the Santacruz computer was flown to the United States and handed over to the DEA for analysis.

No one could possibly suspect what the DEA would find. It was so shocking that the DEA's eventual report was classified.

It was no secret that the drug cartels had embraced technology as the answer to their smuggling prayers. More and more, they relied on high-tech equipment to handle their day-to-day operations. But until the Santacruz computer came along, no one in officialdom remotely imagined exactly *how* sophisticated they had become.

Imagine a database with the names, the addresses, and the work and home telephone numbers of every DEA agent and United States official in Colombia. A database with similar information on every member of the CNP and other Colombian law-enforcement agencies. Imagine a computer able to tap into the Cali phone company, with access to the phone company's own database. Imagine a computer able to tell the Cali mafia who called whom, and when. Imagine a drug cartel with the ability to finger informants almost as quickly as informants appeared. The Santacruz computer had all that capability, and more.

The DEA and the CNP had been wondering why their informants against the Calis had shorter life expectancies than those of fruit flies. Now they knew.

The computer was so important to the Cali's that their tech people operated it 24/7.

About those tech people. America is rightfully proud of its technological strides. Its colleges and technical schools offer courses second to none. The drug lords realized as much, which is why some sent members of their organizations to attend United States schools.

One cartel leader sent his sons to the United States to study. The DEA knew who they were, but since the sons hadn't committed any crimes and weren't wanted, there was nothing the DEA or anyone else could do. When the students finished their schooling, they returned to Colombia and assumed important positions in the family drug syndicate.

Since the early days of the drug war, the smarter drug lords relied on the best technology their money could buy. As technology improved, so did their ability to conceal their activities. Just think of all the great strides in electronics, communications, and computerization in the past few decades. Then think of all that high-tech in the hands of traffickers worldwide, and you begin to appreciate the magnitude of the challenge to the DEA.

Encryption had become commonplace. Messages were sent scrambled, over secure channels, in codes developed by computers. Decrypting them was next to impossible. It could be done, but it was an incredibly time-consuming task.

If computers have been a tremendous boon to civilization, they have been a godsend to traffickers, whose efficiency increased a thousandfold. They could keep track of a packet of drugs from the time it left Cali or Medellín to the moment it arrived at its destination in North America or Europe.

Money transfers became ridiculously easy. A few taps on a keyboard and the exchange was completed.

Drug money was being regularly laundered over the Internet. There were instances of drug rings conducting Internet "auctions" for dirty money—auctions which were encrypted and thus couldn't be penetrated. Experts estimated that billions of dollars were involved.

One of the first to use auctions—indeed, one of the most tech-reliant drug lords of them all—was Archangel de Jesus Henao-Montoya. The Henao family, along with Diego Montoya and Luis Hernando Gomez-Bustamante, were leaders in what became known as the Norte Valle cartel, or North Valley cartel. They had risen to fill the void created by the demise of the early Cali mafia and had taken the businesslike proclivities of the Calis to a whole new level.

The Henao family virtually ran Buenaventura, a main Colombian port. They brooked no interference. According to authorities, their favorite means of disposing of those they killed was to slice the bodies up with chainsaws and dump the bits and pieces in a river.

Henao was not above killing his own people. When a lieutenant reputedly became too friendly with Henao's wife, the lieutenant and about forty of those who worked with him were eliminated in suitably grisly fashion.

The North Valley cartel's drug network stretched from

Colombia to the States. In 1994, one of their underlings in New York fell behind in his payments. Henao's reaction? The dealer and his entire family were wiped out.

By all accounts, Henao was a physically unassuming, heavyset man with a withered arm. Looking at him, no one would suspect that he would turn out to be so crafty and formidable.

It was Henao who elevated the drug war to a whole new level by his use of the IBM mainframe. He turned the North Valley cartel into the most technologically sophisticated cartel ever seen. To paraphrase, he never met a piece of high-tech equipment he didn't like, particularly if the equipment was of any benefit to his operation.

It wasn't as if he couldn't afford it. By 2002, by best estimates, the North Valley cartel was responsible for approximately half the cocaine entering the United States. They were making money hand over fist. They could afford whatever they wanted, up to and including classified hardware, and they could buy the experts to run it.

A few years previous, one of Henao's experts had been arrested. Nelson Urrego was considered something of a communications wizard. From documents and other intel, the DEA learned important details about the intricacies of the North Valley cartel's communications network.

For instance, the cartel had not one, not two, but three (and possibly more) com centers set up, each with a network of more than a dozen computers and a mainframe. Communications were facilitated by relay stations and repeaters. Their com grid covered much of northern South America and stretched north into the Caribbean. All the messages were encrypted, of course.

Although the DEA and Colombian authorities knew what the cartel was doing, and how, they still couldn't intercept a single message. The best they could do was slowly build a case for indictment while hoping that the cartel slipped up.

As if computerization wasn't problem enough, Henao also had a fondness for military and intelligence hardware—again, the best his money could buy, and his money could buy virtually anything. He perfected a system for mapping out the radar coverage of United States spy planes, and then had his drug planes fly routes the radar didn't cover. He also acquired the ability to pinpoint the location of anyone he was after by their cell phone or pager.

Like every other drug ring, the North Valley cartel did all it could to eliminate rivals. Turf wars took place on a grand scale. In one of their more showy stunts, after a rival was arrested, the cartel stole a helicopter and rigged it with a bomb capable of leveling the facility. Fortunately, it failed to detonate.

Henao didn't neglect the shipping end of his operation, either. He set his experts to work constructing boats that would ride so low in the water, they couldn't be detected by radar. The program wasn't the success he had hoped for, but that was okay. The North Valley cartel was working on another means of transporting drugs, one that could elude detection better than anything seen to date: submarines.

Subs were a logical next step. A decade earlier, a Cali cartel had purchased a Soviet sub, but it reputedly sank on its maiden smuggling run. Another sub was seized by Colombian authorities.

The unique thing about Henao's subs was that he was building his own. Not mini-subs, although he had a fleet of them, but full-sized subs able to travel thousands of miles, clear to the United States if need be.

Someone in Henao's organization, perhaps Henao himself, came up with another bright idea. They were tired of having their shipments seized, so they took a good look at the types of ships that were stopped and boarded and realized there was one kind that was never boarded and never searched. Vessels transporting hazardous waste were treated as if they carried a radioactive plague.

Henao began smuggling drugs on those very ships.

Keep in mind that this was just one drug syndicate among many. It had a reputation for being the most technologically advanced, but others were developing the same capabilities or already had them.

It didn't mean that the DEA was ready to throw in the towel. In September, in a joint op, the DEA and the CNP took down a heroin ring based in Bogotá. The ring was smuggling product into the United States using flight attendants on Avianca Airlines. Seven ring members were arrested in Colombia, another eleven in New York.

Two months later, the DEA and the CNP struck again. Operation Matador's target was Rene Robledo-Roman, the reputed head of a heroin ring that transported heroin overland from Bogotá to towns along the Ecuadoran and Venezuelan borders. From there the heroin made its way to Mexico, and from Mexico into Texas.

The CNP took Robledo-Roman and more than two dozen syndicate hirelings into custody while the DEA was arresting suppliers in Texas and three other states. Altogether, sixty-six kilograms of heroin were seized.

Colombia wasn't producing as much heroin as before—perhaps 5 percent of the estimated global total. By 2002, that was about four metric tons. Compare that to the seven metric tons coming out of Afghanistan and the whopping seventy-two metric tons coming out of Burma. But where the heroin out of

Burma was bound for destinations around the world, almost all of the heroin coming out of Colombia was being smuggled into the United States.

A Sensitive Investigations Unit in Medellín brought two top traffickers to ground. The pair had been indicted in Florida for their part in ferrying some twenty-two tons of cocaine.

Over in Venezuela, a trafficker by the name of Juan Sanchez allegedly served as a middleman for the Colombians and was one of the top transporters in all of South America. The police transported him to jail. Fifteen speedboats and high-tech communications gear were confiscated.

Next, a couple of Spaniards and half a dozen Venezuelans, posing as a family, were stopped at the Maiquetia International Airport in Caracas. Officials found heroin hidden in their shaving-cream cans, in their shampoo bottles, and in other effects—fifty-one kilograms, when it was all collected.

Profiles in Ecstasy

Lest one think the DEA's only successes in 2002 were in South America: it was during this period that the DEA was busily investigating an ecstasy ring based in Israel. Once the DEA had all the evidence it needed, charges were filed in Florida against the two Israeli ringleaders.

The pair reportedly used fleshbags and other couriers to transport ecstasy from Israel to Europe and America. Some forty people were parts of the ring, and three dozen of them were arrested in the initial sweep. The ringleaders were apprehended by Israeli authorities and subsequently extradited to the United States.

This case is noteworthy in that it was the first time Israeli citizens were extradited to the United States on drug charges. Some Americans were surprised by the news, but they shouldn't have been. Israel is no different from any other country. In 1998, a U.S. State Department White Paper on Global Narcotics noted that not only had Israel seen a marked rise in drug consumption, but Israeli syndicates were now trafficking in drugs, particularly ecstasy.

The fact is, Jewish rings had what might be considered a monopoly on ecstasy—70 percent of the world's total market, according to the DEA. The Israelis obtained it in Belgium and the Netherlands, two countries where the chemicals needed to manufacture it were not rigidly regulated. Still, making it was against the law, and Belgian and Dutch police, working with the DEA, closed down more than fifty labs in one year.

The Israelis had a variety of routes and means for smuggling the ecstasy into the United States. They frequently used FedEx and UPS. In 2000, two packages being shipped by FedEx were intercepted. Inside each was forty pounds of ecstasy. That same year, an Israeli syndicate tried to send shipments by air. The first, seized in Los Angeles, contained 650,000 tablets. The second contained more than *two million*.

One Israeli ring tried a novel approach: It recruited young Hasidic and Orthodox Jews as couriers. Finder's fees were paid to "recruiters" with access to rabbinical seminaries and yeshivas. Some of the recruits were duped into thinking they were smuggling diamonds. Others knew exactly what they were smuggling. All were in it for the money.

The ring's rationale was that no one would ever suspect an Hasidic or Orthodox Jew of being involved in drugs. And for the longest while, their ploy worked. The mules, as drug couriers are sometimes called, brought in anywhere from 30,000 to 50,000 tablets at a time. Often, the ring sent several couriers on the same flight, so that if one was arrested, the others might still make it through customs.

In Los Angeles, what police described as a major ecstasy ring was put out of commission with the arrest of fifteen people and the seizure of approximately $8 million worth of ecstasy. Once again, most of the suspects were Israelis.

Not content with the market in the United States and Europe, the Jewish syndicates branched out into South America and Asia, as the arrest of a Jewish man trying to smuggle 25,000 ecstasy tablets into Japan demonstrated.

The Israeli syndicates had a good thing going. But it was too good. Ecstasy was so profitable that the Israelis began to see increased competition. The Colombians entered the market on a relatively small but growing scale. Nigerians, Chechens, Albanians, Serbs, and others tested the waters and liked the money they made.

Experts predicted violent consequences. Just as the Colombian and Mexican turf wars resulted in hundreds of deaths and untold gallons of spilled blood, so, too, did the volatile ecstasy scenario promise to reap a dire crimson harvest at some point in the future.

Cruise Control

In Aruba, an illuminating bust was made.

Aruba customs had learned that Colombian heroin was being smuggled into Puerto Rico on a cruise ship—not by passengers, but by five crew members. The five intended to deliver it to an individual in San Juan.

Aruba authorities contacted the DEA office in San Juan. An undercover sting was set up. First, the five crew members on board the *Carnival Destiny* were arrested. Then DEA agents, posing as the couriers, met their contact in San Juan. As soon as he paid them the $2,000 transport fee, he was clapped in handcuffs.

This was a spur-of-the-moment op, if you will; not an involved, long-term countermeasure. In keeping with the fluid nature of the drug war, the DEA had to be ready at a moment's notice to deploy its resources as needed.

Madness of the Method

It should be noted at this point that the DEA's responsibilities weren't limited to investigations and arrests. The DEA was also charged with cleaning up illicit drug-lab sites.

Clandestine labs use dangerous chemicals as a matter of course; chemicals that pose a hazard to people and to the environment.

Quite often the DEA was called in after the fact by local and state officials who had no idea what to do and lacked the resources to clean up the labs even if they did.

Fortunately for the general public, most labs are in rural areas. They have to be. The odors and other activities associated with drug labs tend to give their presence away, especially in urban settings where more people are apt to notice.

Meth labs were some of the worst. They were also some of the most numerous.

Meth also happened to be the focus of a DEA operation called Living Large—or so the DEA thought at first.

For two years, the DEA, in conjunction with the Riverside, California police department and the Riverside County sheriff's department had been investigating a ring that turned out to be dealing in ecstasy as well.

One of the alleged traffickers was the inadvertent inspiration for the op's name. He had a fondness for the good life, especially expensive cars, and had amassed quite a collection of Jaguars, Ferraris, and Mercedeses, to mention a few. More than eighty cars were seized when the warrants were served. Fifty-seven people were arrested.

Meth also figured in a profoundly disturbing link that the DEA uncovered between a large meth ring in the Midwest and Middle Eastern terrorists.

Suspects from Lebanon, Jordan, and Yemen were sneaking the meth into the United States by way of Detroit and Chicago. Some of the proceeds ended up in bank accounts tied to terrorist groups, among them Hezbollah. Exactly how much poured into terrorist coffers before the DEA brought the ring down is difficult to say, but the total had to be well up in the millions.

Syria was already a major transshipment point for hashish when authorities unearthed intel that showed Syria had entered the heroin trade in a big way. One report accused the Syrian government of being directly involved. Some of the profits were allegedly filtered to terrorist groups.

The fact was that by 2002, there wasn't a country anywhere in the world that didn't have a "drug problem" to a greater or lesser degree. The drug plague had gone global. Some countries were more involved in trafficking than others. But then, the lure of big money always produces a flagrant disregard for the law. Politicians, who seldom qualify as founts of ethics and morality, are too often too eager to line their pockets however they can.

Greed was certainly rampant along the United States–Mexico border. To be blunt, the border was a sieve, leaking drugs nonstop. Millions of dollars' worth were being seized each year, but it was still only a drop in the illegal bucket.

To give some idea: cocaine seizures were pushing 90,000 pounds. Heroin was in the neighborhood of 4,000 pounds. For marijuana, the total figure was close to two million pounds.

The traffickers tried every trick they could come up with. They hid their wares in every kind of legal shipment imaginable. In one instance, both cocaine and marijuana were found in a truckload of sand. In another, a huge amount of marijuana was found in a truckload of glass. In a third, about $10 million worth of Mary Jane was found in a trailer filled with fake Christmas trees.

The DEA closed down a ring in El Paso. The smugglers were bringing marijuana across and relaying it to cities like Atlanta and Chicago. Seventeen people were indicted in Texas, another dozen in Illinois.

In North Charleston, South Carolina, the problem was crack. A local gang had laid claim to North Charleston's streets. It was so bad that dealers were selling the stuff in the open in broad daylight.

Working with local agencies, the DEA spent eight months amassing evidence. Their persistence paid off.

More than 300 street-level dealers were arrested. Another thirty higher-ups were charged.

Conquista

Toward the end of the year, another Colombian case made news.

The target of Operation Conquista was a syndicate exporting some 150 tons of cocaine annually to Europe and the

United States. Fifteen bigwigs were arrested, among them a former Colombian senator. The ring used speedboats to transport the cocaine from the Guajira coast region to oceangoing vessels well off shore.

Table Manners

In October, an Israeli ecstasy ring blundered. Two of its members showed up at a warehouse in Belgium. They wanted to purchase several tables. Then, right in front of the warehouse workers, they proceeded to hide ecstasy tablets *inside* the tables. When a warehouse employee asked what the tablets were, one of the ring members replied that they were "horse vitamins."

Needless to say, the workers were suspicious. They reported the incident to the Belgian federal police. The suspects had left after arranging to have the tables shipped to the United States. The BFP confiscated the tables and the tablets and contacted the DEA's Brussels office.

The DEA decided to run a sting. The tables, now empty, were allowed to go on their way but were closely monitored.

The two Israelis who had arranged the shipment arrived in the United States ahead of the tables to await their delivery. The Israelis arranged a sale to a third suspect. As the deal was going down, the DEA closed in.

Dealership Raid

In Hartford, Connecticut, an increase in drug activity caused concern for the chief of the Hartford police department. He asked a DEA Mobile Enforcement Team for help. The team had been aiding police agencies in New England cities and towns for some time, providing crucial resources unavailable at the local level.

A joint op determined that a drug ring was using an automotive company and a market as fronts for drug sales. The gang had its fingers in cocaine, heroin, crack, and marijuana. Undercover buys were made, and eventually forty people were charged with various crimes.

The Nightwatch

In November came more proof that Israeli dominance of the ecstasy market was being challenged. A Dominican ring was unearthed. Its members were mainly *from* the Dominican Republic, at any rate, although they were operating out of Amsterdam and New York City.

The Dominicans were a bit more creative than the Israeli ring that tried to hide ecstasy in tables. They smuggled the drug in shipments of catalytic converters for cars, and, in one noteworthy flight of ingenuity, in the print of a famous Rembrandt painting called *The Nightwatch*. They also relied on couriers.

Loose Ends

An especially complicated case came to fruition at the end of the year. Actually, it was three separate DEA/FBI ops that started out as unrelated to one another but turned out to be interconnected.

Originally, the target was a trafficking syndicate in Los Angeles that was funneling cocaine in from Mexico and relaying it to points around the country. At the same time, another

DEA op was in progress involving a drug ring in Anchorage, Alaska. Soon the DEA discovered that the Los Angeles syndicate was supplying the Alaskan ring. A third op revolved around a cell in Kansas City, which, like the Anchorage ring, was receiving drugs from Los Angeles.

The upshot was that arrest indictments were handed down for close to 100 suspects in three states.

The DEA closed out the year with a bust that had international implications.

As previously mentioned, certain paramilitary terrorist groups in Colombia had become involved in the drug trade. Some ran protection rackets for drug lords. Others trafficked in drugs themselves.

The United Self-Defense Forces of Colombia, or AUC, was one of the latter. Estimated to have some 8,000 diehard members, the AUC was accountable for about 70 percent of the human-rights violations in the country. Among those violations, according to the CNP, were more than 800 murders and 200 kidnappings. That's deplorable enough, but the AUC was also believed to be responsible for close to seventy-five massacres in which some 500 people were brutally and ruthlessly slaughtered.

The one thing the AUC needed was weapons. Lots and lots of weapons. The one thing the AUC had plenty of was cocaine. Lots and lots of cocaine.

A DEA/FBI task force leaped into action when it was learned that the AUC was shopping around for arms. The AUC did not have a lot of money to spend, but they were more than willing to swap cocaine for military hardware.

A pair of AUC commanders found a pair of potential sellers in Houston. Meetings were held in exotic locales like the Virgin Islands and St. Croix. One meet was in London. The last was in Costa Rica, and it was there that the deal was finalized, and where the DEA dropped the net.

2002 had been a busy year. Record amounts of drugs were seized. Arrest totals were higher than ever.

Before an account of 2003, we need to take a look at the overall pattern and examine one aspect that has yet to be touched on.

SHADOWS ON THE WALL

By the start of 2003, one-fifth of all eighth graders in the United States had tried marijuana at least once. Males were twice as likely as females to partake, and also twice as likely to try harder drugs.

Ecstasy, a relative newcomer to the drug scene, had made a major splash and was now available in every state and major city, if not every small town. Ecstasy use among twelfth graders had doubled, as evidenced by the jump in emergency-room admissions and arrests.

The consumption figures for other drugs saw little fluctuation. Despite the DEA's many successes, the number of people using drugs had not fallen off to any appreciable degree.

It was business as usual. Drug syndicates were making as much money as ever, and as long as they did, the status quo would never drastically alter.

Cocaine was still pouring into the United States by the ton.

Approximately 65 percent came across America's southern border. Critics blasted the government for not being able to stem the flow, but they failed to realize the enormity of the problem.

Consider the sheer number of people entering the United States. More than 300 million each year. Many came across America's borders in one of the more than 100 million vehicles that entered at established ports of entry. It was impossible for U.S. Customs to stop and search every one. President Nixon tried, and the resultant furor could be heard clear down in Colombia.

Another 60 million people came to the United States by air. Screening techniques had improved since 9/11, but there were far too many people for each and every one to be searched from head to toe for contraband.

Then there were the 90,000 passengers and merchants ships that arrived at United States ports, to say nothing of 157,000 smaller vessels.

In short, and to be blunt, there was simply no way in hell that the government could stop drugs from being smuggled in. Not all of them. Not even most of them. But that didn't mean the government was ready to give up. That didn't mean the DEA threw in the towel and admitted defeat.

The success of the war on drugs couldn't be measured by the number of seizures. *Every* interdiction counted, whether large or small. Every shipment of heroin confiscated meant less fuel for the fires of addiction. Every ounce of crack seized might mean one less crack baby born to a hopeless addict. Every tablet of ecstasy taken off the market was one less tablet available to be the cause of a lethal overdose.

Drug advocates say that the government has no business being involved in drug suppression. They conveniently ignore the cost in human suffering and focus on statistics that show how pervasive drugs have become. What's the use, they ask, when the war is already lost?

But to say they are biased is a gross understatement. They are more than biased. They are converts to the cause. It's no secret that some of those screaming the loudest for drugs to be legalized are themselves users of illegal substances.

They do have a point, though, in one regard, and it is confirmed by their own lifestyle. As long as there are people willing to use drugs, the drug trade will thrive. It's not the government who feeds the drug beast. It's the insatiable appetite of those who consume drugs.

Market Trends

At the beginning of 2003, the Colombians still dominated the cocaine market along the Eastern seaboard. From Maine to Florida they ruled the roost, as far as product. But a change had taken place. At the street level, the Colombian role had dwindled. Their cocaine was now being distributed by Dominicans and others.

In the western United States, an even bigger change had occurred. The Colombians were no longer the main suppliers. Mexican traffickers had taken over, in large part due to the payment-in-cocaine system that the Colombians had instigated.

The Colombians didn't seem to mind. They were content to function mainly as suppliers. They would let the Mexicans handle the wholesale end and the heightened risks that went with it.

Both the Colombians and the Mexicans had learned from previous mistakes. Losing so many large shipments had taught them to smuggle smaller amounts. That way their losses weren't as great. To compensate, they increased the number of shipments.

The Dominicans had become major crack players. They had intense competition from Jamaican and Puerto Rican rings. Street gangs were also heavily involved in crack, notably the notorious Bloods and Crips. We will take a closer look at all of them in a subsequent chapter.

The heroin finding its way onto United States streets had four sources. The Colombians were increasingly active in heroin dealing but as yet could not compete, volume-wise, with either Southeast Asia or the Middle East. Mexican heroin traffickers had also increased their share, particularly west of the Mississippi River, where black-tar and brown-powder heroin outsold everything else.

As with cocaine, it was largely in the East that the Colombians found outlets for their heroin. And as with cocaine, most of the street-level distribution was left in the hands of Dominicans. An intricate working relationship had developed, with both sides benefitting. For the Colombians, the plus was less risk. For the Dominicans, it was more money.

Every means conceivable was used to sneak the heroin in. Couriers on airplanes were commonplace. Couriers on buses were also being used, as the DEA discovered when they arrested a Colombian with two kilograms in his possession.

The largest seizure of Colombian heroin to date took place when fifty-four kilograms were found in false bottoms to 1,400 boxes of frozen plaintains.

Heroin from Southeast Asia, once dominant in the United States, had declined. One exception was the heroin being brought in by entrenched Chinese syndicates. Their network extended from British Columbia to the northeastern United States, where it put them in direct competition with the Dominicans and others.

Nigerian rings were active in half a dozen cities. The DEA had pinpointed Chicago as a central hub of one of the largest, with cells in Atlanta, Baltimore, Newark, and elsewhere.

Mexican traffickers were now heavily involved in meth. Thanks to them, the drug was more plentiful than ever. Formerly, biker gangs made most of it, but not anymore. For the past couple of years, Mexican super labs had been the trend, labs able to manufacture three to four times as much as an "average" meth lab. But seizures had taught the Mexican traffickers to downscale their operations so they didn't lose as much meth and expensive equipment each time a lab was raided. The DEA and other agencies were hitting more than 6,000 labs each year, but that still wasn't enough to cut down the supply.

The meth crisis was compounded by the growing number of indie outfits, small-time operators out to make a lot of quick bucks. They bought whatever they needed from local convenience stores. As for learning how to make meth, that was easy. All they had to do was get on the Internet. Meth recipes were posted at various sites.

It was a lot easier for suppliers, big and small, to coordinate shipping and other aspects thanks to computers.

The United Wa State Army was now in the meth business, as well. Most of their meth entered the United States via the mail. Originally, they supplied Laotian and Thai populations in the United States. As demand grew, they expanded their share of the meth market into non-Asian areas.

The purity levels of meth varied drastically. In 1994, the DEA had pegged the average purity level at about 70 percent.

A few years later, it had dropped to roughly 30 percent. By 2002, it was up to between 35 and 40 percent.

The most popular drug of choice by far was still marijuana. The DEA believed that there were roughly eleven million regular users. Surveys suggested that at least one-third of the American population had tried marijuana at least once.

In the United States proper, indoor grows now vastly outnumbered outdoor grows, for the simple reason that indoor grows were a lot harder to detect. Five states held top honors for the most indoor grows reported. California, Florida, Oregon, Washington, and Wisconsin. Note that three of those states comprise the entire West Coast.

As for the outdoor grows, once again California held the top slot, followed by Hawaii, Kentucky, and Tennessee.

Mexican marijuana smugglers were pumping as much marijuana to the north as ever. They tried everything they could think of to outwit customs. In one instance, they wrapped the marijuana in cellophane, then smeared the packages with motor oil, grease, and mustard in an attempt to thwart drug dogs. The packages were found anyway, hidden in a tractor-trailer shipment of TV sets.

By 2003, Canadian marijuana was being seen more and more. Cultivated in indoor grows, it was particularly potent and thus favored by users. The DEA estimated that in the province of British Columbia alone, the illicit marijuana trade was reaping a billion dollars each year. Little did the DEA realize, but the Canadian share would continue to rise steadily as time went on.

The use of something else was rising the Internet. Not only could anyone who was interested find recipes for making meth, or instructions on how to use every illegal substance under the sun, but there were also scores of sites devoted to praising the alleged merits of various drugs, and sites promoting the legalization of drugs in general.

The Internet had become a prime propaganda tool for the drug lobby. Some sites attacked the government for its stance. Others portrayed the DEA as a bunch of hired thugs.

Anyone cruising the Net could find just about anything on drugs and any topic related to drugs. Much of it was misleading. Sites that praised the use of LSD or hash seldom pointed out the downside. The risks to life and health, the addiction factor, et cetera were conveniently glossed over. The many emergency-room visits by drug users of all kinds were seldom brought up.

The DEA developed a site of its own. It was a comprehensive site that not only included a history of the agency and its many stellar accomplishments but also related the facts about the substances that the DEA had been created to combat.

One of those substances, ecstasy, had seen a disturbing rise in usage. It had spilled over from the rave and club scene and was now in more general use, especially among the young. The same thing was happening in Europe, where most ecstasy came from.

Domestic labs producing ecstasy had appeared, but only a few, and their output was small. The DEA had made it too hard to obtain the necessary chemicals for any large labs to spring up.

LSD was still being used, although certainly not to the degree of its heyday during the psychedelic years of the late 1960s. Most of it came from the West Coast, particularly California, where there were more holdovers from the hippie days than anywhere else. It was troubling, though, that a small but noticeably growing number of young people were experimenting with acid.

As with meth, recipes for making LSD were available on the Net. Some users made their own and sold it to friends. The quality varied greatly. Large-scale labs were rarely encountered, although the DEA did raid one, a raid that will be recounted in a bit.

PCP was seeing something of a resurgence. Popular in the latter half of the 1980s, it had lost ground to crack and ecstasy. Its comeback took place mainly in the Southwest, where the DEA had seized almost fifty kilograms in the inaugural years of the twenty-first century.

GHB was still much in evidence on the rave scene. Again, recipes were available on the Net. Since it was relatively easy to make, the DEA had seen instances where GHB was being whipped up in bathtubs. The drug continued to figure in a number of sex-assault cases.

So did a newcomer to the scene—flunitrazepam, or Rohypnol. Rophy, as it was commonly called on the street, was used extensively in Central and South America and in Europe as a sedative and for treating insomnia. It was not approved by the FDA for use in the United States.

Mexican traffickers were supplying it, but the Colombians had become involved, too, bringing the Rophy in through Florida.

As with ecstasy and GHB, many users mistakenly believed that Rophy was safe to use. Some found out the hard way that this wasn't true, as Rophy soon became the new "date rape" drug.

This, then, was the overall situation as 2003 commenced and what the DEA was up against.

2003

Candy from Strangers

The year got off to an auspicious start financially for the DEA. The President's budget request to fund the agency was a whopping $1.7 billion, a far cry from the early days when the budget was in the low millions.

By now, the DEA had more than 8,000 personnel. Many were based in foreign countries, where they were particulary at risk.

A four-point strategic plan was developed to coincide with the Department of Justice's own long-range goals. The DEA's primary focus would be in four areas: international targets who supplied drugs that eventually ended up on United States streets; national and regional targets, those who bought drugs overseas for the United States market or manufactured their own within U.S. boundaries; local targets, the small drug outfits that plague so many communities; and finally, the last but perhaps the most crucial focus would be on the DEA itself, on honing its operational effectiveness and streamlining its chain of command.

A substantial chunk of the budget was devoted to combating the newest threat on the international scene, narco-terrorism. Specifically, the aim was to enhance the DEA's intelligence capabilities in that regard, including communications intercepts.

In keeping with the adage "just when you think you've seen it all," the new year was to usher in a new form of an old drug and an old substance turned to illicit purposes.

The former was hallucinogenic candy—chocolates laced with psilocybin mushrooms. Reports of the candy came from Oregon, Ohio, Rhode Island, and Virginia. The scope indicated that the candy was being distributed nationally, and this set off alarm bells among DEA staff.

These were the first incidents of their kind that the DEA had seen. The National Drug Intelligence Center had reported several earlier incidents, but everyone thought they were an aberration. Now it appeared that someone was producing the candy on a steady basis.

On nine different occasions shipments of over 250 pounds were discovered at an airport in Portland, Oregon. That, and other factors, led the DEA to suspect that the ring was operating out of the Pacific Northwest. It was believed that the psilocybin mushrooms were grown in Oregon or Washington. The mushrooms were then ground up and added to the chocolate while it was in a liquid state. The chocolate was then poured into molds and, once it had hardened, wrapped in colorful foil.

To most people the chocolates seemed to be nothing more than ordinary candy. They were molded in all kinds of innocuous shapes: butterflies, eggs, pumpkins. Some were molded to resemble the popular Reese's Peanut Butter Cups.

The Portland seizures had all been shipped via FedEx, although a package intercepted later was sent by UPS. The largest seizure consisted of eleven kilograms, the smallest five kilograms.

The DEA labs found something interesting.

First, the lab techs crushed the samples and soaked them in sulfuric acid. Then they stripped away fatty elements by washing the chocolate with chloroform. The resulting layer was isolated, basified with NaOH to pH 10, and extracted. When the extracts were analyzed, it chemically confirmed the presence of the mushrooms.

The interesting thing was that the amount of mushrooms in the candy varied greatly from one shipment to another. This indicated one of two things: either the people making the mushrooms were doing an imprecise job, or there were several makers involved. It also warned of the heightened possibility of an overdose. A customer used to candy of a certain potency might pop two or three of a different kind into his or her mouth, never realizing that the new candies were much more potent.

A seizure made in Rhode Island proved especially disturbing. South Kingstown police became suspicious when they noticed an individual selling chocolate at a local school. The candy was wrapped in foil, but it did not appear to be ordinary candy, and one of the officers cut a piece in half. The gray flakes of mushroom were visible to the naked eye.

A seizure of candy that came from Virginia provided another example of inconsistent production. Here, the mushroom-laced chocolate was sandwiched between two layers of pure chocolate. Also, the mushroom content was as high as 20 percent, a significantly greater proportion than what had been previously found.

What the DEA didn't realize at the time was that recipes for the mushroom chocolates were being posted on the Internet. Anyone who wanted to could visit any of several sites and get detailed instructions.

Thus it was that soon the Vail, Colorado police department issued an alert to law-enforcement agencies everywhere that dealers were selling the candy at concerts, clubs, and parties. The going rate averaged $10 for a one-inch cube of laced chocolate.

Since then, many more reports have surfaced. Portland, Oregon is believed to be where most of the candy is coming from, but there are other sources.

The candy has certain advantages for the users. A casual observer would never suspect that mushrooms were mixed with the chocolate, and users can ingest the candy in public without arousing suspicion.

The case is still open.

Packaging

Labs were confirming the presence of other drugs in new forms, as well. In Florida, it was injectable vials of Special K. In California, it was green ecstasy pills with a dove logo. In New York, it was cylinders of compressed cocaine hidden in green plastic plantains. Also from New York came another interesting discovery: customs agents at JFK International Airport seized three bottles of Havana Club rum from a passenger who had flown into the United States from Cali,

Colombia. The liquid in the bottles looked like rum, but it didn't seem quite right to the alert customs agent. Analysis showed that it was in fact *liquid heroin*. An alert was issued, warning that authorities were likely to see more such instances.

From Florida came word that cocaine was being sold in brick form. In Texas the authorities wondered about some hard red chunky substances that looked like candy, found wrapped in plastic baggies. On testing, it turned out to be red crack.

From Iowa came tablets that law officers thought might be ecstasy but turned out to be a mixture of three forms of piperazine, an anthelmintic drug used in the treatment of worm infections.

There was no doubt about the ecstasy seized a during a raid in December of 2002 in Pennsylvania. It is worthy of mention for two reasons: first, the suspect had set up a front company to purchase the chemicals he needed. Supposedly, they were being used to flavor fruit juices, but they were really being used to make ecstasy in a lab hidden in an enormous steel drum that had been almost completely buried in the suspect's driveway and then concealed with plants and boulders.

Herbicide

Those who like to get high were always looking for new ways to do it. From sniffing glue to chocolate mushrooms, there wasn't anything they wouldn't try if it had been shown to have the effect they desired.

Imagine the DEA's surprise to find that the latest fad was an herb.

Salvia divinorum is a perennial in the mint family. It looks like sage and can grow to three feet in height. It is native to the Sierra Mazateca area of Mexico, but it can be grown just about anywhere except the coldest and driest of climates.

The Mazatec Indians had long used the herb as part of their religious ceremonies. They ingested it to see visions. Perhaps it was inevitable that someone, somewhere, would strike on the novel notion of trafficking in it.

The herb is versatile. It can be brewed and drunk as tea. It can be chewed like chewing tobacco, or ground up and rolled and smoked. Or, if the user so desires, it can be steeped in a pot until vapors rise, and the vapors inhaled.

The effects are intense and nearly instantaneous. So-called out-of-body experiences are common. So is the sensation of traveling through time and space, or of physically merging with other objects. Some users think their senses are heightened to where they can smell sounds and hear colors. The effect only lasts about an hour. Contrast this to LSD and other drugs, with which the effects' duration is far longer.

Salvia divinorum posed two problems for the DEA. Because it had never been encountered north of the border before, no one had ever done a scientific study of the herb's impact on users. Evidence suggested that the long-term effects were similar to those of LSD: flashbacks, chronic depression, and even schizophrenia. Worse, some people using it for the very first time reported that it had drastically altered their personalities. Extroverts became introverts. It also seemed to affect the user's ability to communicate verbally.

The second problem was that Salvia divinorum wasn't classified as a controlled substance. There had been no need, since no one had ever reported its use in the United States. And since it wasn't a controlled substance, it was perfectly legal to use.

Soon, people were selling it on the Internet. Dealers thought they had a gold mine, but it was eventually found that the effects were so disturbing that few customers became regular users.

Enough people were buying it, though, to induce head shops across the country to start selling it. Grows appeared in Hawaii and elsewhere. Plants were selling for anywhere from $20 to $45. An ounce of crushed leaf cost $15 to $120. In liquid form, it was going for $110 to $300 an ounce, depending on where it was being sold.

It didn't stay legal for long. Australia was the first country to outlaw it. St. Peters, Missouri, became the first United States town to pass an ordinance against it after it was recognized as the latest drug fad.

The DEA was quick to push for Salvia divinorum to be added to the controlled substances list, which would take an act of Congress. And no sooner had the DEA done so than the pro-drug lobby championed a push to keep it legal.

Business as Usual

Elsewhere, it was business as usual for the Drug Enforcement Administration.

In January of 2003, the DEA and other agencies in Hawaii took part in Operation Meltdown. Drug houses in eastern Hawaii were raided and a variety of drugs confiscated, including ice (or crystal meth), cocaine, marijuana, and several kinds of prescription drugs. Twenty-one people were arrested, one a juvenile.

That same month in Florida, the DEA and the Monroe County sheriff's office went after a crack ring. Sheriff's deputies had learned that crack was being sold in the parking lot of a fashionable club in Key Largo. The DEA was contacted and arrests were made. Those, in turn, led to two high-level drug dealers in Homestead, Florida, who were allegedly supplying crack to Homestead and the Florida Keys. Undercover agents met with the dealers to set up a buy, and when the pair offered to sell the agents $4,000 worth of crack, they were cuffed and carted off.

In Puerto Rico, a long-term investigation came to fruition with the arrests of members of a reputed cocaine and heroin ring that had been selling a kilogram of cocaine for $18,000 and 125 grams of heroin for $10,000. The ring was well organized. It operated out of San Juan, Ponce, Toa Alta, Toa Baja, Catano, and Bayamón. On the morning of February 8, more than fifty federal and Puerto Rican officers conducted simultaneous raids in all six cities and towns. Ten warrants had been issued, but only five of the suspects were caught in the sweep.

Guatemala

South of the border, a new player of sorts was on the scene. Usually it was Mexico or Colombia or Colombia's neighbors who were mentioned in news stories pertaining to drugs. Now it was Guatemala's turn.

A new president had been elected three years before. During those years, Guatemala had become a key transit point for drugs shipped from South America to Mexico, especially cocaine. At least five drug syndicates that the DEA knew of sprang up and forged working relationships with the Colombian cartels and Mexican traffickers. By the end of 2003, the DEA projected that 200 tons of coke had passed between Guatemala's borders.

The really remarkable thing was that the Guatemalan government took precious few steps to stop the influx. Drug seizures dropped by half. Those that did take place only seemed to occur after the United States complained about the lax enforcement since the new president took over.

Coincidence? Whispers were heard, rumors that the government was a party to the drug transactions and that certain key officials were being paid huge amounts of money to look the other way.

The DEA did what it could, but as the DEA's chief of operations told Congress, there wasn't a lot the DEA could do when many high positions in Guatemala were being administered by individuals whose complicity in the drug trade was undeniable.

Now that the drug lords had a stranglehold, experts predicted that the situation would be the status quo for years to come. Yet another country was caught in the net of degradation and decline cast by the modern plague called drugs.

Roundup

There was good news from south of the border, although it arrived a bit indirectly. A drug kingpin previously extradited to the U.S. finally stood trial and was convicted.

Fernando Henao-Montoya was related to Archangel Henao, the notorious mastermind behind the Colombian cartels' newfound reliance on high-tech equipment to a degree never before seen.

In the early 1990s Fernando became involved in the family business—drugs. He was put in charge of ferrying cocaine shipments into the United States. The DEA, FBI, and other agencies had their eyes on him, waiting for him to slip up, and he did.

Fernando arranged a 5,000-kilogram shipment of coke that reached the States by way of Venezuela and Mexico. He then sent a trusted underling to pick up the money due; approximately $25 million.

An Organized Drug Enforcement Task Force oversaw the op that resulted in Fernando's extradition to the United States. He ended up pleading guilty in Manhattan Federal court.

In May, another task force, the Cornwall Regional Task Force, made up of the Royal Canadian Mounted Police and other Canadian agencies, with assistance from the DEA, wrapped up an investigation of a ring smuggling marijuana and cocaine into the United States.

The marijuana was being grown in Ontario and Quebec, then slipped through Cornwall and down into the United States, notably New York and Florida.

Ring members on both sides of the border were arrested and the ring was put permanently out of operation, or as permanently as anything can be in the constantly shifting panorama of the war on drugs.

As has been conclusively demonstrated, drugs know no political boundaries.

Witness the last remaining Communist superpower. China had seen a tremendous rise in drug use. The country had an estimated one million drug addicts. Most were hooked on heroin. But in recent years China had seen a spike in the use of synthetic drugs like ecstasy and crystal meth, predictably among the young. Communist or not, China's youth had money to spend, and many were spending it on recreational drugs. A rave culture had sprung up, very much like its capitalist counterpart.

China had signed the 1988 United Nation Drug Convention, which spelled out cooperative efforts that the countries were to make. On a regular basis, Chinese officials turned over samples of drugs they seized, especially samples of drugs from shipments intended for the United States, to the DEA.

Part of China's drug problem stemmed from its proximity to two major drug-producing areas, the Golden Triangle and the Golden Crescent. Internally, China manufactured large quantities of ephedrine and other chemicals that were being diverted to the illegal market.

Initially, critics charged that China was not taking the problem seriously enough. In the early 1990s, the country's budget for fighting drugs amounted to less than one million dollars. But by 2003, that total had risen to almost $20 million, still a far cry from the amount that the United States and other Western countries were spending, but an improvement.

Corruption in China was as widespread as in certain Central and South American countries. Communist officials were often paid to look the other way by Chinese drug kingpins. But China had stepped up its enforcement campaigns and displayed a new attitude of cooperation with other countries.

In regards to the United States, China extended a helping hand to DEA agents and others operating out of the U.S. embassy.

A joint investigation by the DEA and the Chinese in Fujan Province brought about the dismantling of a major heroin ring that was smuggling large amounts of heroin into the United States. China also closed down a meth ring and seized four tons of meth. Chinese officials persuaded Burma to clamp down on drug operations on their mutual border.

The DEA looked forward to more cooperation in the future as the Chinese became even more active in drug enforcement.

✾ ✾ ✾

In Arizona, a shooting took place involving a drug dealer who was robbed of ill-gotten gains. It alerted the police to the presence of a marijuana ring in Phoenix, and the DEA was notified.

Wiretaps and surveillance were undertaken. The ring was smuggling marijuana into Phoenix from Mexico, then passing it on to outlets in Texas, New York, Illinois, Kentucky, Virginia, Michigan, and Ohio.

Arrests were made, but the ring continued to operate. There was always someone ready to take the place of those who were arrested.

In order to penetrate the ring's many levels, a conspiracy investigation was mounted. The results made headlines all across the state when it became known that one of the alleged bigwigs was an Arizona Cardinals football player. The other ringleaders were reputedly from New York City. In all, thirty-four suspects were taken into custody and about 1,500 pounds of marijuana was seized, along with a couple of tractor-trailer rigs and nine other vehicles.

In South Carolina, cocaine was more readily available than ever before, and crack cocaine use was heading for the stratosphere. A new ring based in Walterboro was to blame. They were smuggling the cocaine in from Florida and the New York area.

The DEA launched Operation Casper as a countermeasure. Several prominent ring members were identified and arrested, but they refused to cooperate with authorities for fear of reprisals. In fact, two potential informers were attacked by gunmen while they were at home. One was rendered a paraplegic for life, and the other was shot in the head but survived.

It was estimated that the ring was responsible for distributing some one million dollars' worth of cocaine over a four- to five-year period.

The DEA was able to bring the ring to trial after a ring member agreed to help the DEA in return for leniency. At the man's sentencing, the judge took his help into account and sentenced him to one-third of the time he would otherwise have served.

Up in North Carolina, wide-ranging marijuana eradication efforts were underway. The DEA, working with state investigators and the North Carolina Air National Guard, had instigated an aggressive campaign. Whenever air crews spotted grows, ground personnel were promptly notified and closed in. In one instance, the grower noticed the aircraft and was trying to destroy her own plants when the ground team got there. In another, a sixty-year-old man cultivating more than 700 plants was caught in the act of tending them.

Yaba

Marijuana was old hat compared to some of the new drugs. Of foremost concern to the DEA was a new form of meth.

Up to this point, meth users either injected the drug directly into their bloodstreams, smoked it, or snorted it. But now meth was appearing in tablet form—small reddish-orange or green tablets imprinted with logos, just like ecstasy.

The tablets were traced to Thailand. There, they were known as yaba, and that was how users in the States began to refer to them.

The original source was the United Wa State Army in Burma, which funneled the tablets in large quantities into Thailand, and from there, the tablets ended up in Asian communities in the United States. But now the tablets were being seen more and more outside the cultural confines of the Asian communities as users of other ethnicities became interested.

The rave scene had a new fave.

Yaba had several advantages over other forms of meth: there wasn't any danger of coming down with hepatitis or AIDS from contaminated needles; users avoided the telltale track marks from chronic needle injections; and the tablets were easily concealed and could be inserted into the end of a straw, then slowly consumed by sipping a soft drink or other liquid.

Many regular meth users, though, didn't like the tablets. They felt that the rush they got wasn't as intense, and the rush was a big part of any drug's appeal.

So far, not many tablets have surfaced, but the DEA expects that to change over the next several years as they grow in popularity.

The Dark Crystal

In the meantime, crystal meth was still highly popular, as the suspects involved in making it in a secret lab in Sparks, Nevada were well aware. A tip was turned in to the Consolidated Narcotics Unit, which was made up of the DEA, the Washoe County sheriff's office, and the police departments from Sparks and Reno.

Two of the suspects were shadowed and seen selling the meth at a Reno casino. Nine pounds of the drug was taken from their vehicle. Another man was arrested at the lab.

New York

It should go without saying that New York City has a consistently high level of drug abuse. Cocaine and crack are readily available. Crack, the corpse-maker, had been conclusively tied to more drug-related violence than any other illegal substance, and in New York its use was epidemic, particularly in parts of the city where poverty ran rampant.

By this time, the Dominicans were acting mainly as mid-level distributors and street dealers for the Colombians. They had a lot of competition from Puerto Rican and African-American rings. On the street, gangs like the Bloods and the Latin Kings, the Mara Salvatrucha and the Neta, regularly spread their poison.

The number of outdoor markets and street-corner sales, though, had declined. Close scrutiny by the authorities forced many dealers to sell from their homes or other indoor locations. Drug business was often conducted at nightclubs. Some cocaine and crack was sold through delivery services, a variation of "pizza to go."

The incidence of cocaine use in New York City was well above that of the national average. Cocaine-related emergency-room visits had actually dropped from 1997 to 2000, which was encouraging, but the elation was short-lived. The numbers climbed again the very next year. Cocaine, in one form or another, was the leading drug when it came to sending people to the hospital. Figures showed that twice as many cocaine users were admitted in New York City as the national average.

Buffalo, New York, was in the same disreputable boat. Its stats were way above average, due largely to several extensive and extremely active drug rings of which the city did not care to boast.

One of the rings, known locally as the Del Luiza Boys, was considered the worst of the worst. Many of the gang's members were felons with long criminal records. They had a vast number of home invasions, robberies, shootings and murder to their names. When several were arrested and posted bail, they went right out and sold more drugs. One Del Luiza member was caught and sentenced to home incarceration, provided he wore a monitoring device at all times so the police could ensure he did not violate the terms of the judge's sentence. He stayed home, like the judge wanted—and sold drugs right out of his house.

The Del Luiza Boys were just one of many gangs getting their drugs from Medellín. The DEA and U.S. Customs had the route worked out: the cocaine and heroin were shipped to Puerto Rico and from there to New York City. From the Big Apple it was parceled out to places like Buffalo and Rochester.

Operation Deja Vu involved the DEA and a large task force. Over a span of seven months, evidence was meticulously collected. When the day came for the mop-up, sixty-three suspects were arrested in the United States and four in Puerto Rico, and warrants were issued in Colombia.

It was not the only time Buffalo was in the news in 2003 in relation to drugs. In July, a local trucking company was implicated in a major DEA op. Its owner reputedly operated a transportation cell linked to a Colombian drug lord. The cell brought the drugs in through Mexico and relayed them to various cities and towns around the country.

The lengths to which they would go to was remarkable. In one instance, the traffickers took out the seats and stripped the carpeting from an SUV, then cut secret compartments in the floor. They filled the compartments with coke; welded, sanded, and painted the floor so it looked like it should; replaced the carpet, and were good to go. Or so they thought.

The truck-company owner reportedly had two prior felony

drug convictions. But he was small potatoes in the greater scheme of things.

The DEA was after the Mexican kingpin behind it all.

Ismael Zambada-Garcia and two of his lieutenants were indicted by a federal grand jury in Washington, D.C. The ZGO, as it was known, was accused of smuggling some $17 million worth of cocaine into New York and New Jersey, another $30 million worth into Chicago, and another twenty-three kilograms of cocaine into California. For its large-scale smuggling operation, the ZGO was classified as a Priority Organization Target, and the DEA pulled out all the stops.

Mexican traffickers in the states of Nayarit and Sinaloa were the middlemen in most of the transactions.

The first break came when a fishing boat, the *Macel*, was stopped off the Pacific coast of Mexico. When it was boarded, almost 10,000 kilograms of cocaine were found. Based on information that was gleaned, the full extent of the ZGO operation became clear. Soon more than eighty investigations were underway nationwide.

The FBI, U.S. Customs, the BATF, the IRS, and other federal and state agencies were involved. Nineteen months were spent gathering evidence.

Then came the arrests. Two hundred and forty in the United States and Mexico, and Zambada-Garcia and his top aides indicted. The arrests seriously crippled the ZGO but did not put it out of business—its leaders were still on the loose.

Finding the Friend-Killer

The DEA had better luck with a Mexican cartel boss.

You might remember Osiel Cardenas-Guillen. He had a $2 million reward on his head. Back in 1999, he and fifteen of his hired thugs had assaulted and tried to abduct DEA and FBI agents. He was one of the most wanted drug lords in the entire world, with a drug empire second to none.

Bit by bit, the DEA, the FBI, U.S. Customs, and Mexican authorities had been chipping away at Cardenas-Guillen's Gulf cartel.

In March of 2002, Mexican police nabbed Adan Medrano-Rodriguez, one of Cardenas-Guillen's top men. In May, they nabbed another, Jesus Albino Quintero Meraz, who was fond of bragging that he was responsible for smuggling a ton of cocaine a day into the United States.

But Cardenas-Guillen himself continued to elude authorities. All efforts to snare him proved fruitless despite the reward on his head.

Secretly, some officials began to wonder if maybe there wasn't more to it than simple luck. Their suspicions were confirmed in spectacular fashion when a brigadier general, a captain, and a lieutenant were taken into custody for allegedly aiding and abetting Cardenas-Guillen by suppling him with timely intel on the status of investigations involving him.

What makes this even more ironic is that the three were high-ranking members of an elite airborne unit that was formed to track drug traffickers. Cardenas-Guillen had bought the services of some of the very men the Mexican government had assigned to bring him down.

Almost a year to the day after Adan Medrano-Rodriguez was apprehended, it was Cardenas-Guillen's turn.

Officials had learned that Cardenas, better known as El Loco, or the Friend-Killer, would attend a family function in Matamoros, a party to celebrate his daughter's wedding. On the night of March 13, Mexican troops and police quietly closed in, surrounding the houses where Cardenas-Guillen and his associates were believed to be staying. Before the arrests could be carried out, the drug lord's bodyguards opened fire with automatic weapons and lobbed a grenade. Three soldiers were wounded, two critically. But the bodyguards were overwhelmed and Cardenas-Guillen was finally captured.

Authorities immediately whisked him to Mexico City to be interrogated. The Americans almost as quickly filed papers asking that he be extradited to the United States to stand trial.

With his apprehension, the Gulf cartel was effectively shut down. But it was only one of three major cartels operating in Mexico at the time, the others being the AFO, based out of Tijuana, and another located south of El Paso, Texas.

Accessories

The DEA was attacking the drug crisis from all angles. They were going after the drug lords. They were going after the syndicates. They removed dealers from city streets. They eradicated marijuana grows and raided illegal labs. There was, however, one small but important angle that they had overlooked, an oversight they remedied with Operation Pipe Dreams and Operation Headhunters. The U.S. Marshals' Service, U.S. Customs, and the U.S. Postal Inspection Service took part in the two ops.

Certain drugs required certain paraphernalia. Scales were needed to weigh drugs accurately. Marijuana users favored pipes and bongs. Roach clips were high on any drug user's list of essentials, along with small spoons for cocaine use, et cetera.

Drug paraphernalia was a billon-dollar-a-year business, if estimates were to be believed. Many of the items were sold in head shops, a staple of the drug culture since the 1960s. But more and more, drug paraphernalia was being sold over the Internet. National distributors had online sites where anyone could order any form of paraphernalia they wanted. Even minors could place orders, since few background checks were conducted.

Indictments from Operation Pipe Dreams were handed down against seventeen individuals involved with ten national distributors of drug paraphernalia. Six of those distributors were in California. The others were in Oregon, Arizona, Florida, and South Carolina.

Operation Headhunters specifically targeted head shops in southern Iowa. Search warrants were issued for four shops, and over two million dollars' worth of drug paraphernalia was seized. Indictments were then issued against the national distributors that supplied the head shops, including two distributors in California, one in Detroit, and another in Houston.

New England Kingpin

Out of Massachusetts came a sensational trial capped by a life sentence for the lead suspect in a case that typified the rise and fall of street gangs and the consequences to the community. The case also had the distinction of involving the largest cocaine seizure in Massachusetts history.

The gang was made up mainly of Dominicans. The kingpin was Rafael Yeje-Cabrera. Evidently in the belief that the family that smuggled drugs together stuck together, his father, mother, brother, two uncles, and cousin were also gang members. So was the son of a New Bedford police officer assigned to the drug squad.

The gang's activities were not limited to Massachusetts. It

was also involved in illegal activities in Rhode Island, New York, and Georgia. For ten years, their operation flourished, until a series of lucky breaks on the part of the feds and the gang's own arrogance brought their syndicate crashing down.

The first lucky break for law enforcement came in Memphis in July of 2000, when Memphis police stopped a motor home for speeding. When the police took each of the three men aside for routine questioning, something interesting happened. One of the men said they were bound for Las Vegas. The second man said they were heading for Arizona. The third told the police they were traveling to California.

The police were naturally suspicious. They searched the motor home and found hidden compartments—but no drugs—and a bundle of cash. They let the trio go, but the stop set a law-enforcement steamroller into motion.

One of the men in the motor home had been Rafael Yeje-Cabrera's brother.

The other two, Jose Arcentales and Omi Montanez, would be indicted when the law eventually closed in.

New Bedford and Westport police had been hoping for leads on the local gang, which had a propensity for violence. In 1999, a drive-by shooting took place in broad daylight. A stolen van pulled up to a curb, and the occupants cut loose with autofire, blasting two men.

In April of 2001, authorities had their second lucky break when a truck was pulled over in New York. It was bound for New Bedford, and inside were 319 kilos of cocaine. So was a cell phone, and one of the telephone numbers on the phone's call list was that of Rafael Yeje-Cabrera.

In August, as part of an undercover sting, the Immigration and Naturalization Service arrested Rafael Yeje-Cabrera on immigration charges. In an act of monumental arrogance, he offered the INS agent $100,000 to set him free. The INS agent would get another $30,000 if he would keep Yeje-Cabrera informed of what the DEA was up to.

The INS agent agreed. Yeje-Cabrera was released, and the money along with the bribe, became evidence.

Th DEA and other agencies didn't want Yeje-Cabrera on petty immigration charges. They wanted him on drug charges that would put him behind bars for a long time.

In December another seizure occurred, this time in Massachusetts. The suspects were driving a truck with Arizona plates. They became lost in New Bedford and accidentally blocked traffic on Acushnet Avenue. Anxious to get out of there before they aroused unwanted interest, the driver threw the truck into reverse—and backed into a state trooper.

The two men hopped out. They told the state trooper they were delivering a shipment of eggplant. When the trooper took a look at their tollbooth receipts, he noticed that the receipts didn't match the route the men mentioned they had taken. A search of the truck turned up 600 pounds of cocaine, the largest ever in the state's history.

The trooper had no way of knowing that the DEA and other agencies were aware of the shipment. The seizure was kept a secret long enough for a sweep to be conducted. Ring members from as far afield as Atlanta, the Bronx, and Massachusetts were clamped in handcuffs.

During the course of his six-week trial, Rafael Yeje-Cabrera threatened one of the witnesses. He was convicted of the bribe of the INS agent and for attempting to possess and sell the 600 pounds of coke in the New Bedford seizure. The judge sentenced him to life in prison.

Of the twenty members of the gang who were indicted, fifteen pled guilty. Among them was Yeje-Cabrera's uncle, Jose, who received twenty-two years in prison.

With the convictions, another drug ring had bit the legal dust.

Grosse Point Blank

There was never a shortage of rings and soon enough the DEA would have other organizations to focus their attention on. Witness developments in Grosse Point Park, Michigan that took a somewhat bizarre turn.

It began when the Melvindale, Michigan police department received a reliable tip. A tractor-trailer filled with marijuana was in Detroit, on its way to deliver its load in Grosse Point Park.

The Melvindale PD contacted the DEA. The tip, as it turned out, had a bearing on an ongoing DEA/Michigan State Police investigation into the same ring.

The truck was stopped and searched. Sure enough, inside were some 3,700 pounds of marijuana. The driver agreed to cooperate: the delivery would continue as scheduled. When a Grosse Point Park resident took possession, he was arrested. He was the first of twenty to be taken into custody and charged in a conspiracy indictment as part of a ring that covered five states and had sold as much as forty tons of marijuana since its inception.

The gang had started small. Initially they smuggled in two to four pounds of grass at a time in cars. When that went well, they switched to vans that could hold 4,000 pounds of marijuana. When that went well, they switched to the really big rigs.

The DEA first became aware of the ring in February of

2002, when the State Police in Iowa stopped a car registered to one of the alleged ring members and found $244,000 in cash. The driver had loose lips. He was a courier, on his way to Las Vegas to pay for a marijuana shipment.

The arrests shut down the ring.

Then came the bizarre part. In an unrelated development, more marijuana was uncovered only a few blocks from where the tractor-trailer had delivered the load to the Grosse Point Park resident.

A motorist passing by a residence in the 3900 block of Grayton noticed that a house was on fire. The blaze was called in, and firefighters quickly responded. When they got there, the seventy-one-year-old owner of the residence was calmly sitting on the front porch. The firefighters, and the man's neighbors who had gathered to watch the flames and smoke shoot from an upstairs room, were astounded when the elderly man jumped up, dashed to his car, and sped out of there, driving right across his front lawn.

His hasty departure was explained when firefighters rushed inside to fight the fire.

Drying marijuana hung on clotheslines in the living room. Some of the plants were six feet tall. They were part of an indoor grow found in the basement, complete with a special lighting system so the plants would thrive.

The fire was extinguished, and the pot was seized.

The neighbors were as stunned as the firefighters. They had no idea the man was growing all that marijuana right under their noses.

Boston

In Boston, the DEA, the Boston police department, and other agencies were out to neutralize four violent street gangs. Two of the gangs, from the Dorchester area, were pitted against two others who claimed part of the Uphams Corner/Roxbury area as their turf.

The two sides became embroiled in an ever-escalating war after a gang member from the Uphams area was murdered, allegedly by rivals.

All four gangs were heavy into drugs. When indictments were eventually handed down against twenty-six gang members, among the charges leveled was that of selling crack cocaine within 1,000 feet of a school. Specifically, three schools: two elementary schools and the Community Academy.

One of the suspects had allegedly recruited a minor to sell crack to the school kids.

If it seemed as if the DEA was devoting a lot of attention, and resources, to New England—they were, and with good cause. By this time the six-state region had the dubious distinction of having the highest rate of illegal drug use of anywhere in the entire country.

Massachusetts had the highest rate of all—so high that heroin use had risen a whopping 60 percent in the past few years. Heroin addiction in Massachusetts was three times the national average. Heroin overdoses were up by over 75 percent.

The DEA put part of the blame on cheap Colombian heroin, which was flooding the market. Heroin that was up to 90 percent pure was going for as little as $4 a bag. It was so plentiful that the DEA had received reports of dealers offering free bags of heroin with every sale of eight or more as part of a devious and deliberate campaign to get more people hooked. Kids mainly.

In Connecticut, a dealer was arrested with 300 bags of heroin in his possession near an elementary school.

And it wasn't just the gangs. A schoolteacher was arrested on charges of selling heroin to her students. She reportedly invited them to her apartment to shoot up.

According to a National Drug Survey, 4 percent of New England kids between the ages twelve and seventeen were addicted to drugs. This compared to about 3 percent in the national average.

Dominican gangs, with Colombian backers, were entrenched in cites like Boston, New Bedford, and Springfield.

Police departments were doing all they could, but they needed help, which the DEA was happy to supply.

Kentucky Blue Grass

Down in Clark County, Kentucky, a pair of DEA agents and a deputy sheriff went to a local residence to arrest a woman wanted in North Carolina on drug charges.

When their knock was answered and the front door opened, the agents noticed the strong and unmistakable odor of marijuana. A search turned up nearly 250 mature plants and a sophisticated indoor grow.

The woman and her husband were arrested.

Acid Washed

Back in the days of Timothy Leary, LSD had been the darling of those who saw themselves as the intellectual royalty of the drug set. To them, LSD wasn't "just a drug," it was the elixir of the gods: the wisdom of Zeus, the beauty of Apollo, and the passion of Aphrodite rolled into one. It was a means of expanding consciousness, of altering the very fabric of their being, of launching them on new frontiers of mental and personal awareness.

That same subset still existed, but its numbers were substantially lower than in LSD's heyday. They were a culture unto themselves. Thanks to computers and the Internet, they could network to a degree never before possible.

The tight-knit nature of the LSD culture made it extremely hard for law enforcement to infiltrate it. To compound matters, some self-appointed guardians within the LSD culture made it a point to keep tabs on all efforts by "the man" to erase the culture from existence. Records were kept of LSD arrests, and of the agencies and officers involved.

No doubt about it, the advent of the computer age had been an indescribable boon to criminals of every stripe, but particularly to those in the drug world. We have already seen how Colombian kingpins used the best computers money could buy and other high-tech equipment to nefarious ends.

In truth, the Internet was their "information superhighway." Some encrypted sites were used to auction drugs. Others posted daily updates on drug busts and the latest information on what the DEA was up to.

The LSD culture was part of that counter-campaign. It was small but well organized.

One of the reasons that it was so small had to do with effects of LSD. Or, rather, the lack thereof, in that unlike heroin, meth, and coke, hallucinogens weren't addictive. Not in the traditional sense. By the same token, a lot of potential users were scared off by the effects that LSD *did* produce. It wasn't for nothing that it was known as a mind-altering substance. Common accounts of flashbacks and psychological troubles brought on by sustained use didn't help the drug's popularity any, either.

All of this brings us to William Pickard, sometimes described as the "high priest" of the acid set; his helper, a man by the name of Clyde Apperson; and the largest LSD seizure ever recorded by the DEA.

Everyone has heard of Johnny Appleseed, the quaint gentleman who went around planting apple seeds wherever he went in the hope of turning America into one giant apple orchard. William Pickard might aptly be described as the Johnny Acid Tab of his day, since he singlehandedly did more to spread the use of LSD than anyone else in his generation, and then some.

At one time Pickard was co-director of the Drug Policy Analysis Program at the University of California. How ironic that he should be associated with the largest LSD lab ever found, among others. In its entire history, the DEA had only ever found four LSD labs. Pickard was implicated as being involved in three of them.

That wasn't all.

Back in 1976, William Pickard had been arrested for making LSD. In 1980 he was arrested again, this time for selling ecstasy. Apparently the ecstasy wasn't to his liking, because from then on, it was LSD all the way. In 1996, he was involved with an LSD lab in Oregon. In 1998 he was arrested *again*, this time as he fled an LSD lab in a warehouse in Mountain View, California.

Pickard moved around a lot. He was smart enough to know he couldn't stay in one spot very long. The risk of being caught was too great.

His next LSD lab was in Santa Fe, New Mexico. He and Apperson manufactured about two pounds of LSD every five weeks. That's about ten million doses, which sold for about $10 a dose. Some was sold in the United States. Some found its illicit way to Europe.

On the lookout for a new place to set up shop, Pickard heard about as unlikely a spot as anyone could imagine: an abandoned missile silo.

Enter Gordon Scott Skinner. His family ran a factory in Tulsa, Oklahoma, that produced industrial springs. In 1996, Skinner purchased an abandoned Atlas-E missile base near Wamego, Kansas, from a scrap dealer, purportedly with the idea of setting up a branch of the family business.

In 1998, Skinner ran into Pickard, whom he had met a couple of years previous, at a conference in San Francisco. The pair got to talking and, inspired by his recent purchase, Skinner mentioned that he knew just the spot for Pickard to set up his next LSD lab—not at the missile base Skinner had purchased, but at *another* one, near Carneiro, Kansas, that was owned by a friend of Skinner's. The friend had asked Skinner to fix the base up while he did some traveling.

Unfortunately, the owner of the base committed suicide, and in handling the estate, his father decided to visit the property in question. Pickard and Apperson weren't there, but their equipment was. Skinner panicked and elected to move all their lab equipment to his *own* missile base.

With an abandoned missile base converted into an LSD lab on his property, Skinner did what anyone else would have done. He headed for Nevada to have a high old time at a casino. During the festivities, he got busted for flashing a fake badge and impersonating an officer. A United States district court convicted him. Concerned that it might bring unwanted attention down on his head, Skinner and his attorney contacted the DEA and offered to strike a deal.

Keep in mind that the DEA had absolutely no idea Pickard and Apperson were setting up shop in Kansas and knew nothing about the missile bases. Skinner offered to detail the operation for them in exchange for immunity from prosecution. In common parlance, he was covering his ass—before anyone in law enforcement had the faintest glimmer of a suspicion his ass was involved.

A word about informants: the DEA doesn't offer deals willy-nilly. There is an established protocol for dealing with informants. They must be questioned at length. Their information must be verified. They must be fingerprinted and photographed and have background checks run. Then, and only then, will the DEA agree to work with them, and only after both parties sign a confidential agreement that spells out the conditions.

The DEA went through all of this with Skinner. He told investigators that a person he knew only as Petaluma Al handled shipping the LSD to Europe, and that the money was then laundered through casinos in Nevada. He agreed to wear a wire in a meeting with Pickard and Apperson.

Skinner took DEA agents to the missile base to show them the lab equipment. The DEA then put the base under surveillance and bided its time.

It wasn't long before the two suspects arrived in rented vehicles. It took them two days to load up all the equipment. As Pickard and Apperson were leaving the scene, authorities closed in. Apperson was arrested, but Pickard fled on foot and almost successfully eluded a manhunt. The next day, however, he was discovered, sound asleep, at a local farm.

Fourteen canisters filled with chemicals required to make LSD were seized. Their monetary value alone was over $1 million.

The trial was as fascinating as everything that had led up to it. Pickard claimed that the charges against him were trumped up; that he was a mere researcher, and that his activities were all part of research he was doing in relation to the Drug Policy Analysis Program. He claimed that all the false ID's he had were needed so he could freely move about among those involved in the drug culture. He also claimed that the government once tried to enlist his services in retrieving Stinger missiles from Afghan warlords.

The trial dragged on as the prosecution painstakingly presented its case and the defense did its best to rebut it. In the end, Pickard was given life in prison with no chance of parole.

His supporters cried foul. They made a Web site devoted to his case. They asserted that he was innocent.

Strange, then, that within two years of his arrest, the amount of LSD available in the U.S. dropped a projected 95 percent.

Afghanistan

Afghanistan was once again the world's leading producer of opium poppies. Under the Taliban, heroin sales reaped $40 million annually, much of which went to funding terrorist organizations. The new president had instituted a ban on growing poppies, but for growers in the more remote regions of the country it was business as usual.

The Afghan government tried to induce the farmers to cooperate by offering the princely sum of $1,250 per hectare to destroy their poppies. But the farmers could make as much as $16,000 per hectare if they let the poppies grow and sold them. It didn't take a rocket scientist to do the math.

Accordingly, the DEA was braced for one of the largest poppy crops ever. More than $1 billion worth, by conservative estimates. Among their other concerns were hints that the Afghan growers might be forging alliances with the Colombians, and the undeniable fact that a lot of the money made would go toward financing terrorist activity worldwide.

Mention should be made that some in the pro-drug lobby claimed it was all the U.S. government's fault. That the United States should never have toppled the Taliban. They bought the Taliban lie that poppy production had been eliminated, conveniently ignoring evidence to the contrary.

The DEA zeroed in on one of the Afghan rings. It was made up of Afghani nationals who had taken up residence in New York and were smuggling heroin into the United States from Afghanistan and Pakistan.

A couple of informers proved invaluable. Through them, the DEA learned how the ring operated. Most of the poppies came from fields in the vicinity of Jalalabad. The chemicals used to process the poppies into heroin came from Germany. Other heroin came from Pakistan.

The DEA set up a sting involving a mailbox that the ring used as a drop for heroin sent by mail. They overheard a defendant advise another to be sure to use an "American-sounding" name to avoid arousing suspicion. The defendants believed that Christmas was the best time of year to smuggle heroin because the volume of mail reduced the odds of the heroin being detected.

The ring had other ways of bringing the heroin in, including a trick never before seen. They hid it in the seams of clothes of

Afghan women, in special plastic tubing that could not be detected unless the garments were torn apart.

When the DEA was ready, ten Afghan nationals were arrested and indictments were filed against others. The agents had done their jobs well, but the heroin seized was a drop in the bucket compared to the deluge about to wash over America's shores.

Operation Northern Star

In January of 2003, America's neighbor to the north had taken what the DEA viewed as an overdue positive step. At long last, Canada had imposed restrictions on the sale of pseudoephedrine, which was essential in making meth, and on shipping pseudoephedrine across the border.

The DEA could finally go after Canadians who served as links in the meth chain.

As noted before, Mexican syndicates had a stranglehold on the meth market. So-called super labs in Mexico and California produced about 80 percent of all the meth used in the United States, and much of the pseudoephedrine needed to manufacture that meth came from Canada.

Operation Northern Star, a combined effort by the DEA, the Royal Canadian Mounted Police, and other agencies, targeted Canadian pharmaceutical companies who, despite the new laws, were continuing to supply pseudoephedrine to brokers, who in turn supplied it to meth makers.

It is interesting, and troubling, to note that many of the brokers were of Middle Eastern extraction, and that some of the money was laundered through banks in the Middle East. Given the national state of mind, the link to terrorism was suspected.

Most of the pseudoephedrine was smuggled into the United

States through Port Huron and Detroit. Some was hidden in special compartments in cars. Some was hidden in tractor-trailer trucks, in shipments of things like bubble gum and bottled water.

From one company alone, the DEA seized 14,400 pounds of pseudoephedrine tablets, enough to make 9,000 pounds of methamphetamine.

An eighteen-month investigation culminated in more than sixty arrests. Dozens of indictments were handed down. Among them were six executives with three Canadian chemical companies.

Some of those arrested were Lebanese citizens, who were taken into custody overseas.

Following the Money

As stated, terrorism was very much on the DEA's collective mind. The war on drugs and the war on terrorism were inextricably linked. It had been established beyond any equivocation or shred of doubt that various terrorists organizations were financing their operations in large part through the illicit sales of drugs.

Because of its unique position as America's leading drug-enforcement arm, with branches and agents in many countries around the world, including those where terrorism flourished, the DEA, in the course of its drug investigations, often gleaned important intel about various narco-terrorists.

More than 600 terrorist acts were perpetrated against the United States and its citizens and military between the mid-1990s and the turn of the century. The U.S. Department of State began keeping an official list of foreign terrorist organizations. Within a few years, the list had almost three dozen names. Many, the DEA was to find out, were directly or indirectly involved in drug trafficking.

Everyone knew that the Taliban had done all in their power to aid and abet Osama bin Laden and his al-Qaeda network. The DEA had reason to believe that heroin trafficking helped fill al-Qaeda's coffers.

Intel also confirmed that in southeast Turkey, the Kurdistan Workers Party, or PKK, levied "taxes" on drug shipments passing through territory it controlled, and sold its services to protect drug shipments.

In Colombia, the terrorist situation had worsened. The FARC was bolder and more violent than ever. No one was safe. Presidential candidate Ingrid Betancourt and her chief of staff, Clar Rojas, were kidnapped by the FARC. A congresswoman, Martha Catalina Daniels, an outspoken critic of the FARC, was tortured to death.

By now the FARC controlled whole sections of the country's eastern lowlands, despite the army's efforts to roust them out. Those areas also happened to be major cocaine-processing and coca-cultivation regions, and the FARC was being paid a lot of money to protect labs, shipments, and airports.

The FARC had also become involved in the drug trade themselves. Some units were producing their own cocaine base. Others were selling coke to various international drug syndicates.

Another terrorist group, the National Liberation Army (ELN), conrolled a strip along Colombia's border with Venezuela, including some prime growing regions for opium poppies and cannabis. The ELN, too, was reaping dividends from drug money, although not quite to the same extent as the FARC.

A new element in Colombia complicated the picture even

more. Many Colombians were fed up with the drug cartels. Many were sick at heart about the Communists and their terrorist tactics. They were outraged at the continual rape of Colombian society. Since their government wasn't resolving the crisis fast enough to suit them, they took the law into their own hands and formed vigilante groups. Some were organized by wealthy ranchers and plantation owners. Others were made up of ordinary Colombians. All told, the DEA estimated that there were hundreds of such groups.

It was budding anarchy, made worse by the DEA's discovery that some of the vigilantes were funding their organizations in exactly the same way that the FARC and ELN did—through drugs.

It did not bode well that the FARC now had intellectual brethren in Venezuela and other South and Central American countries. So much violence had broken out in Venezuela that wealthy cattle ranchers had formed their own counter-terrorist groups.

In Peru, the Shining Path had been making life difficult for years. They, too, controlled fertile coca-growing regions. They, too, extracted money from those who grew and processed the coca.

One of the DEA's strategies was to hit the drug syndicates and narco-terrorists where it would hurt them the most—in their wallets. The DEA's financial investigations section was doing an outstanding job of ferreting out drug accounts and seizing financial assets. But, as always, the drug rings, and the terrorists, readily adapted.

In Afghanistan and neighboring countries, traffickers had stopped using conventional banks and were laundering their funds through an underground financial network known as *hundi* or *hawala*. The hundi had been established centuries ago by prominent crime families and businesses and had one distinct and crucial advantage over modern banks: the money couldn't be traced. There was no paper trail for the DEA to follow back to its source. The drug proceeds simply seemed to disappear.

In South America, the cartels and narco-terrorists had a money-laundering network of their own. It was called the BMPE, or Black Market Peso Exchange. It was not quite as detection-proof as the hundi, but it did make tracing money considerably more difficult. The DEA calculated that the BMPE was laundering billions in drug funds each year.

But those plying the drug trade weren't the only ones who could learn and adapt. The DEA was constantly coming up with new ways to deal with the new challenges.

One of those ways were the Sensitive Investigation Units, mentioned earlier. The units were composed largely of seasoned law-enforcement operatives from host countries who worked in close partnership with the DEA. In order to ensure each unit's integrity, those who took part were required to undergo periodic reviews and lie-detector tests.

Having highly skilled and superbly motivated nationals from host countries take such an important part was a strategy that proved itself time and time again. The units were so successful that the DEA now had them in nine countries.

Another step the DEA took was to form an Intelligence Response Team, a special group of intel experts who could be dispatched anywhere on the globe at a moment's notice. Their speciality was narco-terrorism in all its many forms and guises.

At the same time, the DEA was working with Russia, Romania, and Germany to better coordinate their drug-enforcement investigations. It was hoped that by linking their respective databases, information could be shared quickly and effectively.

The DEA's ultimate goal was to create a giant drug-intel network embracing all of Europe and Central Asia as well as the states and provinces that once made up the Soviet Union. A grand plan, but if it became a reality, it might well help turn the tide in the worldwide drug war.

Only time would tell.

Distribution

Another new development concerned cocaine couriers.

For decades, the Colombian cartels had used couriers to transport coke into the United States. Invariably, the couriers were Colombians. But now the DEA was seeing more and more instances of Mexican nationals caught trying to smuggle Colombian coke. Some of the cocaine was sewn into the linings of luggage or clothing. Some was concealed in the footwear that the couriers wore. Some couriers were fleshbags, and swallowed balloons or condoms with the heroin inside.

But why so many Mexican nationals? This was the question that the DEA wanted answered. One possible reason was that more and more Mexican traffickers were directly involved in the cocaine trade.

Another was that the determined and conscientious efforts of the Mexican president to eradicate the Mexican cartels was having a decided effect. One major cartel had already been destroyed, and another was gravely impaired. Lesser syndicates had also been torn apart.

The situation can be described in one word: chaos. It had become so serious, from the Colombians' perspective, that the DEA had gotten word that Colombian traffickers were making an unprecedented number of visits to Mexico to reestablish ties with crippled allies or establish new ties with new middlemen.

The Colombians were suffering setbacks in other areas, too.

For some time, they had been supplying large amounts of heroin to a Dominican gang in Philadelphia. The gang's web had spread into Newark and New York. What made this case notable was that the purity of the heroin they were selling was the highest of any in the country.

The thoroughness with which the DEA built its case was a testament to their persistence. The entire ring was uncovered, from the Medellín supplier to each and every member of their Dominican associates, all the way down to street-level dealers. Often, in a drug case, some of the suspects would slip through the net, but not this time.

The DEA believed that Philadelphia had gone from being a typical user city to a distribution hub. The Santos gang, named after one of the alleged leaders, had a lot to do with it. His two top lieutenants, interestingly enough, were his girlfriends.

During the course of a two-year op, the DEA made several seizures. The first was over three kilgrams of cocaine intercepted on its way to Philadelphia from New York City. The second was six kilograms. The third involved four kilograms seized from a courier en route via bus from New York to Philly. Yet another was of two kilograms on their way from Colombia to the States.

Altogether, forty-five suspects were arrested. They faced life in prison.

* * *

As on the East Coast, so on the West.

A Grand Jury in western Washington brought indictments against eleven members of a heroin and cocaine ring. The links of the chain stretched from Medellín to Seattle. The gang smuggled most of their drugs into the Puget Sound area. From there, some was sent to Chicago and New York City.

Once again, the Colombian supplier was arrested—a hallmark of the exceptional cooperation between the DEA and the Colombian national police. They weren't the only agencies involved. U.S. Customs, the IRS, and a host of state and local departments, as well as Canadian customs, all chipped in.

Farther south, in late June of 2003, a hiker out enjoying the scenic wonders of the Sierra National Forest stumbled on an unexpected sight—40,000 opium poppy plants—and notified authorities.

It was unusual to find them being grown domestically. Smaller grows had been found in Oregon, Washington, Idaho, and Montana, but this was the first instance of poppies being grown in a national forest.

Down in San Jose, more of those chocolate mushrooms surfaced. These were cast in star-shaped molds and wrapped in either gold or silver foil. Pieces of the mushrooms could be seen with the naked eye.

The DEA issued an alert, asking that anyone with any information about the source of the chocolates to contact them.

Worcester

Worcester, Massachusetts, was the hub of two separate ops.

The first centered on a street-level ecstasy ring that dabbled in firearms. Over a span of several months, an undercover operative bought close to 2,000 ecstasy tablets, a couple of vials of Special K, and seventy Oxycodone tablets from the suspects. The agent also bought a rifle and a sawed-off shotgun.

The DEA had more than enough evidence to make arrests, so a final buy was set up in the parking lot of a Worcester pub. Because firearms were involved, the BATF was called in. The Worcester police and the Massachusetts State Police completed the law contingent.

Although they were armed, none of the suspects resisted. The arrest of the suspects effectively put an end to the ring.

The second Worcester investigation involved the DEA with state and local agencies in unraveling a large Jamaican coke ring. Hundreds of hours of surveillance and a wiretap resulted in warrants being issued for the apprehension of eleven suspected members. The ring spanned four states and was implicated in at least one murder that the DEA knew of.

The Four Untouchables

Perhaps the most notable case of 2003 centered on a Chinese heroin ring with the cinematic name "The Four Untouchables." This case was so unusual in so many respects that we will take an in-depth look at how it unfolded.

It began back in 1988 with another case that generated considerable ill will between United States and Chinese authorities. A California businessman by the name of Wang Zong Xiao was arrested in Shanghai and accused of attempting to smuggle one million dollars' worth of heroin into the United States in the stomachs of dead koi. Koi are popular exotic goldfish, the kind commonly seen in fountains at malls and the like.

Wang was brought back to the United States as a material witness against three alleged co-conspirators. But when he took the stand, he claimed that his confession in Shanghai had been forced. He accused the Chinese police of torturing him with a cattle prod until he confessed and of threatening to kill him if he didn't cooperate.

Needless to say, it threw the koi case into disarray. Matters weren't helped any when Wang's lawyer learned that United States prosecutors had been told about the alleged torture but did not say anything for fear of ruining their case.

The judge was not happy. He ruled that Wang's constitutional rights had been violated. Wang was released. Chinese authorities wanted him back, but a United States appeals court refused on the grounds that he faced execution.

The Chinese were not happy, either. Relations between Chinese police and their United States counterparts soured. For years the Chinese would not help the United States in any way during drug investigations.

Fast-forward to 2001. The DEA and FBI began hearing the name Kin-Cheung Wong in connection with heroin smuggled into the United States.

It was a name they were familiar with. In 1988, a shipment of rubber bound for the United States from Thailand was sitting out in the rain when it was noticed that something strange was going on. The bales had cracks in them, and the rain had started a chemical reaction between the rubber and heroin hidden aside.

Kin-Cheung Wong was sentenced in the United States. He got out after only four years and was promptly deported.

Prison hadn't changed Wong's ways—far from it. Soon he was running a combination gambling den and brothel in Fuzhou, the capital of Fujian Province. He was also the head of a powerful heroin-smuggling syndicate that became known as the Four Untouchables because they seemed immune to prosecution. (Part of the reason for their presumed charmed lives came to light when a vice minister of police was arrested for aiding and abetting them.)

In June of 2001, an undercover FBI agent made a heroin buy in New York. He got three-quarters of a pound of horse, and something else: Kin-Cheung Wong's name as the source.

In September, the DEA formally asked China's public-security ministry for assistance. Given the strained relations between the two countries, the DEA and FBI were not overly optimistic, but to their considerable satisfaction, China agreed.

Over the next twenty months, the joint United States-Chinese op uncovered a lot more intel about the wily Mr. Wong and the Untouchables. Wong operated out of his house of ill repute, the aptly named Huamei Entertainment Company. The Four Untouchables were having heroin brought into Fujian Province in China by the truckload from the Golden Triangle. From there, it was smuggled into North America. The quantities were so huge that Canada was awash in heroin, and the United States was witnessing a glut of Homeric proportions.

The Four Untouchables laundered their money through Hong Kong banks. In every respect they qualified as a full-fledged cartel. Bringing them down became a top DEA priority.

But Wong had learned one thing in prison—to be more cautious. He went to great lengths to cover himself, even going so far as to conduct drug deals in his steam bath so that hidden microphones couldn't be used and the conversations couldn't be recorded. He refused to set up deals in the United States. Buyers had to come to him.

So that's what the DEA did. They set up an undercover buy in China. True to the agreement, three-quarters of a pound of heroin was delivered to an address in Manhattan.

The DEA had the goods on Wong, but they wanted more. They wanted to bring down the whole operation. There was a complication: there was no extradition treaty between the United States and China. Charging him in the United States would be pointless. They could charge his accomplices, but they didn't want a repeat of the Wang case. They didn't want to rely on witnesses from China.

The Chinese wanted Wong and the rest of the Untouchables just as bad. But so far they had little direct evidence of his complicity—not enough to put him away for a good long while. So they resorted to a sting. They enticed Wong with a huge chunk of cash into selling undercover agents seventy-seven pounds of heroin.

The wary Wong balked at first. He wanted nothing to do with the deal. But his advisors in the Four Untouchables persuaded him to take the risk.

It proved costly. Wong and more than thirty other members of the Untouchables were arrested—some in China, some in the United States, some in Canada, and some in India.

Why India?

Because police there, acting on intel provided by the DEA, had raided a meth lab in a house in Calcutta, a lab run by the Four Untouchables.

The raid caused a bigger flap than anyone anticipated when

it was learned that the house was owned by Upen Biswas. Biswas was well known in India; at one time he was the senior director of India's criminal bureau of investigation.

Allegations flew thick and fast. Some speculated that Biswas was corrupt; that during all those years when he had been arresting and prosecuting criminals, he had been one himself. It was rumored that he must be on the take and had been all along.

It turned out, though, that the five suspects arrested in connection with the lab, two of whom were Chinese and three of whom were from Myanmar (formerly Burma) were not the ones who had rented the house from Biswas. He had rented it to another gentleman by the name of S. N. Thanga, who conveniently disappeared. Indian authorities found several forged passports and drivers' licenses in that name.

The raid took place on May 18.

On May 22, a delivery truck pulled up with a shipment for Thanga, but Biswas refused to accept it. Indian authorities impounded the shipment at the Calcutta airport and found chemicals intended for the drug lab.

The Indian parliament later cleared Biswas, but some members walked out in protest.

It turned out that one of the Chinese men arrested at the lab was a cousin of a leading figure in the Four Untouchables.

The DEA and Chinese officials met with their Indian counterparts to wrap things up.

For the DEA, the investigation was historic. For the first time ever, DEA agents had been permitted to conduct an investigation on sovereign Chinese soil. The level of cooperation that the Chinese showed was remarkable.

As for Wang Zong Xiao, the one who caused all the earlier

contention, there were indications that the heroin he was accused of trying to smuggle might have been Untouchable heroin. No one would ever know for sure.

Wang certainly couldn't tell them. In January of 2003, Wang and a female friend left a nightclub at 3 A.M. and walked toward his Mercedes. Two men dressed in black sprang from the shadows and hacked him to death with machetes.

New England

In New England, the use of crack cocaine was on the rise. In March, the DEA and officers from four area police departments, acting on intel garnered by the Maine State Police, served warrants on members of a suspected crack ring.

In June, twenty-six people were taken into custody in connection with a different investigation into a different ring. The police chiefs of Lewiston and Auburn had requested the DEA's help.

The Mafia

On the other side of the world, the DEA and Italian authorities were trying to bring down not one but two drug syndicates. One was made up, in part, of members of Sicily's notorious Mafia.

The first drug ring liked to move its drugs by air. Colombians supplied the cocaine, which the Italians then funneled into Europe using couriers. In January, an Italian was arrested for trying to smuggle in twenty-four kilograms at Rome's Fiumicino Airport. In June, the Italian national police and the DEA's Rome office were involved in seizing more than 100 kilograms, again at Fiumicino.

The second drug ring was partial to bringing cocaine in by sea. The Mafia evidently thought that this was safer, but they didn't know that law-enforcement agencies from three countries, including the DEA, were on to them. They found out when a shipment of 220 kilograms of cocaine was seized in Athens. Thirty-three people were arrested. Fourteen were alleged Mafia members. Warrants were issued for others in Colombia, Venezuela, Italy, and Greece.

Extradition

One of the many persistent problems that the DEA had to deal with was the touchy international issue of bringing suspects back to the United States to stand trial. Some countries, like China, did not have extradition agreements with the United States. Others did, but balked at the idea of having their citizens tried in United States courts.

Thus it was that a ruling by the Argentine Supreme Court was greeted as extremely good news by the DEA.

It began with a drug ring based in Buenos Aires. They received heroin from Colombia and had couriers bring it to the United States. In 2001, the Colombian ringleader was arrested and extradited to New York City.

The DEA wanted to try four leading members of the ring's Buenos Aires cell in the United States on charges of importing an illegal substance, but an Argentine federal judge wouldn't allow extradition. They were already being prosecuted by Argentinian authorities, and the judge decided that having them tried in the United States constituted double jeopardy, which violated Argentinia's constitution.

The case was appealed of Argentina's Supreme Court. In a surprising development, the high court overruled the lower court. The Argentine Supreme Court said that the charges against the suspects in Argentina and the charges against the suspects in the United States were in regard to two different crimes—trafficking and importing—and therefore double jeopardy did not apply.

The DEA was free to have the suspects extradited.

Informants

In Colombia, a new tactic was being tested.

Informants, as we have established, were a routine part of investigations. But the DEA, in conjunction with the Bogotá Country Office and the Colombian national police, took it to a whole new level.

Newspaper ads were taken out. Posters were put up all over Bogotá. Leaflets were distributed. Television commercials were aired. Billboards were plastered with the news that new confidential hotlines had been set up. Anyone with information about heroin rings was invited to call. If their information panned out, if it resulted in an arrest or a seizure, then the callers would be rewarded financially.

The rationale was that most people were afraid to contact the authorities for fear of reprisal. It was well known that the cartels had executed hundreds of informants. No one cared to be next on the list.

By assuring informants of complete confidentiality, and with the added incentive of money, the CNP and the DEA were hopeful that important information would be forthcoming.

Intel was getting harder to come buy. The drug syndicates were smaller than in the early days, and infiltrating them wasn't as simple as it had been. Also, syndicate reliance on computerization and sophisticated electronic countermeasures made wiretapping much harder.

The DEA had a lot riding on the pesos-for-info program. If it worked, they planned to expand it, perhaps, into other Latin American countries.

H

2003 was a big year for H.

Residents in Plainsboro, New Jersey, were shocked when they learned that a major heroin ring had a cell operating out of the ironically named Pleasant Hollow Apartments. The ring was pumping an estimated 900 pounds of heroin each year from Cali into the United States.

Three suspects living at the Pleasant Hollow Apartments were pleasant enough. During the four years that they stayed there, the three made no secret of being from Colombia and would often make trips to South America to see their families, or so they claimed.

Some of the residents had noticed that the suspects received an awful of lot visitors at all hours of the day. Some were aware that the suspects received an awful lot of packages. Indeed, neighbors sometimes held the packages in their own apartments when the suspects weren't home. A few people later admitted to the DEA that they had wondered if the suspects were drug dealers, but their suspicions had been blunted by the fact that the suspects never sold drugs to anyone living at the apartments.

The DEA learned of the Plainsboro cell while investigating a major drug ring in Miami. The pipeline stretched from Cali through Argentina and Nicaragua to southern Florida, and from there to the Northeast.

Some of the same old smuggling ruses were used—and one new one. Heroin was hidden in drinking straws, which in turn were hidden in shipments of seafood. When the seafood arrived in Miami, the straws were unpacked and sent north to Plainsboro and other points to be sold on the street.

Fleshbags were employed to bring the proceeds back to Cali. A typical fleshbag would fly south with $100,000 in bills in his or her stomach.

Western Union wire transfers were used, although always in small amounts to avoid unwanted federal interest.

The ring's death knell neared. Twenty-eight people were arrested, in the United States and in several South American countries, and over a hundred pounds of heroin was seized.

Rocky Mountain High

Seventeen was the magic number in Colorado: seventeen suspects involved in a crack-cocaine ring that had taken root in Pueblo.

A DEA Mobile Enforcement Team was in on the bust, in cooperation with the Pueblo police department.

PCP

In southern California, the drug was PCP, and those selling it were hardened career criminals with a record of violence and total disregard for the law.

Two PCP labs, one in Compton and another in Los Angeles, were raided. Agents found small inflatable pools that were used to decontaminate chemicals crucial to making the PCP. A third lab, not yet fully operational, was discovered and prevented from becoming so.

Labs in residential neighborhoods always caused the DEA grave concern. Manufacturing PCP was risky. Ether was among the chemical components, and ether was not only flammable, it was highly explosive. Sodium cyanide, an extremely toxic poison, was another ingredient. There was always the danger of cyanide gas forming, which could wipe out everyone in the lab's vicinity.

Phenyl magnesium bromide was yet another of the chemicals, one that reacted violently if it was accidentally mixed with water.

The potential for a disaster was frighteningly real. PCP makers had a history of not giving a damn about innocents who might be harmed. Routinely, chemicals were dumped where anyone, even children, might come into contact with them.

Surveillance of the latest ring revealed that some of the PCP was being shipped to Texas. DEA agents from the Houston office, with state and local authorities, identified and arrested the perpetrators at that end, all fourteen of them.

Twenty-eight people found themselves staring at the world through cell bars in California. Over eleven gallons of PCP were seized.

"It's the Drugs, Stupid!"

On and on it went. Investigation after investigation, arrest after arrest. The drug lobby liked to say, loudly and publicly, that the war on drugs was a failure. They liked to portray the DEA as a black-booted Gestapo carrying out the failed policies of a corrupt government. The more paranoid among them went so far as to maintain that the government was in league with the drug syndicates, and that the DEA was a smokescreen to trick the gullible American public into believing that the government was sincere about wanting to stamp out drugs.

The lunatic fringe was alive and well, ignoring the evidence before their own eyes. It was delusional to think that the Colombian and Cali cartels were secret government ops. It was insane to imagine that the likes of al-Qaeda or Hezbollah were in any way sympathetic to, and in partnership with, vested United States business and government interests. It was just plain stupid to contend that the ruling elite wanted everyone hopped up on drugs to make the populace that much easier to mold to their will.

The DEA was only doing its job. It isn't the overt arm of a secret society intent on global domination. To coin a popular catchphrase, "It's the drugs, stupid."

The pro-drug crowd made much of the fact that the DEA had arrested some four dozen physicians. The DEA was overzealous, they charged, and picking on helpless, honest doctors.

The truth of the matter was that the physicians arrested had broken the law, either by taking money to write false prescriptions or by dispensing drugs with no prescriptions. The DEA wasn't getting carried away. It had been specifically created to staunch the flow of illegal substances, no matter who was involved.

Over the course of its first thirty-odd years, the DEA had a lot to be proud of. Hundreds of millions of dollar's worth of drugs had been confiscated, and many violent criminals had been taken out of circulation. True, drugs were still pouring across America's borders, but the blame had to be placed squarely where it was deserved: on human nature. Greed and the universal urge for instant gratification were a volatile combination.

A new year was about to dawn, yet another in the unending battle.

2004

In terms of financial resources, the DEA was doing very well indeed.

The new budget authorized a whopping two *billion* dollars, the largest ever for the Drug Enforcement Administration. That was $607 million more than in 2003, and $599 million more than the DEA had asked for.

As the year got underway, two concerns were paramount.

Narco-terrorism was now at the top of the list. The State Department believed that close to twenty of three dozen terrorists organizations that the United States formally recognized were dealing in drugs to raise funds they needed to orchestrate terrorist attacks. Consequently, the DEA was mandated to devote close to $30 million of its budget to fight narco-terrorism.

The other big concern was heroin. Few drugs were as relentlessly destructive. Few accounted for as many lives lost, as many homes and families disrupted or ruined. In many respects, including its addictive properties, heroin was far worse than cocaine and leagues beyond marijuana.

The DEA's heroin signature program established that nearly 80 percent of the heroin entering the United States now came from South America. As recently as 2001, that figure had been 60 percent. The jump was attributed to South American suppliers stepping in to fill the void when the share of Mexican heroin plummeted from 30 percent to 9 percent. The big drop in Mexico had nothing to do with supply and demand and everything to do with the destruction of another leading Mexican cartel.

The N'Drangheta

Early in the year, a four-year op was wrapping up in Europe with one of the largest drug sweeps ever.

Taking part were the DEA's Rome and Cartagena Offices, the Italian Arma dei Carabinieri, the Spanish national police and the Spanish *Guardia Civil*, the French judicial police, the Australian national police, the Colombian national police, and the Venezuelan national police.

The focus was a drug syndicate that regularly shipped cocaine from South America to Europe. Its ringleaders were Italians whose criminal organization was patterned along the lines of the Mafia. Known as the *N'Drangheta,* they controlled Calabria, Italy, and the region around it.

An Italian national living in Monteria, Colombia, was the linchpin of the whole network. He arranged for drug shipments, reporting directly to his superior, the head of the N'Drangheta.

Most of the cocaine was shipped to Italy, but Spain, Germany, Holland, and Australia received their share.

There was no way of determining how much coke the Italian ring had smuggled over the years, but best estimates pegged it in the hundreds of tons.

The six countries timed their sweeps superbly. Seventy-eight suspects were apprehended in Italy, one in Spain, and another fifteen in Colombia, including the Italian linchpin. More arrests would be forthcoming.

Intel gathered during the sweep led authorities to several containers that had recently reached the port of Gioia Tauro, Italy, from Colombia. In the containers were marble blocks used in construction. In the marble blocks was cocaine. Over three tons of coke was seized, altogether, and the N'Drangheta foray into the cocaine trade was derailed.

Chicago

About this same time, Chicago became the focal point of unrelated investigations.

One centered around an assistant station manager for the Royal Jordanian Airlines at O'Hare International Airport. The individual was a naturalized citizen from Jordan, living in Willow Spring, Illinois. He was accused of being the money man for a meth ring, and of using his position at the airline to smuggle cash overseas. Another man who worked with him, another naturalized Jordanian, was taken into custody at O'Hare after United States Customs inspectors found he was trying to sneak out of the country with $615,817 in cash.

The money men, in turn, led the DEA to the meth ring, which was based in California. The ring operated by smuggling pseudoephedrine into the United States from Canada. The pseudoephedrine was stashed at safe houses in Chicago and Detroit until the head of the ring needed some to sell to the

Mexican traffickers who made the actual meth. The money was then sent back to Chicago to be smuggled out of the country by the Royal Jordanian Airlines employee and his companion.

A method they frequently used was to stuff the cash into empty cereal boxes and pack the cereal boxes in suitcases.

The Jordanian Airlines employee was eventually sentenced to forty-one months in prison.

The other Chicago item was vastly more troubling.

The DEA and the Chicago police department were conducting a routine investigation of drug dealings in a Chicago neighborhood when a startling find was made in a trash dumpster near an elementary school. Inside the dumpster were three hand grenades and a thirty-seven-millimeter grenade launcher.

The Chicago PD's Bomb and Arson Unit disarmed the grenades, and the launcher was turned over to the DEA. The DEA brought in the Bureau of Alcohol, Tobacco and Firearms.

Unfortunately, no one knew who had placed the grenades and launcher in the dumpster, or why. Speculation was that a local drug gang had ditched them when the gang noticed police in the area.

The results could have been too horrible to contemplate if schoolchildren had gotten their hands on the live grenades first. All that a child had to do was pull the pin and the aftermath would have been devastating.

Most Wanted

From New York came word that Archangel de Jesus Henao-Montoya had been arraigned in federal court.

The mastermind behind the Norte Valle cartel, which was

the source of over half of all the cocaine smuggled into the United States from South America, was taken into custody earlier in the month in Panama. Panama then expelled him, straight into the eagerly open arms of United States authorities. He was arraigned upon his arrival.

The DEA had long been after Archangel. Almost singlehandedly, he had transformed the North Valley cartel into the most powerful cartel in Colombia, if not the Western Hemisphere. His fondness for high-tech equipment and computers had a lot to do with it, but in the end, neither kept him from being apprehended.

The indictment against him alleged a host of crimes, including working with terrorists. The North Valley cartel relied on Colombia's AUC to protect drug shipments and labs, and the AUC was recognized by the State Department as a terrorist organization.

There would be many more cases like this, and soon—cases in which narco-terrorism figured prominently. A new era in drug enforcement was in full swing.

Another wanted trafficker, though, was still at large.

Ismael Zambada-Garcia, the head of the ZGO, was the rival that Ramon Arellano-Felix had gone to assassinate that fateful day in Mazatlán. Zambada-Garcia was now the most powerful smuggler in all of Mexico, and he was pouring cocaine and marijuana across the United States southwestern border.

Zambada was such a thorn in the United States' side that in February of 2004, the Drug Enforcement Administration announced that a $5-million reward was being offered for information leading to Zambada's arrest and conviction.

Best calculations had it that by now Zambada had smuggled approximately sixteen metric tons of coke into the United

States, but that was a conservative estimate extrapolated from seizures and intel, and the actual figure was undoubtedly much higher.

With the decline of the Tijuana cartel, Zambada had risen to preeminence in Mexico. At first, he concentrated his smuggling efforts along the Arizona border, but as his network and power grew, so did the area of the border under his control. For three years he had been operating with virtual impunity.

It was hoped that the reward would tempt informants. In addition, the DEA had billboards in southern Arizona asking for information as to his whereabouts. The DEA also sent out flyers and hung wanted posters.

In February, Zambada garnered another dubious distinction. He was featured on the popular show, *America's Most Wanted*.

In Florida, the DEA launched an op intended to crush a coke, meth, and marijuana outfit. The ring was smuggling the stuff into Texas from Mexico, then bringing it to cells in Orlando, Jacksonville, and Crescent City.

Nearly 300 officers were involved in the sweep. It was coordinated so that simultaneous raids were initiated at 4 A.M. in all three cities.

Forty-four arrests were made.

Strange Bedfellows

At the same time, the DEA was after another ecstasy-and-marijuana ring based in Canada. What makes this case noteworthy are the nationalities of the culprits.

Up to this point, Israeli and Russian gangs had a lock on the ecstasy trade. But just as the Colombians once dominated the cocaine market only to see others gradually take part of that trade away, so it was with ecstasy. Gangs from Southeast Asia were now showing an interest.

If any identifiable pattern had developed over the DEA's lifespan, it was on display here. Whenever one nationality or group showed that smuggling a given drug reaped large profits, others always wanted to share in the money pie.

Operation Candy Box, as it was dubbed, was initiated through confidential intelligence linking the gang activity. Soon the DEA had identified the ring's leaders, a Chinese and a Vietnamese. It was unusual to see the two working together, but drugs made for lucrative business, and big bucks made for strange bedfellows.

Not only were the pair bringing in large amounts of ecstasy and marijuana, they had a sizeable money-laundering system, a system so deviously clever that by studying it, the DEA's financial investigations section was able to recommend changes that would make it much harder for money launderers to operate in the future.

To give some idea of the ring's breadth of operations: it involved nineteen North-American cities—sixteen in the United States and three in Canada.

By March, the DEA had enough evidence to move in. More than 130 suspects were taken into custody, labs were raided, drugs were seized. The ring was completely destroyed.

In April, an incident occurred that did not directly involve the DEA but showed how pervasive, and insidious, the drug plague had become. It involved one of the United States' South American allies.

Colombia had made great strides in its war to clean up its

national disgrace. The CNP had evolved into a formidable force, and the Colombian government was no longer rife with corruption.

However, not too long ago, the head of Colombia's police force had stepped down after it was learned that officers under him had accepted more than $1 million in bribes to protect a cocaine shipment.

Now came the latest scandal.

A ship called the *Gloria* was about to set sail on a tour of the United States and Europe. An old sailing vessel, she was dubbed Colombia's ambassador of goodwill. Her crew were some of the best in the Colombian navy. Often, trainees went along to literally learn the ropes.

Docked in the port of Cartagena, the *Gloria* was about to embark on another of her goodwill voyages when a routine last-minute inspection revealed a stash of drugs. Hidden in the engine room were ten kilograms—about twenty-two pounds—of cocaine, and 16.5 kilograms—about thirty-six pounds—of heroin. If sold in the United States or Europe, the drugs would reap millions.

The seventy-five crew members were relieved of duty and an investigation was conducted.

It became a national scandal: proof—not that any was needed—that while Colombia might have turned the corner in the drug war, it, like the United States, had a long way to go before victory would be achieved.

Mexico

The flamboyant cartels of yesteryear were gone, but others still flourished, among them the notorious North Valley cartel, so named because it got its start in the Norte Valle del Cauca area. In many respects it was a lot like the old cartels, keeping a higher profile than its contemporaries.

Intel suggested that since its inception, the North Valley cartel had pumped some $10 billion worth of cocaine through Mexico into the United States. It had a strong working relationship with Mexican traffickers. Its labs and routes were protected by the AUC, a recognized terrorist group.

Most of the cartel's coke came out of the port city of Buenaventura. The authorities knew this, but knowing it and stopping it were two different realities. The NVC paid huge amounts of money to have select officials look the other way. They were also so electronically sophisticated that they were able to accomplish something many drug rings could only dream of doing. They tapped into the phones of Colombian police and military leaders and even wiretapped the phones of DEA agents.

In May of 2004, the DEA announced that indictments had been filed against nine of the highest-ranking members of the NVC. Among them was a former officer with the Colombian national police who had gone rogue and now worked as an NVC assassin. Another was a lawyer who represented the NVC.

Between them, the United States, Mexico, and Colombia seized close to 50,000 pounds of NVC cocaine.

The once-formidable Tijuana cartel, the Arellano-Felix organization, or AFO, suffered a setback in June.

The AFO had at least 100 murders to its credit. Among them were the deaths of a Mexican special prosecutor and two of his associates, who were brutally tortured. Policemen, soldiers, rivals in the drug trade, informants, even reporters who aired stories that showed the AFO in an unflattering light, were all victims of AFO savagery.

The governments of the United States and Mexico made the remaining ringleaders priority targets. It was particularly rewarding when, on the morning of June 3, nearly seventy special Mexican federal agents surrounded two top AFO lieutenants and their bodyguards and took them into custody without a shot being fired.

One was Jorge Arellano-Felix, the man who had once been a police officer before he relinquished his badge to join his six brothers and four sisters in the family business and became head of the AFO's security operations.

Two other leaders, Javier Arellano-Felix and Eduardo Arellano-Felix, were still on the loose.

Toronto

In 2003, the DEA had learned of a ring smuggling marijuana from Canada. Word was relayed to Canadian authorities, and in due course more details were uncovered.

Toronto was the ring's base, although the Windsor-Detroit area figured prominently in their operations. They used private vehicles to smuggle the marijuana across. Their distribution network included the cities of Detroit, Boston, Pittsburgh, Minneapolis, and Hagerston, among others. The money was brought back into Canada to be laundered.

The Royal Canadian Mounted Police, Canada's border services agency, and the Ontario Provincial Police handled the investigation up north. The DEA, Homeland Security, the FBI, and the Michigan State Police handled it on the United States side.

Every known member of the gang was arrested. Seven hundred seventy-two kilos of marijuana and 3,000 ecstasy tablets were seized, to say nothing of $750,000 in cash seized by Canadian authorities and over half a million by their American counterparts.

The DEA occasionally worked with other agencies to make up the Organized Crime Drug Enforcement Task Force. This partnership proved most effective by killing two birds with one stone, or, in this instance, bringing down two drug rings whose combined reach extended from Canada to the Caribbean, with concurrent investigations.

One of the rings was headed by a Jamaican who had been put on the Consolidated Priority Organization Target List. This was a list of alleged offenders whose organizations were having the most detrimental impact on the United States. So far the task force had collared four of more than forty priority traffickers, as well as 330 lesser offenders.

The Jamaican's ring had formed back in 2000 and had cells in Jamaica, Colombia, Panama, the Bahamas, the United States, and Canada.

The other ring was smaller, and closely allied with the first. Combined, they brought in about three tons of cocaine per month. This was one-tenth of the all the coke being smuggled in.

Foreign agencies helped in the investigation. It took over two and a half years, but eventually the task force was ready. The Jamaican kingpin, the leaders of the other ring, and more than fifty others were apprehended.

Buffalo

Buffalo, New York, was experiencing a crack epidemic.

The DEA and the Boston police had pinpointed the source,

a Buffalo businessman with a previous drug conviction. The suspect was now ostensibly in the T-shirt business, which must have paid extremely well, since he had a nice home in Buffalo and a penthouse in New Jersey that set him back about five grand a month.

Operation Nine Lives swung into high gear, so named because the ringleader's top lieutenant had been shot nine times in the past several years in disputes with rivals, yet survived.

Surveillance was set up. Wiretaps were authorized. One of the latter incriminated one of the Buffalo P.D.'s own.

The tap was on the phone of an alleged gang member, who was a pusher and a convicted felon. At one point, the suspect was talking to a relative who happened to be a Buffalo police officer. Authorities were stunned when the officer proceeded to give the suspect advice on what to wear and how to drive to avoid arousing suspicion. The officer wasn't directly involved in the ring, but he was later suspended.

Indictments were handed down against forty-two individuals. Thirty-two of them were arrested when nearly 400 law officers, led by the DEA, conducted an early-morning sweep through the city.

Ice

The DEA and ICE, an acronym for the U.S. Immigration and Customs Service, filed drug-trafficking charges against eleven alleged members of a Guyanese ring smuggling cocaine into New York City. Most of the coke was sold either in Queens or Brooklyn.

Also charged were a couple who reportedly laundered the gang's money. The pair had set up a front company, a manufacturing and sales firm that existed only on paper, and through it laundered some $10 million in ill-gotten gains.

During the course of the year-and-a-half-long investigation, almost 400 kilograms of cocaine were seized at JFK International Airport in New York and Miami International Airport.

Tijuana

In Mexico, the Arellano-Felix organization was making headlines again, in spectacular fashion.

It began with the murder of another journalist in Tijuana. Francisco Ortiz Franco, the editor of a weekly newspaper called *Zeta*, was gunned down in front of his two sons. Ortiz had been a harsh critic of the AFO and its bloody reign.

It's not well known north of the border, but Mexican journalists who dare to speak out or write accounts against drug syndicates often find themselves victims of the very violence they denounce.

In Tijuana, there is a running line to the effect that "many people eat an apple a day; Tijuana has a body a day."

Ortiz was the latest body. Four days later, Mexican federal agents surrounded a house in Tijuana and called on those inside to give themselves up. Inside were Mario Alberto Rivera Lopez, who was an alleged AFO assassin, and three colleagues, leading suspects in Ortiz's murder.

A gun battle ensued. The assassin and his companions opened up on the federal agents with a machine gun, but eventually all four were taken into custody.

A minor victory, some might say, in light of the fact that Tijuana had essentially become a killing ground for the AFO. Nor was Tijuana alone in that distinction. Many cities and towns in Mexico, far *too* many, were under the near-total control of one criminal syndicate or another. In some areas, drug rings could kill anyone they wanted to with near impunity.

Corruption had been curbed but not erased. It took a lot of fortitude for a police officer barely making enough to feed his family to say no when a fistful of cash was waved under his nose to entice him into cooperating with those he was supposed to bring to justice.

High School Confidential

In Massachusetts, yet another drug ring came into the DEA's gunsights.

A Mobile Enforcement Team, working with the Gloucester police department, the Cape Ann Regional Strike Force, and the Essex County sheriff's department, had identified the members of a syndicate that offered a smorgasbord of illicit substances: coke, heroin, crack, and oxycodone. Some of the drugs were being sold at a local shopping mall.

Among those implicated and charged were a member of a motorcycle gang and a substitute teacher at a regional high school who also worked as an assistant baseball coach at another.

Cyberspace

The DEA continued to combat drugs on less orthodox fronts, including the Internet. The Net was fertile new ground for those dealing in illegal substances. Often they did so under the mistaken notion that the Net granted them some sort of immunity. Cyberspace, they erroneously believed, was a realm in which they could operate with complete anonymity, and without fear of being caught and prosecuted.

They were wrong.

The DEA could not help but notice that so-called "designer drugs" were the latest hot fad. A number of Internet Web sites had sprung up selling designer drugs under the flimsy guise of research chemicals. Use of these chemicals had resulted in more than a dozen overdoses, two of them fatal.

A bit of background: the substances being sold were either banned under the Controlled Substances Act or rigidly controlled under the Controlled Substance Analogue Enforcement Act (CSAEA).

Why "Analogue"? Because prior to the CSAEA, drug makers would chemically alter or tweak their compounds so that the drug they created was technically different from what was banned under the Controlled Substances Act. By passing the Analogue Enforcement Act, Congress made it possible for the DEA to go after the chemists who made those changes, and the drugs they produced.

Designer drugs are incredibly dangerous. The labs that make them are not renowned for their quality-control standards.

In April of 2002, a New York man died of a designer-drug overdose. He had obtained the drug via the Internet. A friend of his who took the same drug suffered seizures, memory gaps, and problems with his eyes.

In December of 2003, police were called to a home in Fairhaven, Massachusetts. A college student had collapsed on the kitchen floor. Again, he had taken a drug obtained from a site on the Web. He was lucky—he lived. But to this day he suffers from chronic seizures.

The next victim wasn't as fortunate. A young man in St. Francisville, Louisiana ingested what he thought was a designer drug similar to ecstasy, which he had bought from an Internet provider. He became severely ill and asked that his mother drive him to the hospital. He died three days later, after his body temperature had risen to 108 degrees.

Many users were under the impression that designer drugs were somehow safe; that they were just another form of LSD or ecstasy. The word being spread on the Internet was that they weren't as risky as drugs like crack or meth, or as addicting as heroin or cocaine.

Chat rooms were set up in which users could talk about the wonders of their favorite drugs, and about where those selling them could promote their chemical poisons.

Customer lists revealed that the sites had thousands of users worldwide. At one site alone, over $20,000 a week was being exchanged.

The DEA moved in. Five Internet sites were shut down, and those who operated them were arrested.

One was run by a group out of San Diego, another by individuals from Arizona and Georgia.

The operators of a third, based in Baton Rouge, Louisiana, were not only charged with distributing illegal substances but with contributing to the death of a user who had succumbed to an overdose.

The man behind a fourth Internet site tried to screen his activities under the guise of selling landscape supplies. On this case, the DEA was assisted by the U.S. Navy's Criminal Investigative Service. That's because the designer drugs were being sold to Norfolk Navy personnel who held regular rave parties at which the drugs were used. An eighteen-year-old died from an overdose, and three other people were hospitalized.

✧ ✧ ✧

The designer-drug arrests were yet more examples of the DEA coping with new challenges. It was essential for the DEA to keep abreast of the latest technology and the potential for abuse it offered.

For as surely as the sun rose and set each day, as surely as it was simply yet tragically "human" for some people to want to use drugs and others to want to supply that need, cocaine and heroin and meth and ecstasy and all the rest of their nefarious ilk would continue to tear at the fabric of society.

THE CHALLENGE FOR THE FUTURE

If there is one aspect that this book has made clear, it is the fluid nature of the drug war.

Traffickers are constantly adapting, adjusting, shifting, changing. They are always looking for new drugs, for new ways to market drugs, for new routes to smuggle drugs, for new and better profits.

Traffickers are ruthless. They do not play by any set of rules. They scorn the law. They laugh at the idea of any sense of propriety. There are no lengths to which they will not go in order to achieve their ends. They will hurt, maim, and kill, and they do not care if innocents are hurt, maimed, or killed in the process.

Traffickers are a threat to the bedrock of civilization. This might seem a grandiose statement, but consider Colombia, where the Medellín cartel brought the country to the brink of anarchy. Consider the consequences if every country were the same.

Drugs are a modern scourge; a blight on society. They warp perspective, ravage minds, debilitate bodies, destroy personalities. They kill, and they will go on killing.

In order to deal with the crisis, the Drug Enforcement Administration must continue to adapt; to refine and use every legal resource at its disposal. The challenges for the new century are the same as for the last: to anticipate the traffickers' movements in an effort to gain a step on them.

You can't intercept a speedboat with a rowboat. You can't tap a phone line with two tins cans connected by string. In order to do its job and do it right, the DEA must have whatever resources it will need to oppose the traffickers on equal if not more advanced footing.

Critics have a field day with the DEA's budget. "Over a billion dollars!" they exclaim. Money that could be "put to better use elsewhere." But their argument is specious on two fronts. The traffickers have no spending limits. They will expend whatever they must to make and smuggle their wares. IBM mainframes do not come cheap. Cargo ships are not bought out of petty cash. Estimates vary, but it is safe to say that the total annual expenditures of those in the trafficking trade is in the billions.

The second contention is the more sophist. Yes, certainly that billion dollars could go to help the needy or be used for education. But if the DEA were to be eliminated, there would be that many more overdoses, that many more people who must endure chronic wasting conditions for the remainder of their short lives, that much more suffering. And if the DEA were to be dissolved tomorrow, who would protect our children from those who would prey on them? Local and state agencies often lack the resources to cope with drug rings that span the globe.

The drug crisis in America's schools is bad enough. Just think of how much worse it would be if there were a direct pipeline from the drug labs to the classroom.

So long as drugs exist, governments, in the interest of self-preservation, will need to control their use. In America's case, the DEA was created for that specific purpose, as the enforcement arm of America's effort to preserve her way of life.

All this will seem silly to the drug lobby. It will be laughable to those who traffic in drugs. But to the average American, to mothers and fathers struggling to raise their children the best way they know how, it is neither inconsequential nor the result of naïveté. It is a matter of opportunity versus addiction; of hope versus despair.

Instead of being vilified, the DEA should be praised. Yes, it has made mistakes. Yes, overzealous agents have on rare occasions done things that in hindsight they should not have done. But those lapses are few.

The good that the DEA does is inestimable. On that basis alone, its existence is more than justified.

America is often accused of doing things wrong. Her enemies, both external and internal, make much of her alleged mistakes. The Drug Enforcement Administration is something that America has done right. It deserves the wholehearted support of the American people, and of Congress. It must not be made into a political plaything or perverted for sinister ends. It must be allowed to continue to enforce our country's drug laws without undue interference.

The Drug Enforcement Administration has shown itself

worthy of its mandate. The call for the new millennium is for the DEA to continue to wage the drug war by beating the drug traffickers at their own game.

The old saying says that one must fight fire with fire. But the DEA must fight greed with constraint. It must abide by the law even if its enemies do not. It can't combat the traffickers with the same tactics they use, because the tactics they use are illegal, immoral, and unethical.

Drugs can drown a country in the depths of avarice and bloodshed. The DEA is America's promise to herself that it will not happen here.

APPENDIX A
Wall of Honor

During the course of this book, mentions have been made of Drug Enforcement agents who gave the ultimate sacrifice in the performance of their duties. The life of a DEA Agent is a dangerous life. Nowhere is that more vividly illustrated than in the following list of those who died for what they believed in.

The author apologizes in advance for the inadvertent omission of any individuals.

2004

Special Agent Terrance Loftus. Agent Loftus was killed when the Cessna 206 he was piloting crashed. As this list will show, far too many agents have lost their lives in air crashes of one kind or another. It is, in fact, one of the leading causes of death while in the performance of DEA duties.

2003

Telecommunications Specialist Elton Lee Armstead. He died of injuries he sustained from a fall while he was installing surveillance equipment.

2001

Investigator Alice Faye Hall-Walton. Killed in an auto accident.

2000

Special Agent Royce D. Tramel. Struck by a car.

1997

Special Agent Shaun E. Curl. Died in the line of duty.

1995

Secretary Rona L. Chafey. She was with the Cleveland County sheriff's office, working as part of a DEA task force, at the Alfred P. Murrah Federal Building in Oklahoma City when the truck bomb went off.

DynCorp Legal Technician Carrie A. Lenz. She was under contract with the DEA at the time of her death, working at the DEA office in the Alfred P. Murrah Federal Building in Oklahoma City. She was six months pregnant.

DynCorp Legal Technician Shelly D. Bland. She, too, was under contract with the DEA, and working at the Federal Building when the blast occurred.

Office Assistant Carol June Fields. Another of Timothy McVeigh's victims. Ms. Fields had been with the DEA and its predecessor a combined twenty-nine years.

Special Agent Kenneth G. McCullough. As with those above, he died in the explosion at Oklahoma City.

1994

Special Agent Frank Fernandez Jr. He was on a reconnaissance mission in Peru as part of the DEA's cocaine-suppression campaign when the plane he was in crashed.

Special Agent Meredith Thompson. She was on the same plane.

Special Agent Jay W. Seale. He, too, was on the plane.

Special Agent Juan C. Vars. Yet another agent on the aircraft that went down.

Special Agent Frank S. Wallace Jr. The last of the five who were killed. This was one of the worst crashes in DEA history.

Special Agent Richard E. Fass. He was shot during the course of an undercover investigation in Arizona. The day he was killed, his fellow agents had treated him to a luncheon because he was due to leave soon for his next duty assignment in Mexico.

1993

Detective Stephen J. Strehl. Detective Strehl was with the St. Louis, Missouri, police department. He was part of a DEA task force involved in airborne surveillance of a possible indoor marijuana grow when the helicopter he was in went down.

Special Agent Becky L. Dwojeski. Killed in an automobile accident.

1992

Special Agent G. Douglas Althouse. He was slain while trying to stop a car theft in Alabama.

1991

Special Agent Alan H. Winn. He had been a helicopter pilot in the U.S. Marines. He was taking part in an air op in Hawaii when the copter crashed.

Special Agent Eugene T. McCarthy. He had been called to active duty during the Persian Gulf War. He died in Saudi Arabia in a helicopter crash.

1990

Police Investigator Wallie Howard Jr. Howard was with the Syracuse, New York, police department. He was taking part in the Central New York Drug Enforcement Task Force and was shot while working undercover when drug dealers tried to take the $42,000 he was to use to make a coke buy.

Criminal Investigator Joseph T. Aversa. Aversa was working with the DEA on the New York Drug Enforcement Task Force. When an undercover officer was fired on by suspects,

Aversa and others members of the task force rushed to help, and Aversa was fatally wounded.

1989

Special Agent Rickie C. Finley. He was involved in a jungle op in Peru when the aircraft went down.

Special Agent Everett E. Hatcher. He was taking part in an undercover assignment on Staten Island, New York, when he was shot and killed.

1988

Special Agent Paul S. Seema. He was shot during an undercover investigation in Los Angeles and died a day later.

Special Agent George W. Montoya. Shot with Special Agent Seema, he was pronounced dead at the scene. A special Paul Seema–George Montoya Golf Tournament was organized to raise funds for their children.

Detective Terry W. McNett. McNett was with the Sedgwick County, Kansas, sheriff's office. He was helping to execute a search warrant in Wichita when he was shot and killed.

1987

Special Agent Arthur L. Cash. He died in a traffic accident in Arizona while engaged in transporting prisoners.

Special Agent Raymond J. Stastny. He was shot while working an undercover assignment in Atlanta, George, and died six days later.

1986

Special Agent William Ramos. While making an arrest in Las Milpas, Texas, he was shot by a suspected trafficker.

Office Assistant Susan M. Hoefler. She was with the Guadalajara, Mexico, field office, when she died of injuries she sustained in a car accident.

Criminal Investigator Charles M. Bassing. A member of the Arkansas State Police, he was taking part in a DEA Marijuana Eradication Spotter School when the helicopter he was in crashed in Mount Ida.

Deputy Sheriff James A. Avant. He was with the Pulaski Country, Arkansas, sheriff's office, and joined the DEA's Little Rock task force. He was in the same copter as Investigator Bassing.

Criminal Investigator Kevin L. Brosch. Brosch was with the Jefferson Country, Arkansas, sheriff's office. He, too, was taking part in the DEA's Marijuana Eradication Spotter School.

1985

Special Agent Enrique S. Camarena. Possibly the most widely publicized DEA death ever. The subject of numerous articles and a book. He was with the Guadalajara, Mexico, Resident Office when he was abducted and tortured to death. Every October, millions of Americans wear red ribbons in honor of his sacrifice. A yearly golf tournament in his name raises money for the DEA Special Agents Survivors Benefit Fund.

1984

Detective Marcellus Ward. A member of the Baltimore, Maryland, police department, Detective Ward joined a DEA task force and was shot while working undercover.

Special Agent Larry N. Carwell. He was on a DEA flight in the Bahamas when the helicopter went down.

1982

Special Agent Thomas J. Devine. In 1972, he was shot during an undercover assignment in New York City. He survived but had to use a wheelchair. Special Agent Devine continued to work despite complications from the wounds that necessitated several operations. A decade after the shooting, he finally succumbed.

1977

Special agent Robert C. Lightfoot. He died as the result of a firearms mishap in Bangkok, Thailand.

Special Agent Francis J. Miller. Killed in a car accident in New York while on his way home from work.

1976

DEA Country Attaché Octavio Gonzales. Gonzales was the head man at the DEA's Bogotá, Colombia office. He was shot by an informant.

Special Agent James T. Lunn. Lunn was a pilot. He was involved in an opium eradication operation in Mexico when his aircraft went down north of Acapulco.

Special agent Ralph N. Shaw. He was on the plane with Special Agent Lunn.

1975

Special Agent Larry D. Wallace. Assigned to the DEA's Tokyo District Office, he was shot during an undercover investigation and later died at the Naval Regional Medical Center in Guam.

1974

Clerk-typist Mary P. Sullivan. She was in the Miami Regional Office Building when it collapsed in August.

Supervisor Clerk–typist Martha De Skeels. Another victim of the collapse. Before working for the DEA, she had worked for the Bureau of Narcotics and Dangerous Drugs, the DEA's predecessor.

Fiscal Assistant Anna J. Pope. A third life lost in the collapse.

Secretary Anna J. Mounger. Only twenty-four, she had planned to leave the DEA at the end of the week to marry a Marine.

Secretary Mary M. Keehan. She, too, had worked for the BNDD before coming to work for the DEA.

Special Agent Charles H. Mann. Special Agent Mann has just been transferred from the DEA's Ankara, Turkey office to Miami. His first day on the job was the day the building collapsed.

Special Agent Nickolas Fragos. It was not only his first day at the Miami office, it was his very first day as a DEA Special

Agent. He had spent three years in Vietnam as a medic, earning a Silver Star, two Bronze Stars, a Purple Heart, and two Army Commendation Medals.

Investigator Leslie S. Grosso. A member of the New York State Police, and the DEA's Joint Task Force, he was shot during an undercover operation.

1973

Detective Gerald Sawyer. A Los Angeles Police Detective, he was working undercover with the DEA when he was shot by a drug dealer. Detective Sawyer was the first LAPD undercover drug officer to be slain in the line of duty.

Special Agent Emir Benitez. He was shot in Fort Lauderdale, Florida, during an undercover investigation and later died at Broward County General Hospital.

Special Agent George F. White. White was a pilot with the DEA's predecessor, the BNDD. He was killed when his plane struck a power line.

Special Agent Richard Heath, Jr. He, too, was with the BNDD. He was shot during an undercover buy in the Netherlands and died two months later from complications in Quito, Ecuador.

1972

Special Agent Frank Tummillo. BNDD. He was shot and killed in the same incident in which Special Agent Thomas J. Devine was paralyzed and subsequently confined to a wheelchair. Devine was Tummillo's supervisor at the time.

A well-known figure in law enforcement, Special Agent Tummillo was honored in one of President Nixon's weekly radio addresses.

1971

Police Officer Gene A. Clifton. Clifton was with the Palo Alto, California police department. He was assisting BNDD agents in executing a search warrant when a suspect fired through a door, striking him.

1970

Special Agent Hector Jordan. BNDD. Assigned to the Chicago Office, he was jumped by seven members of a gang and died from the injuries he sustained.

1967

Special Agent Mansel R. Burrell. An agent with the Federal Bureau of Narcotics, Burrell was murdered in Gary, Indiana, the victim of a drug ring. Only twenty-three, he is the youngest federal narcotics officer to be slain while in the performance of his duties.

Narcotics Agent Wilson Michael Shee. With the Federal Bureau of Narcotics, he was killed by an informant.

1950

Special Agent Anker M. Bangs. He was chief of the FBN's Twin Cities office. Acting on a tip, he had gone to an opium den in St. Paul, where he was murdered.

1944

Agent Andrew P. Sanderson. Federal Bureau of Narcotics. Died when the tire on his government vehicle blew out and the vehicle overturned.

1935

Narcotic Inspector Spencer Stafford. He was with the Bureau of Narcotics in the U.S. Department of the Treasury. Stafford was investigating a veterinarian in Post, Texas, for dispensing illegal substances. As he came out of the veterinary hospital the vet owned, the local sheriff opened fire on Inspector Stafford with a Thompson sub-machine gun. It turned out that the sheriff, a deputy, the vet, and a doctor were all involved in a narcotics ring. Only the year before, Congress had passed a law making it a federal offense to kill a federal officer while in the line of duty. Stafford's killers were the first to be charged under the new statute.

1934

Agent John W. Crozier. Bureau of Prohibition, Narcotics Department. Died when his vehicle collided with a lumber rig.

1928

Narcotic Agent James E. Brown. Bureau of Prohibition. Murdered in California by an opium trafficker.

1924

Narcotics Inspector Louis L. Marks. Bureau of Internal Revenue, Prohibition Service. Died in a bus accident.

Narcotic Agent James T. Williams. Prohibition Service, Department of the Treasury. Shot in Chicago during a scuffle when his partner's revolver went off. The slug struck Williams in the head. Only twenty-five, he was on his first assignment.

1922

Narcotics Inspector Bert S. Gregory. He went to a hospital to visit another inspector and while there his revolver fell out of its holster and went off. Gregory died the next day.

Federal Prohibition Agent Joseph W. Floyd. He was serving a search warrant in Houston, Texas, when he was shot and killed.

1921

Federal Prohibition Agent Stafford E. Beckett.

Federal Prohibition Agent Charles A. Wood.

The two agents were slain during a raid on whiskey smugglers along the Texas border with Mexico. The raid capped a series of gun battles between the smugglers and federal agents. Agent Beckett had killed a smuggler the day prior to his own death.

APPENDIX B
Crack Cocaine

An Overview of Crack Cocaine

No single drug has had more of an adverse impact.

The first reported instances of anyone smoking any form of cocaine occurred in Peru in the 1970s. A number of users started to smoke coca paste, and before long the practice had spread to Bolivia, Colombia, Ecuador, and other countries in South America.

Coca paste is actually an extract produced during an intermediate stage of cocaine production.

The word that eventually came to be commonly used to refer to smoking cocaine is "freebase." There are two ways of freebasing. The first is the way it was first done in California, which entailed using ether as part of the process. This incurred a high risk of a fire or explosion. The second way, which involves mixing the cocaine hydrochloride with either ammonia and water or baking soda and water, eliminates the risks of the first. Needless to say, the second way became more popular.

The word "crack" itself comes from the crackling sound that is made when it is being heated.

Crack use was initially seen in 1981 in Los Angeles, San Diego, and Houston. By 1985, it had leapfrogged to New York City, and once crack hit the Big Apple it exploded like a stick of TNT onto the drug scene.

By 1988, there were more than one thousand crack houses in Detroit, seven hundred in Miami, and seventy-five in Dallas, where Jamaican traffickers had a lock on the trade. Jamaicans were also responsible for introducing large amounts of crack into Camden and Kansas City. In Philadelphia, it was the Dominicans who had the lion's share; in Phoenix, it was the Bloods and the Crips.

Since then, of course, crack has spread everywhere, even to small towns in America's heartland. Not as much is heard about it in the news these days, but that's not because crack use has dried up. It's because the media tends to focus on hot drug fads of the moment, and once a drug has been around awhile, it's relegated to old news and only mentioned in passing.

People often wonder why crack had such an exceptionally devastating effect. Why did so many become users so fast?

As previously noted, crack is tremendously addictive. Many are hooked the very first time they use, and once hooked, a Catch-22 develops.

Users like the high crack gives. For a while they feel absolutely euphoric, but only for a short while. A typical crack high lasts about ten minutes, give or take. Once a user has floated back down, there is often an emotional backlash. It's a shock to return to reality from paradise. Moodiness, depression, or worse can result.

Users naturally don't like that. They would rather stay high all the time. But that takes money. A lot of money. As cheap as crack is, to feed a regular crack habit is expensive—thousands of dollars over the course of a year. Since few crack users have that kind of money in the bank, they have to get it somewhere else. So they steal, or invade homes, or sell their bodies—anything and everything they can think of. But it's a doomed effort. So the crack user is forced to turn to other drugs, like heroin, or alcohol, to ride out the low spells between hits.

Today crack use has stabilized, but it is still widespread. According to the latest National Survey on Drug Use and Health, about 4 percent of the United States population tries crack at least once.

That same figure holds roughly true for college and school-age users. It's interesting to note, though, that while crack use among eighth graders held steady last year, crack use among tenth and twelfth graders dropped. For those who scoff at programs like DARE and "Just Say No," there can be no disputing that such programs have an effect on drug awareness. About half of all high school students say they know that they run risks when they use certain drugs, crack among them.

Looked at conversely, over 96 percent have never tried crack and never intend to. That alone is encouraging.

The DEA makes more than 5,000 arrests for crack-related offenses each year. Close to half of those arrested are between the ages of twenty-one and thirty. It should be remembered that far more arrests are made for drug offenses at the state and local levels, which means that the nationwide total for crack arrests is much higher.

Based on information gathered by the Arrestee Drug Abuse Monitoring Program, about a third of all adult male arrestees and about 35 percent of all adult female arrestees test positive for cocaine at the time of their arrests. Close to 20 percent of the males and 25 percent of the females are crack users.

On the national level, over 40 percent of all federal charges filed each year are for drug offenses. Crack cocaine accounts for one-fifth of those.

Crack-related emergency-room treatments total approximately 12 percent of all drug treatments, but another encouraging note is that the number of crack treatments has progressively declined since 1992. The average age of those seeking treatment is thirty-seven.

It wasn't long after crack was introduced that someone thought to mix it with other drugs. When mixed with marijuana, the combination is known as an *oolie*. When mixed with PCP and marijuana, it's called a *wicky stick*. Crack is also mixed with heroin on occasion, resulting in *moonrocks*.

Although the usual way to ingest crack is to smoke it, there are instances where users inject it. They do so because the high lasts longer.

Nearly all the crack in the United States is made domestically. The number of crack houses had dwindled, but crack will continue to be a persistent blight for years to come.

APPENDIX C
Sinister Brotherhoods

No book on the DEA would be complete without mention of the gangs who provide drugs at the street level.

Americans have long had a perverse fascination with gangs. In the Old West, outlaws like Jesse James and Butch Cassidy, prototypes of the phenomenon, were extolled as heroes. The minions of the law out to bring them in, such as the Pinkertons, were belittled and scorned.

Mobsters became all the rage in the 1920s. During the Great Depression and immediately afterward, there were the likes of John Dillinger and Baby-Face Nelson, Bonny and Clyde, and Machine-Gun Kelly—members of criminal gangs whose exploits were glorified in the press and in the movies.

After World War II, the public became interested in two other types of gangs; biker gangs and street gangs. Marlon

Brando in *The Wild Ones* did more to glorify bikers than any publicity agent ever could. Street gangs had been around longer—witness the Bowery Boys—but they received a real-life and cinematic makeover that transformed them from packs of mischief-makers into cold-blooded criminals.

Never mind that movies made bikers seem like noble rebels. Never mind that you rarely saw street gangs burst into spontaneous song while dancing down the street, à la *West Side Story*. With Hollywood, image was everything. Whether the image was true or not didn't matter.

The Hells Angels were the most notorious example of glorified bikers. A whole series of Hells Angels movies glossed over their criminal underbelly and portrayed them as party animals who occasionally went astray. Sure, they were violent, but they were only having fun, and they never *really* wanted to hurt anyone.

The reality was much different. It was ugly, bloody, and littered with bodies. It was the reality that the DEA and other law-enforcement agencies had to deal with on an ongoing basis.

Onscreen, street-gang members were portrayed as misguided innocents who didn't want to do bad things, but who were tragic victims of circumstance, or of society. Once again, the darker elements were glossed over.

The truth is that street gangs willingly and wholeheartedly became involved in all aspects of the drug trade. They embraced it with open arms. Many used drugs, but that's a given. What they liked most was cramming their pockets with greenbacks from the sale of drugs.

For many gangs, of bikers and otherwise, drugs were more than a means to make ends meet. Drugs became a way of life. Nearly everything the gangs did revolved around either using drugs or selling drugs. They were a subset of the corporate structure, high finance in microcosm. They were also incredibly violent. Where a corporation might initiate a hostile takeover of a rival company, biker and street gangs preferred to rub the competition out.

Biker Gangs

Big bikes. Leather jackets. Hot babes. The appeal of being a biker isn't hard to fathom.

How many bikers are there? The exact number depends on who you ask. Most, it must be stressed, are law-abiding. Most are ordinary citizens who like to get away on weekends or whenever they can to enjoy the freedom of the open road.

The American Motorcycle Association once made a public comment to the effect that 99 percent of its members are honest citizens and only 1 percent are outlaws. Not long after the distinction was made, outlaw gang members began wearing 1 percent patches, and proudly called themselves "one percenters."

One estimate has it that there are upwards of 900 outlaw biker gangs in the United States. That figure seems inflated, but whether it is or it isn't, there is no doubt whatsoever that certain gangs are criminal enterprises through and through and have been formally recognized as organized crime elements by the courts, the FBI, and the DEA.

In recent decades, the bigger outlaw gangs have spread their wings and gone international. They now have chapters throughout Canada, Europe, and Australia. Interpol has recognized them as a formidable threat.

The image of outlaw bikers as basically harmless, carefree,

oversized kids couldn't be more wrong. They are incredibly violent. Witness the motto of the Hells Angels: *Three people will keep a secret if two are dead.*

Contrary to their image, many of the gangs are also incredibly sophisticated. Their bikes aren't the only technology they're involved with these days. They are into computers, and many gangs have their own Web sites. They use state-of-the-art surveillance equipment and countermeasures, and, of course, the best armaments their ill-gotten gains can buy.

The bigger outlaw gangs are run like businesses. They have constitutions and bylaws and recognized chapters. They trademark their insignias. They keep financial records, they pay bills. Many members attend college to earn degrees in fields that will directly benefit the gang's criminal ends. They hire attorneys with expertise in organized-crime cases. They develop their own intelligence files on rivals, as well as on law-enforcement agencies and personnel.

Outlaw gangs like to put on a happy face for the public. They hold rallies to raise money for charitable purposes. They hold blood drives. They let average joes join and showcase them at public events. But at their core, outlaw bikers are just that: outlaws. The range of illegal activities they engage in runs the gamut from murder to extortion, from prostitution to arson. But the one activity they all engage in, the one that brings them the most money, the one that concerns the DEA, is drugs.

Best estimates have it that biker gangs at one time were responsible for three-fourths of the meth sold in the United States. With the inroads made by Mexican traffickers and others, that figure has fallen, but biker gangs still push a lot of meth. In recent years, they've branched out into other drugs, thanks to contacts their international clubs have made with established syndicates like the Colombian cartels and the Italian Mafia.

The Criminal Intelligence Service of Canada had shown that biker gangs are now as organized as the Mafia. Indeed, an FBI report rated them as #2, right behind *La Cosa Nostra,* in terms of the threat they pose to the general welfare.

How did it come to this? Why didn't the authorities clamp down on them sooner?

Police and federal budgets aren't limitless. Often, resources are tight and must be allocated on a priority basis. Biker gangs and street gangs were both evolving toward their present criminal state at the same time, but it was the street gangs who drew most of the heat from law enforcement because they were perceived as the greater of the two evils. It was the street gangs who made the nightly news day after day, week in and week out, with accounts of drive-by shootings and other violence. As a result, the public, and the politicians who serve them, were demanding that something be done.

Law-enforcement agencies had no recourse but to allocate more of their resources to dealing with street gangs, leaving the bikers in the enviable position of being able to do pretty much as they pleased. It was a situation that they were quick to take advantage of.

So who are these biker gangs? The Hells Angels are the most infamous. Others include the Bandidos, Outlaws, Pagans, Mongols, Hessians, Satan's Choice, Sons of Silence, and the Ku Klux Klan Motorcycle Club, to name just a few. The list could go on and on. The Big Four, as far as law enforcement is concerned, are the Hells Angels, the Bandidos, the Outlaws, and the Pagans.

The Hells Angels got their start in 1947. A bunch of bikers known as the Pissed Off Bastards of Bloomington decided they needed a new name and chose one formerly used by fighter pilots during World War II. The Bandidos were formed in Houston, Texas, in 1966. For the Outlaws it was Chicago in 1959. That was also the year the Pagans started, in Prince George County, Maryland.

Exact membership numbers are subject to debate. The Hells Angels are supposedly pushing the three-thousand mark, but it could be much higher by the time all affiliates are included. The Bandidos have somewhere between two and three thousand. The Outlaws, about 1,500. The Pagans have about 500, although one expert pegs their membership as high as 900.

The Hells Angels, as noted, have been endlessly glamorized. In 1967, no less an actor than Jack Nicholson starred in *Hell's Angels on Wheels*. They like to present themselves as bad boys with good hearts. But according to law enforcement, the Angels are involved in meth, cocaine, and marijuana.

The Bandidos are considered one of the fastest-growing gangs. The Bandido Nation, as they are also called, are heavy into meth, prostitution, and weapons smuggling.

The Outlaws, or the Outlaw Motorcycle Club, as it is sometimes designated, derive most of their money from drugs. Meth and cocaine, especially, although they are heavily involved in the valium black market. Their insignia is supposedly copied from the skull emblem on Marlon Brando's leather jacket in *The Wild Ones*.

Interestingly, the Bandidos and the Outlaws have an unusual relationship. They actually get along, and they work together in various aspects of the drug trade.

The Pagans are considered the most violent. Not that the others are pacifists, it's just that the Pagans have strong links to the Mob and are known associates of Mafia families in the Northeast. They work as enforcers and hit men. Their drug dealings include meth, PCP, marijuana, and cocaine.

To further dispel the image of outlaw bikers as good ol' boys on wheels, mention should be made of their hit squads. Each gang has a small elite group dedicated to eliminating "problems." With the Hells Angels, it's their Filthy Few. The Bandidos have what they call their Nomads. The Outlaws have dubbed their enforcers the SS. The Pagan kill squad is comprised of thirteen members known as the Black T-shirts.

For the longest while, a truce existed between the Big Four except for the Hells Angels and the Outlaws, traditional enemies. Each side blames the other for presumed slights, and the harvest of their hatred has been a bounty of lifeless bodies.

Then, tensions between the Big Four began to mount. Drugs were the cause. There is only a limited amount of turf, and each gang eyed that of its rivals with envy. In February of 2002, at a biker gathering on Long Island in New York, those tensions spilled over. The Hells Angels and the Pagans went at it. One Pagan died, five others were shot, and five more were stabbed.

At a swap meet in California, the Hells Angels and a smaller outlaw gang called the Vagos became embroiled in a bloody fight.

But it was the deadly melee at a casino in Nevada that has threatened to consume the bikers in a conflagration of their own making. This time it was the Hells Angels and the Mongols who traded bullets, blades, and blows. A Mongol and two Angels died in the casino, and another Angel was shot to death later elsewhere.

Now the Mongols, the Pagans, the Bandidos, the Outlaws,

the Vagos, and others all have it in for the Hells Angels. Rumors have run rampant that a major war is imminent, but so far it hasn't materialized.

The DEA has done what the DEA is supposed to do, and gone after biker drug operations. In many localities, the DEA joined task forces targeting bikers. RICO statutes were brought to bear in successful conspiracy prosecutions.

Biker gangs are extremely close-knit. Only members who have been with a gang for years are admitted into the inner circles. Infiltrating them is next to impossible.

Informers are also hard to come by. Gang members have sworn vows of silence under penalty of death, and they know full well that if they break that vow, a kill squad will stop at nothing to silence them.

Money will often loosen lips, but outlaw bikers already receive their share of the gang's income and value their lives more than a few more dollars.

Still, the DEA never gives up. In November of 2002, two members of the Ku Klux Klan Motorcycle Club were convicted of drug trafficking, money laundering, and weapons violations. Several times a year, the pair would drive from New England, where their club was based, to Arizona, where they picked up crystal meth, which they then took back to New England and sold.

More recently, the DEA raided sixteen homes and businesses in New York and arrested three members of the Hells Angels and a lawyer affiliated with the club for their alleged involvement in a meth ring. The DEA relied on wiretaps and surveillance to build their case. The raids were conducted in Waterford, Troy, Albany, and Cohoes, among other locations. The clubhouse in Troy was reinforced with cinder blocks and had a thick steel front door rigged with cameras.

These are only a couple of instances among many.

Outlaw bikers will continue to be heavily involved in drugs for the foreseeable future.

Street Gangs

In the last two decades of the last century, street gangs became society's bogeymen. On the nightly news, Americans were regaled with horrific tales of street-gang atrocities: bloody accounts of drive-by shootings that claimed innocents, reports of cold-blooded murders and drug dealings. Americans routinely heard how street gangs had taken over neighborhoods, or how formerly quaint parks had become open-air drug markets.

There was no evil that street gangs would not commit, no depths to which they would not stoop.

They had names like the Bloods and the Crips, the Black Gangster Disciples, the 12th Street Crew, the Almighty Latin Kings Nation, Zulu Nation, the Vice Lords, Sisters of the Struggle, the Norteños. Hundreds of names for hundreds of gangs.

Some gangs went national and had affiliates, or "sets," throughout the country. The Bloods and the Crips are two of the more infamous examples.

The Bloods were originally known as Compton Pirus from West Pirus Street. Their gang color is red, supposedly because many of the founding members were from Centennial High School in Compton, California, and red was a school color. Initially, they were more concerned about their turf than about making money, but that soon changed.

Today, some sets are run like any business. Older Bloods buy legitimate establishments like liquor stores or car washes to launder drug money.

The Crips got their start in California, too. Their gang color was also taken from the colors of a Los Angeles high school.

Both gangs tend to favor certain clothes and certain ways to wear them. Both gangs have hand signs and code words. The early Crips wouldn't use the letter "b" in conversations because it's the first letter of "Bloods"; the Crips used "c" instead.

For the longest while, the Bloods and the Crips were bitter rivals. They killed one another with abandon. In recent years, that has changed to a limited extent. Today, the two will sometimes work together.

Not all gangs are national. Some are based in a single city. Others control a few measly blocks of precious turf.

By 1980, the majority of large American cities reported gang problems. By 1990, the problem had become pervasive. Every city with a population of more than 100,000 had gangs.

To give some idea of the astounding growth in gang numbers: in 1989, it was estimated that there were 1,439 gangs with a combined membership of about 120,000. By 1991, there were 4,881 gangs with 249,324 members.

Between 1991 and 1993 there was another quantum leap, to 8,625 gangs with the total number pegged at 378,807. But that didn't paint the total picture. Many localities did not have the resources to engage in an in-depth study. Consequently, it was felt that the numbers were considerably higher. One estimate put the gangs at 16,643 strong and their membership at over half a million.

How many are there today? No one really knows. One survey estimates 26,000 gangs with 840,500 members. Another places the number of gangs at 31,000 with only 816,000 members.

Trying to arrive at a definitive number is like trying to count the shifting grains of sand in an hourglass. Gangs constantly add and lose members. More pertinent, they generally don't advertise how many members they have unless it's to brag to impress their enemies. Gang members avoid, as much as possible, being identified by the police and the feds, for obvious reasons.

One fairly reliable study by the National Drug Intelligence Center gives perhaps a better picture. It found 7,400 gangs. Gang activity was reported in 98 percent of cities with populations of more than 100,000 and 78 percent of cities with populations under 50,000.

Of the national gangs, the Bloods and the Crips were in forty-two States. A Chicago-based gang, the Black Gangster Disciples, was reported in thirty-five states.

Originally, location was the determining factor in the birth and membership of most gangs, but that changed. Ethnicity became a dominating influence. Gangs were formed according to race. Today, however, there are a growing number of what are called "hybrid" or "mongrel" gangs in which the color of the member's skin is less important than complete loyalty.

The growth of gangs overall seems to have peaked. Back in the '90s, it was reported that gangs were spreading like measles, and that new affiliates were being organized as fast as the gangs could create them. The news stories made it sound like a deliberate, well-thought-out campaign.

Several studies showed differently. Many new chapters were started by gang members who had moved from one city to another, not as part of any grandly devious scheme, but simply because their families had relocated. This was especially true in smaller cities and towns. Parents tired of gang-bred violence and rampant drug use in the big city packed up their families, many of whom were gang members, and moved to smaller communities that didn't have a gang problem. But the first thing the transplanted gang members did was to organize a gang, or an affiliate, of their own.

This is not to say that the some gangs weren't opening chapters in other cities as part of a master plan to increase their memberships and their income. They were. And they were remarkably successful. So successful that a few have gone international.

Today, no city, no town, no locality can call itself safe. Not even Indian reservations. On the Navajo reservation in Arizona, for instance, authorities estimated that there were more than fifty gangs, some with ties to larger gang "nations," as the biggest gangs like to call themselves.

The average age of most gang members is seventeen. But they can be as young as ten and as old as sixty.

Degrees of organization vary. Some gangs consist of a bunch of locals who hang out together for a fun time and dabble in crime as a sideline, mainly for the thrill. Others are structured like a business and are vastly more sinister.

Gangs and crime go hand in hand. To be more precise, gangs and serious crime are synonymous. A gang forms and a rash of crime results.

The crime that receives the most media attention is murder, with ample justification. In Chicago alone, between the mid 1980s and the mid-1990s, there were close to one thousand gang-related homicides. The Illinois Criminal Justice Information Authority found that three-fourths of these involved gang members killing members of rival gangs, which was to be expected. What wasn't expected was that more than 10 percent involved gang members killing members of their own gang. Only 15 percent percent involved gang members murdering individuals with no gang affiliation whatsoever.

The media bombardment notwithstanding, most cities do not rack up large numbers of gang killings each year—Los Angeles and Chicago being two of the two most notable exceptions. They are among a handful that have anywhere from 150 to more than 200 gang-related homicides annually.

To put that in better perspective, consider that annually, about ten cities have fifty gang homicides each. Fifty cities have anywhere from ten to fifty. And 436 cites have ten or less.

Words like "more" and "less" are hardly relevant when we're dealing with human lives, but it should be apparent from the statistics cited that gang killings in most states are not as common as many would think given the degree of media attention.

An illustrative point is that gang killings, like the growth of gangs overall, appears to have reached it nadir—with a notable exception.

In recent years, the number and membership of Asian gangs have seen a marked rise. The Department of Justice has pegged the total at about 15,000 Asian street gangs in California alone. Most are Vietnamese, Cambodian, or Laotian. They have adopted names like the Tiny Rascal Gangsters or the Street Killer Boys.

Some have taken the names of existing gangs regardless of their lack of affiliation. Thus we see gangs like the Asian Bloods, with no relationship to the "Blood Nation."

Asian gangs show a definite affinity for violence, especially against non-gang members of the communities in which they live. Home invasions have become a speciality of certain Asian gangs. They make their money through extortion, burglaries, robbery, and drugs.

The general consensus has been that the street-gang culture is steeped in drugs; that their entire existence revolves around the use and sale of illegal substances. However, several recent studies, including one by the FBI, show that while drug trafficking is indeed a means that gangs employ to make money, it is not the only one. They engage in other illegal activities, too.

To put this in perspective, about one-third of all the arrests for cocaine sales in Los Angeles involve gang members. For other drugs, that figure is even less. It suggests that their share of the drug market is far less than had been assumed. But that doesn't mean the mistake should be made of downplaying the adverse impact they have on society as a whole.

The DEA hasn't ignored the threat. Playing a vital role in a multitude of regional task forces, the DEA has taken part in the arrest of hundreds of gang members. Wiretapping, surveillance, and, to a lesser degree, informants are the main techniques used to acquire evidence. Infiltration is out of the question, particularly with regard to ethnic gangs. A forty-year-old white DEA undercover agent, no matter how good he might be, can hardly waltz up to the Crips or the Bloods and ask to be a member. Ethnicity is a barrier that law enforcement can't penetrate.

That didn't stop the DEA and a multi-agency task force from taking down a crack ring in southern Nevada with ties to a Los Angeles street gang. After conducting an eight-month investigation, the task force raided three homes in Las Vegas and environs. Twelve suspects were arrested.

Then there were the Mafia Insane Vice Lords.

Based in the Windy City, the gang got its start in 1958, when it was known as the Conservative Vice Lords. Over the next two decades, the gang grew until there were various factions operating under the Vice Lord banner. These included the original Conservative Vice Lords, the Mafia Insane Vice Lords, the Cicero Insane Vice Lords, the Imperial Insane Vice

Lords, the Traveling Vice Lords and the Unknown Vice Lords. Together, they comprised the Vice Lords Nation.

The Nation went national, with affiliates in close to thirty states. Membership swelled to a peak of about 30,000.

The Mafia Insanes were founded by Troy Martin. Exactly how many members they have is unknown, but a good indicator is the fact that about 1,700 prison inmates were known to be Mafia Insanes. With that many behind bars, authorities estimated there had to be another two to three thousand loose on the streets. And that was in Chicago alone.

Some gangs are known for their business savvy. Some are known for keeping a low profile. The Mafia Insane Vice Lords were known for being almost fanatical about protecting their turf. They brooked no intrusions, ever, by anyone, especially rival gangs.

Their primary source of income? Drugs. They sold lots of drugs, openly and brazenly, in open-air markets. Cocaine, crack, heroin, marijuana—they sold it all.

Lower-ranking members were required to pay higher-ranking members monthly or weekly "taxes" for the privilege of selling drugs at selected spots. It was estimated that the Mafia Insanes had at least fifty markets in operation at any one time, each garnering between $3,000 and $5,000 per day in drug sales. They had it down to a science. While one or two Mafia Insanes kept the customers lined up and took orders, others dispensed drugs.

In order to entice users to buy their product, the Mafia Insanes would employ the underworld equivalent of promotional giveaways for potential buyers to try new substances. Needless to say, they had all the customers they could handle, and then some.

In September of 2002, the DEA and Chicago police

launched Operation Day Trader to bring the Mafia Insane Vice Lords down. Informers were cultivated. Wiretaps were authorized. Surveillance units sprang into action.

The surveillance and wiretaps revealed a hierarchy within the gang. The founder was known as the King. Under him were five members who had the title of the Five Star Universal Elite. The "Five Stars" showed how high they ranked. The "Universal" meant that other Vice Lord factions were required to acknowledge their positions of authority. Under them were the Three Star Universal Elite, and so on.

It is safe to say that the Mafia Insane Vice Lords were a drug operation from top to bottom. Drugs were more than an entrepreneurial enterprise; drugs were their life. They sold, breathed, and liberally used drugs.

The results of the op exceeded all of the DEA's and Chicago P.D.'s expectations. Despite repeated warnings by Troy Martin not to talk about drug deals over the phone, his underlings did so with a remarkably reckless disregard for who might be eavesdropping.

It's not surprising, then, that the DEA was able to build an impressive case against the Mafia Insanes.

Warrants for over 100 Mafia Insane Vice Lords members and associates were issued. Forty-eight, including Troy Martin, were taken into custody in the initial sweep. Interestingly, with all the arrests, the authorities only confiscated seven guns. When it came to dealing with rival gangs, the Mafia Insanes preferred baseball bats.

In New Jersey, an informant alerted the State Police Street Gang unit to a shipment of marijuana. The Mary Jane had been brought by tractor trailer from California, and the truck was parked at a warehouse in Elizabeth, awaiting offloading.

The state police contacted the DEA, and the resources of the DEA–Newark Task Force, as well as the Elizabeth police department, were brought to bear.

The shipment was believed to be destined for the Champagne Posse, a Jamaican street gang that dominated the marijuana market in New Jersey. Previously, the New Jersey State Police had intercepted another tractor-trailer, intended for the Champagne Posse, in which 1,575 pounds of marijuana had been hidden. Now, the truck at the warehouse was surrounded. Agents and police closed in. Dogs were used, and sixteen boxes of marijuana were found in a load of lettuce. That amounted to 690 pounds.

Both seizures followed on the heels of the arrests of sixty-five alleged Champagne Posse members. The gang was crippled but still very much in business.

That was often the case with regard to the larger gangs. They were too well organized, and had too many members to be taken off the streets in one fell swoop.

Jamaicans like to call their gangs "posses." As best as can be determined, the first posses were organized in Kingston, Jamaica, in the 1970s. By 1974, two posses, the Dunkirk Boys and the Raetown Boys, had made their presence known in New York City. Originally, the posses made their money from extortion, and from freelancing as hit men. But that changed when crack hit the scene.

Today, some of the biggest posses are the Shower Posse, the Spangler Posse, the Waterhouse Posse, and the Montego Bay Posse. The Shower Posse alone has chapters in New York, Philadelphia, Miami, Boston, Pittsburgh, Cleveland, Washington, D.C., Los Angeles, Dallas, Kansas City, Atlanta, Detroit, and Denver. The others are almost as widespread.

Posses have earned justifiable reputations for being violent. Many deal in guns as well as drugs. They are impossible to penetrate, as they only admit Jamaicans.

Perhaps the single most startling development in the war on street gangs was the discovery that a member of a Chicago gang had ties to the terrorist organization al-Qaeda.

He was not the only one with terrorist links.

In the 1980s, members of a Chicago gang known as El Rukins were convicted of conspiring to commit terrorist acts for Libya. Not that they had any great love for Libya or its leader. They were doing it for money. It was the first time in United States history that this had happened.

APPENDIX D
Foreign Terrorist Organizations

The war on drugs and the war on terror overlap. Since the DEA has a pivotal role to play in regard to narco-terrorism, a brief review of recognized terrorist organizations and their drug activities is warranted.

Some narco-terrorists are drug traffickers who rely on terror to maintain their power and their territory. A classic example is Pablo Escobar, who was responsible for the deaths of thousands of Colombians, but to whom terror was a means to an end, not an end in itself.

Then there are certain terrorist groups, some would say *true* terrorists, who engage in the drug trade to finance their terrorist activities. The most blatant example would be al-Qaeda. Although much was made in the media of Osama bin Laden's personal fortune, al-Qaeda still derives a considerable portion of its finances from heroin and other drugs.

As far as the DEA is concerned, it doesn't really matter why a terrorist organization is involved in drugs. All that matters is it is involved, and its members must then be treated like any other drug violators.

This isn't a new concept. During Prohibition, various crime syndicates applied the same tactics, although not on the same scale.

It should be noted that the Drug Enforcement Administration does not target terrorist organizations per se. That is the job of other agencies. The DEA is specifically and exclusively interested in terrorism only so far as it pertains to and impacts the drug trade. That's not to say that the DEA won't pass on timely intelligence to appropriate parties when the occasion calls for it, but for the sake of clarity the distinction needs to be made.

So how many terrorist organizations dabble in drugs? Estimates vary. It's believed that fourteen of the current thirty-six terrorist organizations formally recognized by the U.S. State Department are involved in drugs to varying extents.

How much money is devoted to terrorist activities by these groups? It depends on the group, and estimates vary with the expert. Critics of the war on drugs claim that the total is relatively small and that the government exaggerates the amount to exaggerate the threat. Enforcement advocates argue that the amount is irrelevant. It doesn't take much money to build a bomb, or to finance an operation that produces devastating and tragic results.

The designation for these groups is FTO's, or Foreign Terrorist Organizations. It should be mentioned that certain domestic groups who regard the United States government as a perversion of the constitutional principles on which the government is based would very much like to bring the government down and start over, and a few of them have drug ties, as well.

What follow are capsule summaries.

Revolutionary Armed Forces of Colombia (FARC). The most ruthless and bloodthirsty FTO in the world, bar none. They have slain thousands and there is no end in sight. Men, women, even children—it makes no difference. Their ties to the drug trade are well documented. Initially, they were hired by drug lords like Pablo Escobar to protect labs and drug routes. Then it dawned on them that they could make a lot of money by selling drugs themselves. The FARC is a Marxist organization and was formed in 1964 by the Colombian Communist Party. Cuba has lent the FARC aid.

The National Liberation Army (ELN). Another Colombian Marxist group.

They, too, are involved in drugs. Their speciality, though, is kidnapping. The ELN has kidnaped hundreds of people for ransom. They particularly like to kidnap foreigners, Americans most of all. Since those who formed the ELN regard Fidel Castro as their idealized hero, it should come as no surprise that the ELN, too, has ties to Cuba.

The United Self-Defense Force of Colombia (AUC). It was perhaps inevitable that, once the situation in Colombia deteriorated to the point of near-anarchy, some Colombians would say "enough is enough" and form vigilante groups. The AUC is one such group. It sees itself as a counterinsurgent force and is waging war against the likes of the FARC and the ELN. That in itself is commendable. However, in setting itself up as judge, jury, and executioner, the AUC has wiped out hundreds of FARC supporters, including women and children. And by its own admission, the AUC generates income from drugs.

Sendero Luminoso. Or the SL, or Shining Path. Based in Peru. Another Communist arm, only Maoist, not Marxist. They are responsible for a staggering 30,000 deaths, tried to car-bomb the United States embassy, and have tenuous links to the drug trade.

Tupac Amaru Revolutionary Movement (MRTA). Their goal is to overthrow the Peruvian government. They are yet another Communist group, but Marxist-Leninist, which has resulted in ironic if fitting incidents of the MRTA and SL fighting each other. No known ties to drugs.

The Taliban. Afghanistan. Their government was overthrown, but the Taliban are still active and still involved in the heroin trade.

Al-Qaeda. Osama bin Laden's brainchild. Responsible for the 9/11/01 attacks on New York and Washington and many other atrocities. Bombed the United States embassies in Kenya and Tanzania, killing more than 300 and injuring about 5,000. Planned to assassinate the Pope in 1994 and President Bill Clinton in 1995 while Clinton was on a trip to the Philippines. Avowed purpose is to purge the world of non-Islamic governments. Has proclaimed that it is the duty of all Muslims everywhere to kill Americans wherever Americans are found. Receives an unknown but sizeable amount of money from drugs, mostly heroin.

Al-Jihad. Egyptian-based. Established ties to al-Qaeda. Shares the same extremist philosophy. Born out of another group known simply as Jihad, which was responsible for the assassination of Egyptian President Anwar Sadat. Might be involved in drugs, but to a limited degree.

Kurdistan Worker's Party (PKK). Marxist-Leninist, the PKK wants to establish a Kurdish state in Turkey. In the 1990s they bombed Turkish hotels and kidnapped tourists, but in recent years they have toned down their violence. Definitely, and heavily, involved in drugs. They produce some sixty tons of heroin annually.

The New People's Army (NPA). Communists who want to overthrow the Philippine government. Maoists, they finance their violent operations largely through the cultivation and distribution of marijuana. In recent years, they have branched into crystal methamphetamine.

The Moro National Liberation Front and *The Moro Islamic Liberation Front.* Both of these are based in the southern Philippines. Both are Islamic-inspired extremist groups and are involved in drugs, principally marijuana, but there is also evidence to suggest that, like the NPA, they have taken an interest in crystal meth. The latter group has ties to al-Qaeda.

Abu Sayyaf Group. The ASG has a unique distinction: it got its start in one country and then moved to another. Originally formed in Afghanistan, its operatives relocated to the Philippines to lend support to the Moro Islamic Liberation Front. Like that group, the ASG has close links with al-

Qaeda. And like that group, the ASG has been involved in drug smuggling.

Jaish-e-Mohammed. JEM, or the Army of Mohammed. An Islamist organization that wants to unite Kurdistan and Pakistan. Proven ties to the Taliban, al-Qaeda, and Osama bin Laden. Possibly involved in drugs.

Hezbollah. The Party of God. Out to destroy Israel and hates the United States. Involved in the truck bombings of the United States embassy and the U.S. Marine barracks in Beirut in 1993, among many others. Based in the Bekaa Valley in Lebanon but has cells in North America, Europe, Africa, Asia, and South America. (See HAMAS.)

HAMAS. The Islamic Resistance Movement. Out to overthrow Israel. Runs candidates for political office while at the same time conducts terrorist activities. Based out of the Gaza Strip, but it is now known to have cells in South America.

Many experts have long believed that "traditional" terrorist groups like HAMAS and Hezbollah got most of their money from private backers and countries like Syria, Iran, and Saudi Arabia.

Unknown to those experts was a profoundly disturbing development: at least half a dozen Middle Eastern terrorist groups now have cells in South America.

Brazil, Argentina, and Paraguay are home to a sizeable population of transplanted Arabs, a number of whom operate front companies for terrorist groups and funnel money from marijuana and cocaine trafficking back to them.

Paraguay has the largest population. Its lax immigration laws make it easy for terrorists to relocate there.

The full extent of this new problem has not yet been defined. It has been established that drug money from South America is adding to the coffers of HAMAS and Hezbollah. As time goes on, that list will surely grow.

Al-Gama'a al-Islamiyya. The Islamic Group. The largest terrorist group in Egypt, their stated goal is to replace Egypt's government with an Islamic state. One of its leaders joined in Osama bin Laden's call for attacks on Americans worldwide.

Other members said they want nothing to do with bin Laden. The Islamic Group appears to be on the verge of splintering. In 1995, they tried to assassinate Egyptian President Hosni Mubarak. Marginal if any involvement with drugs.

Islamic Movement of Uzbekistan. Yet another Islamic fundamentalist group whose goal is to turn its country into an Islamic state. To no one's great surprise, it is also anti-United States and anti-Israel. Like other Islamic groups, it is supported by Iran. Like the Taliban, some of its funds may be derived from drug deals, but not to the same degree.

Lashkar-e-Tayyiba. The Army of the Righteous. Based in Kashmir, its campaigns are waged principally against India and Indians, especially Hindus. The Army of the Righteous is made up largely of Pakistani and Afghanistani nationals. They run a chain of religious schools in which future Righteous are indoctrinated. No direct links to drug traffiking, but they do have ties to the Taliban, known dealers in heroin.

That a certain ambiguity attaches itself to various FTO's is inevitable. It's not as if they take out ads in the *Wall Street Jour-*

nal announcing to all and sundry that they are in the drug business. Quite the opposite: they do all they can to disguise the fact. Not just because they know it is illegal, nor even in instances where they might concede it is immoral. They want it kept secret to protect their public image.

That might seem ludicrous, but consider that many terrorist organizations routinely embark on public-relations campaigns to bolster their acceptance level among the gullible.

You don't hear HAMAS or Hezbollah calling press meetings to announce that they are involved in drugs, but they are.

Which brings us to similar groups operating out of Palestine whose drug affiliations cannot be fully ascertained at this time:

The Popular Front for the Liberation of Palestine. Started by a member of the Palestine Liberation Organization in 1967. No known drug connections at this time.

The Popular Front for the Liberation of Palestine-General Command. A disgruntled splinter group that broke away from The Popular Front for the Liberation of Palestine. They brook no middle ground with Israel. Equal-opportunity haters, they eliminate Palestinians who think otherwise.

The Palestine Liberation Front. It broke away from the General Command group. Made up of three autonomous factions. The pro-PLO faction, under Abu Abbas, was responsible for the attack on the *Achille Lauro* in which a wheelchair-bound tourist was murdered.

The Palestine Islamic Jihad. Rabidly wants a Palestinian state. Rabidly wants Israel destroyed. Because the United States has supported Israel, the PIJ has gone on record as recognizing the United States as its enemy but it has not, to date, attacked United States installations or civilians. Other enemies include any and all Arab governments tainted by Western influence.

Abu Nidal Organization. The ANO has a number of aliases. Among them are Black September, the Revolutionary Organization of Socialist Muslims, the Arab Revolutionary Brigades, and the Fatah Revolutionary Council. Different names, pretty much the same animal. The ANO is embroiled in a war of more than words with the PLO. It allegedly assassinated two top-ranking PLO members. When it is not killing other Palestinians, it is attacking other countries, or their interests. Responsible for the attacks on the Neve Shalom synagogue in Istanbul and on the Vienna and Rome airports and for the hijacking of Pan Am Flight 73. Also involved in the killing of Israeli athletes at the 1972 Olympics. Received support from Iraq, Syria, and Libya.

There is hardly a region of the world that does not have a terrorist organization somewhere within its boundaries. Every continent except Antartica is home to an FTO or a cell.

Americans are accustomed to hearing about various Palestinian groups, al-Qaeda, the Taliban, and a few others. But there are many more. Many raise funds through drugs, although most to nowhere near the extent to which the Taliban or the FARC do.

Some are hardly, if ever, mentioned by the United States media because their activities do not directly pertain to the United States or its citizens. But those who live in the countries in which these groups have been spawned known them only too well.

The Revolutionary United Front. Based in Sierra Leone. Out to overthrow the Sierra Leone government. Unfazed by political ideology or religious fervor, they have motives linked to the diamond trade. Sierra Leone has one of the highest diamond productions in the world, and the RUF funds its campaign through the sale of diamonds from regions it already controls. Their revolution could be passed off as simple thuggery were there not a darker element to their uprising: they are backed by the government of neighboring Liberia, which does not produce nearly as many diamonds.

First of October Antifascist Resistance Group. The violent arm of the Communist Party in Spain. They oppose the Spanish government and are in favor of a Marxist variant. No known drug links.

Army for the Liberation of Rwanda. Made up of the Former Armed Services of Rwanda and the Interahamwe. The latter was to blame for the genocide of half a million people. Why were all those people killed? Because they were Tutsis, and the ALR's predecessors, like the ALR, are Hutus. In 1991 they abducted eight foreign tourists, two of whom were Americans, from a game park, and later killed them.

Revolutionary Nuclei. Their mission is to overthrow the government of Greece. Born of the vestiges of a former organization called the Revolutionary People's Struggle. No known drug links.

Revolutionary Organization 17 November. Another Greek group. Their preferred targets are United States officials in an effort to remove the United States military presence from Greece.

The Liberation Tigers of Tamil Eelam. They want a Tamil state in Sri Lanka. Already, they virtually control much of the coast county. The LTTE has a number of front organizations: the World Tamil Movement, the World Tamil Association, the Ellalan Force, the Sangilian Force, and the Federation of Association of Canadian Tamils. More commonly called the Tigers, they regularly set off bombs and murder Sri Lankan officials. They also deal in drugs, as do Tamil groups in Europe and elsewhere.

Mujahedin-e-Khalq Organization. Amazingly, the MEK or MKO—it is called by both acronyms—believes that *Iran* is too Westernized. They want Iran to be even more Islamic than it is. They have attacked and killed Iranian officials and targeted any American unfortunate enough to walk into their crosshairs.

The Japanese Red Army. The media has made the JRA out to be a formidable world presence. Quite a feat, given that it has six members. But there is no denying that this splinter group of the Communist Red Army Faction has a flair for making itself known. Two JRA members are in prison in the United States. One was arrested in New Jersey after explosives were found in his vehicle, explosives that were to be used in the bombing of the USO club in Naples. No known drug ties.

Harakat ul-Mujahidin (HUM). Another Islamic group, this one based in Pakistan. Most of its terrorist activities take place in neighboring Kashmir. Has publicly called for attacks on United States interests. Has ties to Osama bin Laden. Possible drug involvement.

The Irish Republican Army. One of the more famous groups. A U.S. General Accounting Office study purported to show that the IRA is not in any way, shape, or form engaged in drug trafficking. However, IRA members have traveled to Colombia and elsewhere to share their expertise with other terrorist organizations. It could well be that a drug connection will surface in the future.

Finally, we come to a terrorist organization that makes no bones about where it stands on the drug issue.

People Against Gangsterism and Drugs. Also known as Muslims Against Illegitimate Leaders, and as Muslims Against Global Oppression. PAGAD got its start as a small vigilante group fighting rampant crime in Cape Town, South Africa. As it grew, it became not only increasingly more violent, but more virulent in its verbal attacks on the South African government and the West in general. It does not like moderate Muslims, it does not like Jews, it does not like gays. PAGAD has a special strike team, called the G-Force (Gun Force), which is responsible for dozens of shootings and bombings. Among the bombing targets have been gay nightclubs, synagogues, and any restaurant or tourist attraction that caters to Westerners. PAGAD made headlines when the Cape Town Planet Hollywood was bombed. Despite all this, and in keeping with its name, PAGAD shuns any involvement with drugs.

ADDENDUM
Drug Trends and the Future

Some in the pro-drug lobby like to say that if United States drug users were to stop using drugs tomorrow, the illicit worldwide market would dry up. They mention this to illustrate their point that we have met the enemy and he is us. In other words, America is to blame for the drug cartels and the money that FTO's make from drugs.

Their assertion is blatantly false. Yes, the United States consumes a lot of drugs, but the rest of the world consumes more. Take heroin as only one example: United States users pump less than 10 percent of the global heroin output into their veins. Which means the rest of the world is abusing the other 90 percent plus.

Cocaine use peaked in the late 1980s and has held fairly steady ever since. Synthetic drugs, however, have witnessed an upswing, thanks largely to younger users who mistakenly see synthetics as a safer alternative to other drugs. No one can say whether synthetic use has peaked yet. Evidence suggests that it is still on the rise.

As with heroin, the total number of United States users of synthetics is small compared to the global total, which has been pegged at 30 million and climbing by the United Nations.

The United States will most likely continue to see heavy marijuana use. Heroin, never as popular because of its destructive qualities, probably won't see much if any change.

Canada has a burgeoning problem on its hands—biker gangs—that is spawned in part by the drug trade (See Appendix D). Widely perceived as being less rigid in regard to drugs, Canada has become a motorcycle-gang magnet. As a result, its drug statistics have spiked.

Mexico has made great strides, but it will continue to be a trafficking conduit into the United States. Its geographic proximity alone is the main reason. The Mexican government has clamped down on the syndicates, but as we have learned, every time a drug syndicate is crushed, another arises to replace it. A prominent member of the Arellano-Felix Tijuana cartel was recently arrested, yet the AFO chugs on.

Mexican traffickers are a persistent bunch, and they are notoriously contemptuous of authority. It will take an intense countrywide effort to bring about anything approaching stability.

When it comes to stability, or, rather, *in*stability, Colombia is the hands-down leader of the Western Hemisphere. The situation there is worse than in Venezuela, worse than in Brazil, worse than in Argentina, worse than in Paraguay. Colombia has not merely been through hell, it *is* a hell of competing drug interests and widespread corruption. The Medellín cartels, the Cali cartels, the FARC and other narco-terrorist organizations—

all have transformed this once-peaceful country into a war zone.

The amount of Colombian heroin being pumped into the United States will rise. So will the amount of synthetic drugs. The Colombians are no longer content to deal only in cocaine and marijuana. Their cartels are nothing if not deviously astute and and opportunistic businessmen.

Peru, Bolivia, Argentina, Venezuela, Brazil—they will all see a steady increase in drug production and the problems associated with it. If current trends continue, other South American countries will find themselves in the same sinking boat with Colombia.

As Colombia continues to cultivate more and more of its own coca, traffickers in Peru and Bolivia (traditional coca sources) are selling their own cocaine in ever larger amounts. If this continues, they might eventually rival Colombia's output. If that happens—if they lay claim to a bigger slice of the cocaine cake—look to see new regional rivalries develop, accompanied by the inevitable high body count.

Europe, particularly the industrialized countries of Western Europe, use almost as much cocaine as the United States does. That will most likely continue at about current levels. Synthetics are the drugs to watch. Europe is experiencing a rise of unprecedented proportions in synthetic use. Part of the blame must be laid at Europe's own doorstep. The Netherlands is now the world's leading supplier of ecstasy.

In the Middle East, there is a high probability that more and more terrorist groups will turn to drugs as a steady source of income. The growing Islamic populations in South America will be the conduits.

Africa, the so-called Dark Continent, is not nearly as dark as

Europe and North America when it comes to the proliferation of drugs. Not that there isn't drug use. There is a lot of it. But comparatively speaking, Africa is a poor continent, and people can't buy drugs if they don't have money to pay for them. Many in Africa are rightfully more concerned about staying alive to see the next day than they are about where their next toke or fix will come from.

It is anticipated that Asia will continue to be a hotbed of drug activity. Afghanistan and other countries will go on producing heroin, despite government crackdowns. There is only so much the governments can do in countries where nine-tenths of the populations live in remote villages and regions that can take weeks to reach.

Southeast Asia has witnessed two crucial changes with long-term consequences. The first was the surrender of the Mong Tai Army in Myanmar and the partial neutralization of warlord Khun Sa. This was effected by the DEA persuading Thailand to seal its border with Myanmar so that Khun Sa couldn't obtain the chemicals he needed. Once again, though, another entity arose to fill the vacuum, in this instance the United Wa State Army.

The second significant development has been the rise of China as a heroin exporter. Communist or not, China has a sizeable criminal element, and that element is thriving as never before, thanks to China's growing worldwide trade market. Chinese traffickers will make their presence felt more and more as time goes by.

Little has been heard from Russia in regard to drugs, but with the collapse of the Soviet Union, Russian syndicates are making more inroads.

Historically, traditional syndicates like the Mafia, the N'Drangheta, and the Sicilians have also become more active in drugs. The time when, as in a popular Hollywood movie, mafiosi refused to deal in drugs on general principles are long gone, if they ever truly existed. Italy has already witnessed a rise in trafficking, and the end is nowhere in sight.

Increasingly, drug traffickers will turn to alternative means of laundering their proceeds. They have learned the hard way that virtually any money can be traced, and they do not want that. Systems like the Black Market Peso Exchange in South America and the hundi system in Hawaii will thrive.

All of this means, of course, that the Drug Enforcement Administration must work that much harder. But then, that's always been the case.

SOURCES

Primary attribution is due the Drug Enforcement Administration. The bulk of the resource material came from DEA files. However, corroborating accounts, and sometimes conflicting evidence, were culled from other sources.

Herewith a list of those sources:

The Office of National Drug Control Policy
The Bureau of Justice Statistics
The Drug Policy Information Clearinghouse
The Fannie May Foundation
The Los Angeles Times
The Drug Abuse Warning Network
The National Drug Threat Assessment 2002
The National Institute on Drug Abuse
The Federal Bureau of Investigation

Sources

Kansas State University Alcohol and other Drug Education Service
The Associated Press
The Las Vegas Review-Journal
The National Drug Intelligence Center
USA Today
The United States Coast Guard
The Department of the Treasury
The United States Attorney's Office
The New York Times
NewsMax.com
The Danish Drug Users Union
The Orlando Sentinel
The Miami Herald
The Boulder Daily Camera
The Boulder Weekly
The Puerto Rico Herald
New York Magazine
DrugSense Weekly
cannabisnews.com
Stars and Stripes
The National Highway Traffic Safety Administration
Massachusetts Attorney General Office
newswire.com
The U.S. State Department
The Seattle Post-Intelligencer
The United Nations Office for Drug Control and Crime Prevention
The Washington Post
cannabisculture.com
The Guardian
Frontline

The Union-Tribune (San Diego)
The Christian Science Monitor
csmonitor.com
Money Laundering Alert
The L.A. Weekly
The BBC
The Washington Office On Latin America
The Ozark Alabama News
The Jewish Journal of Greater Los Angeles
The Washington Times
The Arizona Department of Public Safety
bikernews.com
Gangs Or Us
SafeYouth.org
The New Jersey State Police
Drug Rehabs.org
The Hawaii County Police Department
The Royal Canadian Mountain Police
The Bureau for International Narcotics and Law Enforcement Affairs
The Arizona Attorney General
The Internal Revenue Service
The Charleston Post and Courier
freepress.com
The Detroit News
The U.S. Marshal Service
The Boston Globe
The Daily Illini Online
The Wamego Times
The Drug Reform Coordination Network
The Massachusetts State Police
The Asian Pacific Post

The Portsmouth, New Hampshire, Police Department
The U.S. Department of Homeland Security
amednews.com
The Buffalo News
The Grim Reaper
crimsonbird.com

ACKNOWLEDGMENTS

The producers of this book would like to acknowledge the following people for their cooperation and service: William Glaspy, William Grant, Sean Fearns, Director of the DEA Museum, and Chris Eagan.

The *Heavy Traffic* companion CD contains excerpts from the National Symposium on Narco-Terrorism, recorded on December 4, 2001, at DEA headquarters in Arlington, Virginia. A full transcript of the entire proceedings can be found at http://www.usdoj.gov/dea/ongoing/narco-terrorism.html#3, or through Miller Reporting. Permission granted by DEA Museum; Copyright © 2001, 2005 DEA Museum.

We would also like to thank the following panel participants: William Alden, Asa Hutchinson, Mark Souder, Robert Novak, Raphael Perl, Steven Casteel, Larry Johnson, General Jose Rosso Serrano (Ret.), and Stephen Pasierb.

INDEX

Abu Nidal Organization (ANO), 323
Abu Sayyaf Group (ASG), 319–20
ACF. *See* Amado Carillo-Fuentes Organization
Adel Ibrahim, Tamer, 116–17
Afghanistan
  drug money laundering in, 242–43
  heroin supplied by, 188, 238–39
  hundi financial network, 242–43
  opium supplied by, 149–50
  Taliban and poppy production in, 237–38
  Taliban as narco-terrorists in, 149–50
AFO. *See* Arellano-Felix Brothers Organization

Amado Carillo-Fuentes Organization (ACF), 68, 82, 93–94, 122
American Motorcycle Association, 299
Anabolic Steroid Enforcement Act, 61
ANO. *See* Abu Nidal Organization
Anti–Drug Abuse Act, 44
Apperson, Clyde, 234–36
Arellano-Felix, Benjamin. *See* Arellano-Felix Brothers Organization (AFO)
Arellano-Felix Brothers Organization (AFO)
  Arellano-Felix, Benjamin, as leader of, 170
  decline of, 265, 268

Arellano-Felix Brothers
Organization *(continued)*
family involvement, extent of,
67, 169–70
as Mexican drug syndicate, 67,
100–101, 170–75
violence by, 272–73
Arellano-Felix, Jorge, 269
Arellano-Felix, Ramon
AFO security headed by, 170
death of, 172–74
Army for the Liberation of
Rwanda (ALR), 324
Arredondo, Arturo, 94
ASG. *See* Abu Sayyaf Group
Assassin Hunter. *See* Yanez
Cantu, Jamie
AUC. *See* United Self-Defense
Forces of Colombia
Avelar, Alfredo Zavala, 40–43
Avianca Flight 203, 73

Bandidos, 301–3
Barnes, Leroy "Nicky"
conviction of, 17
Gallo and drug connection
with, 16
heroin trade controlled by,
16–17
Belgium, 116, 195
Beltran, Alberto, 82–83
Benitez, Rene, 85–86
Big Four as biker gangs, 301, 303
biker gangs
Canadian problem with, 327
criminal syndicates connection
to, 302–3
description of, 299–305
drug use of, 300–301, 302,
303, 304, 305

hit squads of, 303
image of, 299–300, 302
international chapters of, 299
number of in U.S., 299, 302
sophistication of, 300
violence by, 300, 302–3, 304
bin Fawwaz al-Shaalan, Prince
Nayef, 179–82
bin Laden, Osama, 146, 315
jihad, declaration by, 149
as narco-terrorist, 318
Taliban's support of, 241
Black Market Peso Exchange
(BMPE), 243, 331
black tar. *See* heroin
Black Tuna Gang, 17–19
BMPE. *See* Black Market Peso
Exchange
BNDD. *See* Bureau of Narcotics
and Dangerous Drugs
Bolivia, 45, 152, 168
Brownlee, Rickie, 76
Bureau of Narcotics, 2
Bureau of Narcotics and
Dangerous Drugs (BNDD)
abolished, 4
activities of, 2–5
budget of, 4
Controlled Substances Act
influencing, 3
Burma
drug trafficker influence in,
58–59
heroin supplied by, 58–59, 75,
188–89

Cali mafia
as cocaine smuggling
organization, 10, 32, 39, 58,
62–64, 79

as drug money laundering organization, 89–91
investigation and breakup of, 62–64, 69–70
power in other countries by, 57
California, 135
Camarena, Enrique, 40–43, 64
Campuzano Zapata, Oscar Eduardo, 180
Canada, 327
 drug problems in, 328
 ecstasy supplied by, 265–66
 marijuana supplied by, 204, 216, 265, 269–70
 as pseudoephedrine source, 111, 158–60, 239–40, 262
cannabis, 14
Caracol organization, 92
Cardenas-Guillen, Osiel, 117–18, 223–25
Caribbean countries and cooperation in drug control by, 14–16, 19, 35
Carillo-Fuentes, Amado, 68
Caro-Quintero, Rafael, 68
North Valley cartel. *See* Norte Valle cartel
Chambers, Andrew, 133
China
 ecstasy use in, 216
 ephedrine produced by, 80, 217
 Four Untouchables heroin ring, 247–52
 heroin supplied by, 59, 70, 202–3, 217, 247–52, 330
 meth use of, 216–17
 pseudoephedrine supplied by, 80

coca paste, 293
cocaine
 attitudes toward, 45
 biker gangs as suppliers of, 302–3
 Bolivia as major producer of, 45, 152
 Cocaine Wars, 21
 Colombia as supplier of, 21–23, 32, 33, 50–51, 55, 59, 92, 93, 112, 118, 119–21, 152, 153, 177–79, 186, 201, 244, 261–62, 267, 328–29
 deaths attributed to, 44
 Dominican Republic as supplier of, 78–79
 freebase processing of, 293–94
 Guyana as supplier of, 271
 HCI converted from, 29
 Irish mob as suppliers of, 74
 Italy as supplier of, 252–53, 261–62
 Jamaica as supplier of, 270
 mafia as supplier of, 252–53
 Mexico as supplier of, 50–51, 82, 176–77, 196, 210, 223, 264, 268
 Puerto Rico as supplier of, 78–79, 124, 160, 214
 street gangs as suppliers of, 310, 311
 U.S. use of, 20–21, 28–30, 221–23, 245, 246
 Venezuela as source of, 112, 181
coke. *See* cocaine
Colombia
 Cali mafia in, 57–58, 89–90

Colombia *(continued)*
   cocaine supplied by, 21–23, 32, 33, 50–51, 55, 59, 92, 93, 112, 118, 119–21, 152, 153, 177–79, 186, 201, 244, 261–62, 267, 328–29
   cooperation with authorities, 17–19, 33, 36, 169
   as drug money laundering outlet, 89–90
   ecstasy labs found in, 160
   Escobar as narco-terrorist in, 148, 315
   FARC and cocaine involvement in, 152, 153, 167, 241
   heroin supplied by, 59, 107, 168, 188–89, 191, 245, 253
   marijuana smuggling in, 19–20
   Medellín cartel's political influence in, 54–55, 55–57
   narco-terrorist groups in, 146–47
   paramilitary terrorist groups in, 197–98, 263, 268, 317–18
the Commission, 109–10
Communications Assistance for Law Enforcement Act, 72
Comprehensive Methamphetamine Control Act, 80–81
Consolidated Priority Organization Target List, 270
Constantine, Thomas A., 76
Controlled Substances Act
   Congress passage of, 3
   GHB added to, 101
   Internet sales governed by, 274
   Supreme Court ruling concerning, 161

Controlled Substances Analogue Enforcement Act (CSAEA)
   Internet drug sales governed by, 274
corruption, 123
   AFO successes through, 171
   in China, 217
   in Puerto Rico, 124–25
Costa Rica, 140
crack
   addiction to, xii, 30, 294–95
   countries as suppliers of, 202
   "crack babies," rise of, 31–32
   emergency-room treatments for, 30
   street gang trafficking of, 311
   U.S. use of, 30, 31, 194, 213–14, 221, 252, 256, 270, 294, 296
   violence associated with, 31, 221
   women's use of, 31
"crank." *See* methamphetamine
CSAEA. *See* Controlled Substances Analogue Enforcement Act
Cuba
   cocaine supplied by, 21
   Colombian-based traffickers' cooperation with, 22
Czech Republic, 80

date rape, 101–4
Davila-Jimeno, Raul, 17–18
DAWN. *See* Drug Abuse Warning Network
de Jesus Henao-Montoya, Archangel, 185, 263–64
de Jesus Henao-Montoya, Fernando, 215–16

De La Vega, Ivan, 112–13
DEA. *See* Drug Enforcement
  Administration
Delafield Mob, 96–97
Delta-9-Tetrahydrocannabinol
  (THC), 48
designer drugs, 274–75
Digital Telephony and
  Communications Privacy
  Act, 71
Domestic Cannabis Eradication
  and Suppression Program,
  24, 60
Dominican Republic
  cocaine supplied by, 78–79, 201
  crack supplied by, 202
  heroin supplied by, 202–3
Drug Abuse Warning Network
  (DAWN), 10, 91, 115
drug combinations, 296
"Drug Czar" Office of National
  Drug Control Policy, 48
Drug Enforcement
  Administration (DEA)
  air wing, 9, 25, 26, 52, 87
  budget for, xiii, 207, 260
  challenge for the future for,
    277–80
  death of, 281–92
  education of public by, 84–85,
    143
  FBI combined with, 17–19
  formation of, 4
  headquarters location, 52
  informants policies of, 133,
    236, 254
  intelligence analysts training
    by, 10, 52
  Mexico and restrictions placed
    on, 64–66

Priority Targeting System,
  organization of, 169
Purple Heart Award, creation
  of, 81
Sensitive Investigation Units,
  169, 189, 243
Survivors' Benefit Fund, 86
technology used by, 8–9, 26,
  48, 52, 60–61, 86, 205
Drug Enforcement Task Force,
  131
drug money laundering, 89–90
  in Afghanistan, 243
  Black Market Peso Exchange
    and, 243, 331
  Cali mafia, activities of, 89–90
  in Colombia, 243
  Four Untouchables, activities
    of, 249
  Ku Klux Klan Motorcycle
    Club and, 304
drug paraphernalia, 225–26
Drug Policy Analysis Program
  association with William
  Pickard, 234
drug syndicates, xiii, 119–21. *See
  also* Mexican drug syndicates
drug-use statistics. *See* statistics
  on drug use
drugs
  harm to society, xi–xiv, 5–6
  predictions of future use of,
    327–31
  as status quo, 96
Duarte, Jose Ivan, 85–86
"Durango drive shaft," 14

ecstasy
  Canada as supplier of, 265–66
  Caribbean seizures of, 160

ecstasy *(continued)*
  Colombian labs of, 160
  countries as smugglers of, 116, 191, 195, 196, 265–66
  crime syndicates' smuggling of, 116
  Equator as distribution point, 161
  Israel as source of, 189–91
  Operation Green Clover seizure of, 127–29
  statistics on use of, 136–37, 199
  U.S. use of, 114–17
Ecuador
  cooperation with authorities, 86, 161
  ecstasy distribution by, 161
  heroin supplied by, 188
ELN. *See* National Liberation Army
ephedrine, 80
  China as producer of, 217
Escobar, Pablo, 91
  imprisonment and death of, 55–57
  as Medellín cartel member, 22, 47
  as narco-terrorist, 148, 315

FARC. *See* Revolutionary Armed Forces of Colombia
Fass, Richard, 80
FBI
  Black Tuna Gang conviction by, 17–19
  DEA combined forces with, 17–19
  drug control involvement in, 116, 269
  Justice Department combines DEA with, 33
  Marquis organization investigation of, 122–23
  Operation Impunity role in, 94
Federal drug enforcement, 1
Federal Express, 100–101, 106, 138, 190, 209
Felix-Gallardo, Miquel Angel, 67
First of October Antifascist Resistance Group, 324
Flores, Marco, 94
Florida, 18, 23, 29, 35
flunitrazepam (Rophy). *See* Rohypnol
Foreign Terrorist Organization(s) (FTO), 316–26
  Abu Nidal Organization as, 323
  Abu Sayyaf Group as, 319–20
  ALR as, 324
  AUC as, 317
  ELN as, 317
  FARC as, 120, 317
  First of October Antifascist Resistance Group as, 324
  al-Gama'a al-Islamiyya as, 321
  HAMAS as, 320
  Hezbollah as, 320
  HUM as, 325
  Irish Republican Army as, 326
  Islamic Movement of Uzbekistan as, 321
  Jaish-e-Mohammed as, 320
  al-Jihad as, 319
  JRA as, 325
  Lashkar-e-Tayyiba as, 321
  Liberation Tigers of Tamil Eelam as, 325
  MEK/MKO as, 325

Moro National Liberation
  Front as, 320
MRTA as, 318
NPA as, 320
number of engaged in drugs,
  316
PAGAD as, 326
Palestine Islamic Jihad as,
  322–23
Palestine Liberation Front as,
  322
PKK as, 319
Popular Front for the
  Liberation of Palestine as,
  322
al-Qaeda as, 147, 241, 315,
  318, 323
Revolutionary Nuclei as, 324
Revolutionary Organization 17
  November as, 324
RUF as, 324
Shining Path as, 318
in South America, 320–21
Taliban as, 318
Four Untouchables
  Chinese heroin ring, 247–52
  Kin-Cheung Wong as head of,
    249
  money laundering activities
    and, 249
Fox, Vicente, 178
freebase. *See* cocaine
French Connection, 3–4, 34–35
"Friend-Killer." *See*
  Cardenas-Guillen, Osiel
FTO. *See* Foreign Terrorist
  Organizations

Gallo, Crazy Joe, 16
al-Gama'a al-Islamiyya, 321

gamma hydroxybutyric acid
  (GHB), 101, 135, 206
gangs
  attitude to, through media,
    297–98
  bikers as, 299–305
  Hells Angels as, 298
  relation of, to drugs, 297–99
Garcia-Abrego, Juan, 68, 122
Germany as chemicals supplier
  for heroin processing,
  238
GHB. *See* gamma
  hydroxybutyric acid
Gonzales, Gerardo, 83
Great Satan, xi, 146, 148
Guadalajara mafia, 39
Guatemala, drug smuggling in,
  214–15
Guyana, cocaine smuggled by,
  271

HAMAS, 320
Harakat ul-Mujahidin (HUM),
  325
Harrison Narcotics Act, 1–2
hashish, 193
hawala. *See* hundi
HCI, 29
Hells Angels, 301–3
hemp, 162, 164
heroin
  addiction to, xii
  Barnes control of, 16–17
  black tar, 39, 104–8, 125, 132,
    142
  Burma as supplier of, 58–59,
    188
  Chicago as major hub for,
    14–15

346 | Index

heroin *(continued)*
   China as supplier of, 59, 70, 202–3, 217, 247–52
   Colombia as supplier of, 59, 107, 168, 188–89, 191, 202, 243, 253
   Dominican Republic as supplier of, 78–79, 202–3
   Ecuador as supplier of, 188
   horse heroin and Golden Crescent as suppliers of, 34
   Laos as supplier of, 59
   medical treatments for, 85
   Mexico as supplier of, 12, 13–14, 19, 105, 131, 142, 188, 202
   Nigeria as supplier of, 59, 70
   Pakistan as supplier of, 238
   Puerto Rico as supplier of, 78–79, 125
   Southeast Asian campaign against, 12
   statistics on, xx, 327
   street gang trafficking of, 311
   Turkey as supplier of, 3
   types of, 34, 132
   U.S. use of, 142, 231–32, 246, 255–56, 327
Heroin Signature Program, 19, 261
Herrera-Buitrago, Helmer "Pacho"
   Cali mafia founding father, 70
   as drug supplier, 63
Herrera-Nevares family, 15
Herrera-Nevares, James
   arrest and imprisonment of, 14–16
   as leading Mexican drug trafficker, 14–15

Hessians, 301
Hezbollah, 320
   narco-terrorist group in Lebanon as, 150
hit squads. *See* biker gangs
Homeland Security, xiii
horse heroin, 34
HUM. *See* Harakat ul-Mujahidin
hundi (hawala) as Afghanistan financial network, 242–43

India
   ephedrine supplied by, 80
   meth lab in, 250–51
   pseudoephedrine supplied by, 80
informants
   DEA advertisements for, 254–55
   DEA protocol for, 236
intelligence analysts, training of, 10
Intelligence Response Team, 243
International Association of Police Chiefs, 83
Internet drug sales, 204–5, 225–26, 233, 273–75
Iowa, 211
Irish mob, 74
Irish Republican Army, 326
Islamic Movement of Uzbekistan, 321
Israel, 189–91
Italy, 252–53, 261–62

Jairo Garcia-Giraldo, Jose, 167
Jaish-e-Mohammed (JEM), 320
Jamaica, 270
Japanese Red Army (JRA), 325
JEM. *See* Jaish-e-Mohammed

de Jesus Henao-Montoyo, Archangel, 185, 263–64
al-Jihad, 319
JRA. *See* Japanese Red Army
Juan Garcia-Abrego Organization, 68
"Just say no!" campaign, 143
Justice Department, 33

ketamine (Special K), 90–91, 95, 210, 247
Khun Sa, 58, 75
Kin-Cheung Wong, 248–50
Kosovo, 136
Ku Klux Klan Motorcycle Club
  as biker gang, 301, 304
  as drug traffickers, 304
Kurdistan Worker's Party (PKK), 319
  as narco-terrorist group in Turkey, 150
  taxes on drug shipments by, 241

laboratories
  DEA use of, 9
  drug smugglers' use of, 120, 132
Laos, heroin supplied by, 59
Lashkar-e-Tayyiba, 321
Leary, Timothy, 29
Lebanon, narco-terrorism in, 150
Lehder-Rivas, Carlos Enrique
  Colombian sovereignty and, 46
  extradition and imprisonment of, 47
  as informer, 50
  M-19 guerrilla group and, 46
  Medellín cartel organization by, 22–24

Operation Pisces and, 38
  violence by, 32
Liberation Tigers of Tamil Eelam, 325
Loiaza-Ceballos, Henry, 69
Los Greenes, 160
Los Pepes, 57
LSD
  Special K comparison to, 91
  U.S. use of, 61, 128, 205–6, 232–34
  William Pickard's influence in use of, 234

Machain, Humberto Alverez, 64–66
Madrigal, Alejandro Bernal "Juvenal," 92–93
mafia, 252–53
Mafia Insane Vice Lords
  description of, 310–12
  drug trade involvement in, 311–12
  Troy Martin as founder of, 311
Mahdi family (1-4 Mob), 96–98
marijuana
  biker gangs as suppliers of, 302–3
  California as source of, 135
  Canada as suppliers of, 204, 216, 265, 269–70
  cannabis seed drug control operation, 48
  Colombians as suppliers of, 20, 33
  Domestic Cannabis Eradication and Suppression Program, 24, 60
  home-grown use of, 24–25, 204

marijuana *(continued)*
  indoor production of, 60, 230, 232
  as leading substance in drug arrests, 156
  as medical treatment, 48, 83–84
  Mexico as supplier of, 12, 19, 82, 100, 204
  Operation Green Clover seizure of, 128
  Proposition 215 pro-drug lobby support of, 165–66
  statistics on use of, 24, 60, 156–57, 199, 204
  street gang trafficking of, 311, 312–13
  Supreme Court decision to outlaw, 161–65
  U.S. distribution network of, 269–70
Marquis organization, 122–23
Martinez, Charles, 85–86
McCullough, Kelly, 85–86
McVeigh, Timothy, 78
Medellín cartel
  Colombia operation by, 38, 49
  end of, 57
  Fabian Ochoa as leading member of, 130
  heroin supplied to U.S. by, 245
  Lehder-Rivas as leader of, 22, 46
  Noriega's involvement with, 49–50
  organization of, 22
  political involvement in Colombia, 46–47, 54–55
"meth." *See* methamphetamine
methadone clinics, 106–7

methamphetamine
  biker gangs as suppliers of, 300, 302–4
  distribution network of, 79–81, 104, 108–11
  with GMB, 103–104
  Mexico as suppliers of, 203, 239
  Operation Green Clover seizure of, 128
  terrorist smuggling of, 193
  United Wa State Army as suppliers of, 203
  U.S. as producer of, 134–35, 220
  U.S. meth ring smuggling of, 262
  yaba as form of, 219–20
methaqualone, 33–34
Mexican black tar, 132
  Guadalajara mafia smugglers of, 39
  Operation Tar Pit and, 104–8
  Puerto Rico, availability in, 125
Mexican drug syndicate(s)
  Amado Carillo-Fuentes as, 68, 82, 93–94, 122
  Arellano-Felix Brothers as, 67, 100–101
  Juan Garcia-Abrego as, 68, 122
  Miguel Caro-Quintero as, 67–68
Mexico
  cocaine supplied by, 50–51, 82, 176–77, 196, 201, 223, 264, 267
  cooperation with authorities by, 14–16, 19, 35, 94, 122–23, 142, 177–78, 328

DEA restrictions imposed by, 64–66
heroin supplied by, 12, 13–14, 19, 105, 131, 142, 188, 202
marijuana supplied by, 12, 19, 82, 100, 204
methamphetamine supplied by, 79–80, 202, 239, 263
morphine supplied by, 13
Norte Valle cartel operations in, 267
poppy cultivation in, 131
middleman cell, 140
Miguel Caro-Quintero Organization, 68
Mobile Enforcement Team (MET) program, 76–77
Molina Caracas, Tomás "Negro Acacio," 167
Mongols, 301, 303
moonrocks. See drug combinations
Morant, Mark, 100–101
Moro National Liberation Front, 319
MRTA. See Tupac Amaru Revolutionary Movement
Mugniyah, Imad, 146
Mujahedin-e-Khalq Organization (MEK/MKO), 325
Munoz-Mosquera, Dandeny, 73

narco-terrorists
Colombian groups as, 148–49
definition of, 148
Escobar as, 148, 315
FARC as, 120
as FTO, 319
Hezbollah in Lebanon as, 150
importance of, to DEA, 260
IMU in Uzbekistan as, 150
New People's Army as, 319
PLK as, 150
Taliban as, 149
in Turkey, 150
UWSA in Burma as, 150
Narcotics Control Board, 75
National Highway Traffic Safety Association, 140–41
National Liberation Army (ELN)
as Colombian terrorist group, 241
as FTO, 317
National Ribbon Week, 43
National Training Institute, 7–8, 26
Nayarit gang, 107–8
N'Drangheta, 261–62
Negro Acacio. See Molina Caracas, Tomás
The Netherlands, 116
New People's Army (NPA), 319
Nigeria, 59, 70
Nixon, Richard M.
Drug Enforcement Administration creation by, 4
Operation Intercept implemented by, 14
Noriega, Manuel, 49–50
Norte Valle (North Valley) cartel
AUC protection of, 268
cocaine involvement by, 186, 263–64
in Colombia, 185
in Mexico, 267
technology used by, 186–88, 268
NPA. See New People's Army

Ochoa, Fabian
  extradition from Colombia, 125, 130–31
  Medellín cartel, member of, 55, 92–93
Office of Intelligence, 9
Office of National Drug Control Policy, 47–48
Oklahoma City bombing and DEA offices, 77–78
1-4 Mob. *See* Mahdi family
Ontiveros-Rodriguez, Jorge, 93–94
oolie. *See* drug combinations
Operation(s)
  Banco, 18–19
  Candy Box, 266
  Conquista, 194–95
  Day Trader, 312
  Deja Vu, 222
  Face Off, 130
  Global Sea, 70
  Green Air, 99–101
  Green Clover, 127
  Green Ice, 62
  Headhunters, 225
  Immunity, 94, 117
  Immunity II, 118
  Intercept, 13–14
  Juliet, 167
  Juno, 89
  Leyenda, 43
  Limelight, 83
  Living Large, 192
  Matador, 188
  Melt Down, 213–14
  Millennium, 93
  Mountain Express, 110, 158
  Nine Lives, 271
  North Star, 239–40
  Pipe Dreams, 225, 226
  Pipeline, 36–37
  Pisces, 38
  Platforma, 153
  Purple, 153
  Red Tide, 114, 116
  Sanctuary, 129
  Seis Fronteras, 153
  S.O.S., 130
  Stopgap, 20
  Swordfish, 33
  Tar Pit, 104–8
  Tiger Trap, 75
  Triple X, 135
  Trizo, 19
  White Horse, 120
  Wipe Out, 60
  Zorro II, 82
opium
  Afghanistan as supplier of, 149–50
  Mexican poppy cultivation and, 131
  unrestricted sale of, 1
Organized Crime Drug Enforcement Network, 270
Orlandez-Gamboa, Alberto, 91–92
Ortiz Franco, Francisco, 272
Outlaws, 301–3

PAGAD. *See* People Against Gangsterism and Drugs
Pagans, 301–303
Pakistan, 238
Palestine Islamic Jihad, 322–23
Palestine Liberation Front, 322
Panama
  cartel member sanctuary, 49
  as cocaine shipping point, 49
  invasion of by U.S., 49

Paredes-Ortiz, Nelson, 168
Patino-Fomeque, Julio, 69
PCP. *See* phencyclidine
People Against Gangsterism and Drugs (PAGAD), 326
Peru
   cocaine production, drop in, 168
   cocaine supplied by, 120, 152
   Paredes-Ortiz arrested in, 168
   Shining Path as FTO, 318
   Shining Path as narco-terrorist group, 149, 242
phencyclidine (PCP)
   biker gangs as suppliers of, 303
   U.S. as source of, 206
   U.S. use of, 256–57
Pickard, William
   conviction of, 235–37
   Drug Policy Analysis Program involvement in, 234, 237
   LSD's use influenced by, 234
piperazine, 211
PKK. *See* Kurdistan Worker's Party
Policefax DD-14 system, 26–27
poppy cultivation
   in Afghanistan, 237–38
   in Mexico, 131
   in U.S., 246
poppy-eradication program, 19
Popular Front for the Liberation of Palestine, 322
posses, 313–14
Priority Targeting System, 169
Prisco, David Ricardo, 55
pro-drug lobby
   attitude to drug use by, 45, 164–65, 166, 257–58, 279, 327
   attitude to the DEA by, 162–64
   "Just say no!" campaign attitude by, 143
   marijuana legalization efforts by, 48
   Proposition 215 supported by, 84, 161–62
   U.S. invasion of Afghanistan, reaction to by, 238
Proposition 215
   marijuana for medical use under, 84
   pro-drug lobby support of, 84, 161–62, 165–66
   Supreme Court ruling nullifies, 161
pseudoephedrine
   Canada as source of, 111, 158–60, 239–40
   meth-making chemical, use of, 80, 85, 108–11
psilocybin, 208–10, 246
Puerto Rico
   cocaine supplied by, 78–79, 124, 160, 214
   cooperation with U.S., 124
   corruption in, 124–25
   heroin supplied by, 78–79, 124, 125, 214
   homicides in, 175
Pure Food and Drug Act, 1

al-Qaeda, 147, 241, 315, 318, 323
Quaaludes, 34
Quintanilla, Jesse, 94

Ramirez-Abadia, Juan Carlos "Chupeta," 70

Ramon-Magana, Alcides "El Metro," 94
Revolutionary Armed Forces of Colombia (FARC), 148
   Colombian cocaine, involvement in, 152, 153, 167, 241
   federal indictments against, 167
   as FTO, 317
   influence of, 242
   as narco-terrorist group, 120
   Surinam arrests of, 167
   terrorism against the U.S., 151–52
Revolutionary Nuclei, 324
Revolutionary Organization 17 November, 324
Revolutionary United Front (RUF), 324
Robledo-Roman, Rene, 188
Rodriguez-Gacha, Jose, 22, 47
Rodriguez-Orejuela, Gilberto, 58, 69
Rodriguez-Orejuela, Miguel, 58, 69
Rohypnol (Rophy), 206
Royal Canadian Mounted Police, marijuana seizure by, 269
RUF. *See* Revolutionary United Front

Salazar-Izquierdo, Fernando, 72
Salinas-Doria, Gilberto (Gilberto Garza-Garcia), 93–95
salvia divinorum, 211–13
Santacruz-Londono, Jose, 58, 69, 183
Satan's Choice, 301
scandals, 126–27, 133

Seis Fronteras operation, 153
Sendero Luminoso (SL). *See* Shining Path
Sensitive Investigation Units (SIU), 189
   host country operatives working with, 243
   organization of, 169
Shining Path (SL), 149, 242, 318
SIU. *See* Sensitive Investigation Units
Skinner, Gordon Scott
   as informant, 235–36
   involvement in LSD lab, 235
SL. *See* Shining Path
Sons of Silence, 301
South Caicos island, 23–24
Southeast Asian heroin campaign, 12
Southeast cartel, 176–77
"Special K." *See* ketamine
"speed." *See* methamphetamine
statistics on drug use, xii, xiii
   alcohol-related arrests, comparison to, 155
   boys and girls compared by, 156–57, 199
   cocaine, 296
   crack, 295, 296
   date rape and, 101–2
   ecstasy, 136–37, 199
   heroin, 125–26, 327
   marijuana and, 24, 60, 156–57, 199, 204
   New England and, 231, 232
   Puerto Rico and homicides and, 175
   U.S. use of and, 20–21, 24, 115
steroids, 61

street gangs
  Asian, 309
  Bloods, 305–307
  Crips, 305–307
  drug involvement by, 305, 307, 309–10, 311–12
  gang names of, 305
  on Indian reservations, 308
  Mafia Insane Vice Lords, 310
  posses, 313–14
  terrorist groups' ties to, 314
  violence by, 305–309
Supreme Court, 2
Survivor's Benefit Fund, 86
swallowers, 120
Switzerland, 80
Syria, 193

Taliban
  as bin Laden supporter, 241
  as FTO in Afghanistan, 318
  as narco-terrorists in Afghanistan, 149–50
  poppy production by, 237–38
TARA. *See* Trans America Ventures Services
technology
  biker gang use of, 300
  Cali mafia use of, 183–84
  DEA use of, 8–9, 26, 52, 60–61, 86, 205
  drug world use of, 36, 70–72, 119, 138
  Internet use of, in drug abuse, 204–5, 225–26, 233, 273–75
terrorism. *See also* narco-terrorists
  al-Qaeda and U.S. embassies, 147

terrorist groups
  AUC as, 197
  and methamphetamine ring, 193
Thailand
  as supplier of heroin, 12, 74
  as supplier of yaba, 219
THC. *See* Delta-9-Tetrahydrocannabinol
Thermal imaging technology, 48, 60–61
Tijuana cartel. *See* AFO
Trans America Ventures Services (TARA), 62
Tupac Amaru Revolutionary Movement (MRTA), 318
Turkey
  heroin supplied by, 3
  narco-terrorism in, 150

United Nation Drug Convention, 216–17
United Parcel Service and psilocybin transport, 209
United Self-Defense Forces of Colombia (AUC)
  Colombian paramilitary terrorist groups, 197–98
  de Jesus Henao-Montoya, interaction with, 263
  as FTO, 317–18
  Norte Valle cartel protection by, 268
United Wa State Army (UWSA)
  methamphetamine supplied by, 203, 219
  narco-terrorists in Burma as, 150
  yaba supplied by, 219
Urdinola, Ivan, 63

U.S. Border Patrol, xiii
U.S. Coast Guard, 33, 36, 129
U.S. Customs Service, xiii, 99, 116
  Colombian cocaine seizure by, 23
  Marquis organization investigation by, 122–23
  Operation Impunity role by, 94
  Puerto Rico drug decline and, 175
  South Caicos island investigations by, 23–24, 36
U.S. Department of State, 34
U.S. Military, 35
U.S. Navy satellites in drug investigations, 20
U.S. Postal Service
  drug arrests involved in, 138
  personnel as drug dealers, 139
UWSA. *See* United Wa State Army
Uzbekistan, and IMU, 150

Vagos, 303, 304
Venezuela
  as cocaine source, 112, 181
  cooperation with U.S. government, 112–14
violence, drug-related, xii, 21, 29, 31, 32, 35, 40
  biker gangs as cause of, 299, 304
  crack associated with, 31, 295
  date rape and, 102
  methamphetamine associated with, 80
  murder numbers related to, xiii

Wang Zong Xiao, 247–52
  as heroin smuggler, 249
WTC. *See* World Trade Center
"wicky stick." *See* drug combinations
World Trade Center (WTC), 147–48

yaba, 219
Yanez Cantu, Jamie "the Assassin Hunter," 121–22
Yeje-Cabrera, Rafael, 226–29

Zaghmot, Hassan, 110
Zambada-Garcia, Ismael, 223, 264–65